Journalism in Britain

Es war einmal ein Kind
Das wusch sich nie das Ohr.
Da wuchs ihm aus dem Ohr, o Schreck
Ein kleiner Baum hervor.
(Brecht)

Für Lara Mathilda (nicht mehr ein Kind!)

Journalism in Britain

A Historical Introduction

Martin Conboy

⑤SAGE

Los Angeles | London | New Delhi
Singapore | Washington DC

First published 2011

SAGE Publications Ltd
1 Oliver's Yard
55 City Road
London EC1Y 1SP

SAGE Publications Inc.
2455 Teller Road
Thousand Oaks, California 91320

SAGE Publications India Pvt Ltd
B 1/I 1 Mohan Cooperative Industrial Area
Mathura Road
New Delhi 110 044

SAGE Publications Asia-Pacific Pte Ltd
33 Pekin Street #02-01
Far East Square
Singapore 048763

Library of Congress Control Number: 2010928842

British Library Cataloguing in Publication data

A catalogue record for this book is available from the British Library

ISBN 978-1-84787-494-8
ISBN 978-1-84787-495-5 (pbk)

Typeset by C&M Digitals (P) Ltd, Chennai, India
Printed and bound in Great Britain by TJ International Ltd, Padstow, Cornwall
Printed on paper from sustainable resources

Contents

Acknowledgements

This book is the fruit of a combination of solitude and solidarity. The manuscript itself may have been written in solitary confinement last Spring in the seclusion of a sabbatical semester amidst a particularly leafy Nether Edge. However, despite the isolation which marked the production of the book, it has been accompanied by the sort of collective camaraderie which I have had the good fortune to experience in all of my creative ventures. The Department of Journalism Studies which has provided me with such a stimulating professional environment over the last five years, granted me the gift of study leave which I hope is repaid by this publication and, if nothing else, will continue to fuel collegial debate on the role of academic investigations of journalism's history. Colleagues and friends John Steel and Adrian Bingham have shared enthusiasms and ideas which have emerged in the fabric of this book as well as in the shared project of the Centre for the Study of Journalism and History whose launch accompanied the completion of the manuscript. The library support staff, especially Alastair Allan, have demonstrated once again that it is the confluence of expertise, provision and plain old-fashioned friendliness which makes the library service at the University of Sheffield such a wonderful research tool. Down the years which have seen this project develop, I have learnt much from the combined wisdom of many, including Anthony Delano, John Tulloch, Jane Chapman, Brian Winston, Rob Melville, Jane Taylor, Richard Keeble, Bob Franklin, and from the patient advice of the many former and current journalists involved in the Association for Journalism Education. Beyond these shores, I must thank many colleagues especially Elliot King, Bridget Griffen-Foley, Penny O'Connell, Simon Potter, David Culbert, Jason McElligott and Annik Dubied for demonstrating the growing relevance of historically informed accounts of journalism internationally and for broadening my horizons. Mila Steele at SAGE provided the initial encouragement to develop the idea for publication and Imogen Roome brought it to fruition. I trust that the combined support of all those above is captured in these pages. If it is not, then the usual conditions apply! Students on a variety of courses have patiently watched these ideas germinate and will, I hope, find this publication of use in engaging with the historical sedimentations within contemporary journalism in Britain. For breaking the silence of each day's labours with news from the outside world, my thanks go to Simone for her ultimate demonstration of the value of solidarity intruding into solitude.

Nether Edge, October 2010

Introduction

This introduction will do two things. First, it will outline a working definition of journalism. Second, it will make the case why the history of journalism is important to our contemporary understanding of its role in society. Throughout the book, the history of journalism over the twentieth century will be assessed against the definitions of this opening chapter as it has adapted to and been shaped by political, economic and technological pressures.

Distinguishing Between News and Journalism

First, we need to be able to distinguish between news and journalism. We can ask a friend if they have any news. We don't ask if they have any journalism, and despite the common use of the word 'news' as a synonym for 'journalism', the latter is a very particular set of traditions for the dissemination of news. Journalism must have an institutional framework for its engagement with the facts about and opinions on the contemporary world. It is varied in its form, technological platform and genre. Its forms can range from hard news or a commentary on contemporary politics to satirical reviews or celebrity gossip, to name but a few. It has also changed significantly over time in both its content and its emphasis under political, cultural, economic and technological pressures. Journalism is very much of its time and therefore also very much rooted in its own history.

News is an essential lubricant in human affairs and is certainly as old as social interaction itself. In centuries gone by, travellers, soldiers, merchants, even farmers returning from market, might be asked what news they had heard. Such news did not depend upon formal modes of transmission such as print and later broadcasting and could be equally well exchanged in public meeting places, both official and unofficial – the church, the tavern or the village pump! Journalism, as a commercially structured, periodically produced extension of the older patterns of informal dissemination of information and commentary, is a more recent practice. The features of journalism which distinguish it from the more malleable concept of 'news' lie in the regularity of its publication, which is sometimes referred to as its 'periodicity', and the consistency of its commercial and professional packaging. This means that journalism takes on a shape and an identity which remain recognizable and therefore saleable over time. The point at which we can begin to distinguish it from the more general term of 'news' may be coupled with the introduction of the word 'journalism' into the English language in 1833, when it was first used in the *Westminster Review* in a discussion of the changes in periodical publications of the time. It has been claimed that this neologism was required to encompass the linkage between high cultural forms such as the periodical *Edinburgh* and *Westminster Reviews* and the commercial daily press. Campbell describes how the new word came to signify the yoking of higher and lower cultural forms which was a challenge to existing cultural distinctions (2000: 40). Journalism became structured around the commercialization and ultimately the popularization of the flow of information and opinion about events in the world (Conboy, 2004: 122).

To corroborate the comparatively recent distinctiveness of journalism, in contrast to news, Chalaby (1998) claims that it was as late as 1855, with the final lifting of taxes on newspapers – the so-called 'taxes on knowledge' – that journalism as we understand it today began to take shape as a commodified form of public address, a product that could be conceived and designed primarily to be sold at a profit to a regular market. Others such as Briggs and Burke (2002), Sommerville (1996) and Raymond (1996) have argued that all the ingredients necessary for journalism had been present within British society for a lot longer, even if it took the economic and political convulsions of the mid-nineteenth century to bring them into something approaching this consistently marketable and profitable form. Indeed, there had been a variety of successful periodical publications since the seventeenth century which had provided a wide range of experiments in disseminating information about the world to a paying audience. All this makes a strong base-line for arguing that to understand journalism we need to grasp both its antecedents and the way in which it was created as a response to radical changes in the flow of information. These two observations have a particular importance for the challenges and opportunities which are impacting upon it in the present as it seeks to navigate turbulent economic and technological changes.

Different Traditions of Journalism

By the end of the nineteenth century, the productive dialogue between high and popular culture had reached a particularly fertile moment, as demonstrated by a note sent from one giant of Victorian journalism, Newnes, to another, Stead, in 1890 on their parting as collaborators on the *Review of Reviews*:

> There is one kind of journalism which directs the affairs of nations; it makes and unmakes cabinets; it upsets governments, builds up navies and does many other great things. It is magnificent. This is your journalism. There is another kind of journalism which has no such great ambitions. It is content to plod on, year after year, giving wholesome and harmless entertainment to crowds of hardworking people, craving for a little fun and amusement. It is quite humble and unpretentious. This is my journalism. (Friederichs, 1911: 116–17)

This division of the goals of two distinct forms of journalism is a neat encapsulation of the point of departure for the modern period of journalism, where journalism could be located either as a politically charged form of communication whose goal was to challenge and change society or as a form of populist entertainment which aimed principally to distract a majority of the population from their daily cares. It had become a kind of textual spectrum which stretched from absolute entertainment to an impassioned attention to political affairs.

Some have argued – in company with the second President of the United States of America, Thomas Jefferson – that given a choice between government without newspapers and newspapers without government, they would prefer the latter. Carey (1996) has made a strong contemporary argument, for instance, that journalism is in fact synonymous with democracy:

> *Journalism is another name for democracy or, better, you cannot have journalism without democracy. The practices of journalism are not self-justifying; rather, they are justified in terms of the consequences they engender, namely the constitution of a democratic social order.*

The Importance of Miscellany for Journalism

Yet, beyond these somewhat exaggerated claims for the primacy of one variety – one main function of journalism, we might say – the journalism which emerged after the lifting of taxes in 1855 has been constituted as a commercial mixture whose contribution to democracy combined altruism with anarchy, investigation with innuendo, and social concern with sensationalist tub-thumping. It is only in its broadest contribution to public understanding that it can, rightly, be considered as one commentator has proposed: 'The primary sense-making practice of modernity' (Hartley, 1996: 12). Journalism contributes to the needs of the modern society precisely because of its ability to engage with the multiple levels of our daily lives, which are sometimes occupied by serious social or political questions and at others are lightened by gossip, witty commentary or observations on the merits of newly released films and music or recently published books. Journalism's miscellany assists us in dealing with the complexity of modernity, and because of its need for mass markets in the twentieth century, it responds on a genuinely popular level by providing this miscellany for mass consumption.

The miscellany across what we might call journalism's spectrum has been complicated still further by the fact that in all its forms it has been defined – and indeed judged – from a variety of perspectives, meaning that it is expected to perform several (sometimes incompatible) tasks simultaneously. These perspectives include its relationship to democracy; its publication of information of contemporary importance; its ability to provide topical and popular entertainment; its ability through critical intervention and commentary to monitor the activities of the rich and influential; and through these activities, to monitor also the extent to which it has acted as a stimulus to the constitution of an interrelating series of public spheres by its ability to foster public discussion. These public spheres range from an austere intellectual forum to the rowdy knockabout of political mockery, and from the interests of those intent on monitoring the policies of MPs to those who prefer to scrutinize the tastes and lifestyles of celebrities. In many expressions of journalism's repertoire, levity and good humour have had a part to play, whether this has meant the incorporation of an element of entertainment either in its content – such as human interest or a witty writing style – or through the juxtaposition of more distracting trivial matters along with the serious.

The building blocks of all journalism are the report, the news bulletin and the feature article whether in a written or broadcast format. To these we might add the opinion piece, the commentary, the interview and the editorial, together with interactive features such as letters to the editor and more recent additions such as vox pops, phone-ins, live studio debates and e-mails. It is this range of interaction between genre and audience which has distinguished journalism from mere 'news'. Moreover, within the basic configurations of contemporary journalism there are many combinations and crossovers that challenge more traditionalist distinctions between hard news and soft news, fact and opinion, information and entertainment. Journalism has within this variety always enabled conflicting views of its functions to co-exist without closure around any one of them. It is, in fact, an extraordinarily flexible set of communicative practices. Good journalism has always been able to accommodate a variety of genres, styles and intentions – as we can witness today from the serious analysis of *Newsnight* to the mass appeal of the *Sun*'s well-honed reactionary iconoclasm; from the agenda-setting *Channel 4 News* to the alternative voice of *Indymedia*. Journalism needs to encompass this variety as it seeks to maintain an engagement with the facts of events in the modern world. There are still however hierarchies of believability within journalism, from BBC News and the so-called 'newspapers of record' to the *Sunday Sport* and Kelvin MacKenzie's late and unlamented News Bunny, from the gossip columns of celebrity magazines to the probing of anarchist online publications. Even these hierarchies are problematized by an 'informed scepticism about what is read, seen and heard in the journalistic media' which McNair (1998: 39) assumes is a common, and we might add healthy, feature of journalism's contemporary reception environment.

Journalism as a Discourse

Given the multi-faceted nature highlighted above, journalism can best be described as a form of discourse. In a first sense of the word, this means that it can only be understood as a series of debates and even disagreements concerning what can and cannot be considered as journalism and, as one might expect, these debates ebb and flow over time. Journalism has emerged both as consisting of the claims and counter-claims of a variety of speakers on its behalf – meaning that we must always keep in mind a multiple set relationships for the practice of journalism, with society, with its commercial requirements, with politics, and also as a relatively autonomous cultural practice with its own traditions and history. Journalism can be viewed as an intersection of many conflicting interests, with some of these, at various points

4

in history, having clearer priority than others. Furthermore, it is a set of practices which is structured by the constraints of time, space, money and competition. Within these constraints, Deuze (2005a) argues that it is, to a large extent, the way in which journalists themselves have come to talk about their practice which defines contemporary journalism, while the nature of these same constraints was instrumental historically in the structuring of journalism as a form of language that was confident enough to be able to distinguish itself from its sources through editorial interventions in Matheson's (2000) account of early twentieth-century British newspapers.

Discourse – according to the second sense in which it is often used in contemporary debates around language and culture – is a term influenced by the writing of Michel Foucault (1974). Discourses, according to Foucault, are intrinsically bound up with questions of power since they give expression to the meanings and values of institutions or practices and, in doing so, claim authority for themselves. The discourse of journalism defines, describes and limits what it is possible to say with respect to journalism, whether at its margins or at its institutional core. It describes the ways in which it is possible to think about and criticize the characteristic practices of journalism. One advantage of considering journalism in this way is that it denaturalizes certain common-sense assumptions that are made about it and enables us to criticize these and question their logic. For the purposes of this historical overview, it also assists us in assessing how the dominant opinions in debates over journalism's power and value have altered over time. Certainly, from a historical perspective, many of the expectations which we have come to associate with journalism can be regarded discursively, such as the freedom of the press, the news media as a 'Fourth Estate' and its objectivity, the political functions of journalism and the often obscured economic imperative of journalism – its political economy.

Another advantage of considering journalism as a discourse is that it enables us to view it as creating new forms of power as well as new forms of access to representation. This suggests that journalism has never simply contested the power which lay outside its own sphere of influence – for instance, political power – but that it has instead always been deeply involved in the creation of power structures themselves and particularly, but not exclusively, those power structures which operate within public communication. One of the most widespread fallacies, the so-called 'Whig account of journalism' (Curran and Seaton, 2003), sees it as the triumphant march of the political emancipation of Western societies through their news media (Siebert, 1965). Journalism itself has contributed to this account and drawn upon it as a way of legitimating its relationship with the political status quo. Most recently this underpinned many attempts by Western journalism agencies, including the BBC, to provide journalism training to Eastern European countries based on a tacit assumption that Western free market or public service models of journalism were an inevitable evolutionary step for newly democratized states. Considering journalism as a discourse disrupts any inevitability in the direction which it has taken or the milestones on this trajectory and highlights instead the ways that its development has always been accompanied by disagreement and political preference. In addition, it encourages us to emphasize the variety of practices which it has incorporated over the centuries and demonstrates how much of journalism's resilience and vitality come from its ability to adapt to changes in cultural and economic conditions.

Why History Matters

One of the main reasons for understanding the history of journalism is that it provides us with a clearer context in which to explore claims concerning the inevitability of change or conservatism within journalism today. For instance, when considering whether the internet will consign the newspaper, radio journalism or television journalism to history's scrapheap, we might do well to bear in mind the fact that no media technology has as yet been obliterated by an innovation and so, despite anxieties and prophecies to the contrary, newspapers have not been forced out of business by the power of radio, the cinema was not ousted by television, radio was not displaced by television, and the internet has done nothing so far but add to the richness of the journalistic spectrum. History can help us to appreciate the diversity and the adaptability of journalism and to discourage any view of a simple trajectory, either downhill from a golden peak or uphill towards a state of technological or professional perfection. If anything, its movement across time can best be described as a zig-zag which according to Briggs and Burke (2002) has characterized most of the communication media's history.

Writing specifically about newspapers, Black sees journalism's history as being profoundly informed by the changes necessary within a competitive market:

> Change is therefore a central theme in newspaper history, not only because of its occurrence, and the speed of its occurrence, but also as the awareness of change creates a sense of transience and opportunity. Each period of English newspaper history can be presented as one of transformation, shifts in content, production, distribution, the nature of competition, and the social context. (2001: 1)

By focusing on journalism's history, we can begin to address whether we are really witnessing the final countdown for this particular form of public communication; how journalism has reacted to previous crises; and how today's debates can be illuminated by an appreciation that what we understand by journalism and its main functions has changed over the last hundred years and will, no doubt, continue to change over the next century.

The contours of contemporary journalism had been set long before the dawn of the twentieth century. In the next chapter, we will consider some of the more pertinent changes of the late nineteenth century which enabled journalism to emerge and develop as such a robust and influential form of public communication. These will focus on the continuities which have allowed journalism to maintain a coherence over the last hundred years during an unprecedented period of cultural and technological change. Providing such a historical context, it is hoped, will better enable us to understand the nature of those challenges it faces in the present.

Conclusion

No single-sentence definition of journalism is really adequate to describe the complexity and variety of its output. It encompasses a wide range of practices which together share an overriding concern with the public communication of contemporary affairs and the discussion of those affairs. Journalism, in mapping the contours of the contemporary world, does so across what we might term a textual spectrum. It has developed as a commercial product which depends as much on the regularity of its appearance as on the stability of its character within a highly differentiated market. The specifics of its expression have been shaped over time by a variety of cultural, technological, economic and political factors, and the present forms of journalism bear all the hallmarks of these historical influences. That is why history is so important to understanding the journalism of the present day.

FURTHER READING

Briggs, A. and Burke, P. (2002) *A Social History of the Media*. Cambridge: Polity. In its early chapters, this provides an illuminating account of the ways in which journalism grew out of a range of technological, cultural and political motivations from the Early Modern period to the dawn of the modern age.

Raymond, J. (1996) *The Invention of the Newspaper: English Newsbooks, 1641–1649*. Oxford: Oxford University Press. This provides a collection of very specific and detailed accounts of the publications of this radical period in English history, which saw the emergence of practices that were to help in defining the contours of what later came to be called journalism.

Smith, A. (1979) *The Newspaper: An international History*. London: Thames and Hudson. This is a colourful and engaging account of the rise of the newspaper as an international medium for public communication.

Sommerville, J. (1996) *The News Revolution*. Oxford: Oxford University Press. This explores the radical changes in understanding the contemporary world which were necessary for the practices of newsgathering and dissemination to gain value in the sixteenth and seventeenth centuries. It also proposes that the development of 'news' is a truly revolutionary moment in social developments in Western Europe.

1

Journalism and the Coming of Mass Markets

Introduction

It would be no exaggeration to say that modern journalism began in 1896 – on 4 May 1896, to be precise. This was not because of any single innovation in format or technology but in the way that Alfred Harmsworth's *Daily Mail*, launched on that day, managed to draw a complex range of technical, commercial and textual features into one publication. An astute awareness of the requirements of advertisers, a recognition of the social aspirations of a class of new reader, an ability to produce economies of scale in production, and the organizational genius to be able to distribute this rapidly and effectively, enabled it to become the first truly mass circulation paper, to the extent that by 1900 it was selling in excess of a million copies per day. Chalaby has claimed that with the *Daily Mail*, Harmsworth brought the daily newspaper into the twentieth century and modernized journalism in the process (Chalaby, 2000: 34). However, none of this emerged from a vacuum. Harmsworth was simply a brilliant co-ordinator of these various elements.

This revolution also ushered in what we may call the popular century, where developments in the popular newspaper began to drive the practices of the entire press and where these commercial concerns consolidated their dominance as ever more channels of communication became available. Yet the *Daily Mail*, which was to have such a profound effect on the structure of the journalism of the next century, was the culmination of a sequence of events that had started with a government decision to abolish taxes on newspapers in 1855. This chapter will set out the chronology and debates around the emergence of mass popular markets from the late nineteenth century and show how these were to influence all subsequent mainstream journalism.

Picking Up the Commercial Pace

The abolition of taxes on newspapers in 1855 had begun to release the full force of competition into newspaper production. Elements of sensationalism and entertainment which had hitherto been prominent in the Sunday market were now to be included in the most successful launch of the period, the *Daily Telegraph*, in the very same year as the taxes were lifted. Henceforth newspapers would survive as commercial concerns or not at all. They would do so by maximizing their profits through targeting a topical miscellany aimed at specific readerships that were to be addressed with increasing efficiency. Of course this did not occur overnight, but the process which would lead to a full appreciation of the commercial potential of journalism had nevertheless been unleashed.

This commercialization contributed to a longer-term shift from a genteel view of journalism as an occupation for men of letters to one which saw it as predominantly to do with the satisfaction of market needs. Yet journalism has moved in a complex and sometimes surprising fashion since 1855 and its liberalization after the lifting of taxes to the twenty-first century, despite the fact that certain patterns have remained persistent. The economics of the market, for example, have combined with technological innovations to produce significant changes in journalism's organization, distribution and content. However, this is no straightforward narrative of either triumph or decline, as these changes continue to pose profound challenges – particularly for print journalism – even today. Taking this perspective on the centrality of change to any history of journalism, Smith sees it as being determined by its own structural shortcomings in reaching its self-declared goals:

> In the course of four hundred years the newspaper press has not finally dealt with the issues into which it was born. Its methods of production and distribution are always inadequate to the ideals and purposes which appear to rise from the activities of collecting news. Every century or so they undergo a major alteration ... (1978: 183)

If the contemporary age can provide evidence of an on-going major reassessment of how the commercial needs of journalism continue to match its 'ideals and purposes', then one must stress that these were first highlighted in the mid-Victorian era. This continuity from 1855 to the present has been remarked upon by Negrine, who observed how, according to the great historian of political journalism, Koss, there were concerns in the Victorian era about issues which still have a very contemporary ring to them: ' ... the commercialism of the press, the effect of advertising, the trend to sensationalism, concentration of ownership, and the reduction of political coverage' (Negrine, 1994: 39).

While some would characterize the changes which followed on from 1855 as the decline of a golden age of journalism (Ensor, 1968), others would argue more pragmatically that what had hitherto provided a discourse of public dialogue was from that point onwards replaced by a much more systematically commodified discourse which created what we now recognize as the modern variety of journalism (Chalaby, 1998: 66) – one which targeted the public only insofar as the public constituted a market that could be exploited commercially. Some nineteenth-century commentators applauded these developments and saw this period as providing a rejuvenation in journalism:

> ... in the early sixties ... journalism was at a turning point. A poor order of things was passing away; a better order of things ... by the attraction of many fresh, bright, strong, and scholarly minds to journalism as a power – was coming in, and coming in on well prepared ground. (Greenwood, 1897: 708)

Driven by the improved climate for commercial newspapers after 1855, the penny press of the middle Victorian era was beginning to experiment with a lighter style and more human interest, perhaps best characterized by the 'Telegraphese' of George Augustus Sala and the influential gossip column 'The Flaneur' by Edmund Yates in Samuel Lucas's penny *Morning Star*, founded in 1856. At the same time the respectable, upmarket papers such as *The Times* and the *Morning Post* maintained a sober and anonymous gravitas in their journalism, bringing 'a heavy overdose of politics' (Herd, 1952: 222) with verbatim accounts of Parliament that were composed in blocks of solid and unbroken type and without the sort of banner headlines with which we are familiar today. The tradition of anonymous authorship in journalism was gradually being eroded via the naming of writers in the more popular magazines, and by the 1870s correspondence columns, signed articles and personal details were being used at the cheaper end of the daily newspaper market as well. This had the effect of introducing an apparent pluralism made up of many authors and spokespeople in place of a single authority and the voice of the newspaper as an institution, which had been the implicit norm up to this point in Victorian journalism (Jackson, 2001: 145).

A transatlantic cable was laid in 1866 and telegraphed dispatches then became an accepted part of a more internationalized news-gathering operation, meaning that 'henceforth daily journalism operated within a new tense ... of the instantaneous present' (Smith, 1978: 167). In fact it was the increasingly efficient exploitation of the telegraph in combination with the newly created category of the sub-editor that signalled the only substantive improvement of these years through the extinction of the old 'penny-a-liner', 'a very inferior race of reporters' (Lee, 1976: 112) who provided cheap copy to make up pages, often copied from secondary sources and with little journalistic merit. A sub-editor was employed to shape, reduce and revise reports to fit within the spaces left by advertisements and bolder headlines while matching the identity of the particular paper.

By the 1880s, a combination of stylistic experiments, technological innovations, political advances such as the extension of the franchise to enable a larger proportion of the working population to vote, and improved economic conditions after the recessionary 1870s were to transform the ambition and content of journalism and orientate it irretrievably to mass audiences via the New Journalism. The Foster Education Act of 1870 which made education compulsory and freely available to primary-aged children also helped to fuel a new level of literacy which would soon translate into increased sales of popular publications. The introduction of the telegraph, telephone, typewriter, high-speed rotary press and half-tone photographic block began to change the look of printed material as journalism became a more visualized practice. After 1875, there was a reconstruction of the newspaper industry following a more economically integrated pattern, which encouraged a more considered and methodical capital investment in technology and more attention being paid to circulation figures and advertising revenue. The technological advances which promised a more attractive and profitable product for a wider audience brought new commercial entrepreneurs into an industry which offered increasing returns on their investment through wider distribution and a more astute harnessing of advertising. Above all else, it was the broadening of the franchise through the Third Reform Act in 1884 which meant that this New Journalism was able to address the people as having a stake in public affairs like never before, meaning that ' ... the New Journalism acquired a political resonance which had been largely lacking in press discourse during the previous 50 years' (Jones, 1996: 132).

Newnes – Preparing the Ground for Mass Market Papers

George Newnes was the first to draw together these strands, testing and creating new territories for journalism in a wide range of journals including *Tit-Bits* (1881), *The Strand Magazine* (1891), *The Million* (1892), *The Westminster Gazette* (1893), *The World Wide Magazine* (1898), *The Ladies' Field* (1898) and *The Captain* (1899). Of these, it was the first, *Tit-Bits*, which was to become the model that would have the most profound influence on the daily press.

Tit-bits from all the interesting Books, Periodicals, and Newspapers of the World was launched as a penny weekly on 22 October 1881, with competitions, statistics, historical facts, bits of news, editorials, correspondence columns, fiction, anecdotes, jokes, legal general knowledge, competitions and lots of adverts. Portraits of and interviews with celebrities were also a prominent inclusion in each edition. It was a triumph of promotion, formatting and editorial flair and soon boasted 400,000 to 600,000 in weekly sales, leading Jackson to claim that: '... far from lowering the standards of popular journalism, it undoubtedly raised them' (2001: 55). It was widely imitated because of its success, most notably by *Answers to Correspondents* from Harmsworth, who had learned his trade on Newnes' paper, and by *Pearson's Weekly* which was published by the future proprietor of the *Daily Express*, both of which were aimed at the same market and towards securing similar sales figures, demonstrating the potential for this type of journal. Most importantly, Newnes developed a popular community within his paper though a 'sympathetic intimacy' (Jackson, 2000: 13) with his readers which anticipated much of popular journalism's subsequent rhetorical appeal. He even found ways of extending that projection of community into other areas of his readers' lives and he embarked upon an astute commercial branding of his product that went beyond simply selling papers. In May 1885, for example, he used the paper to launch a life insurance scheme for anyone found dead with a copy of *Tit-Bits* on them in a railway accident and in 1889 at the Paris Exhibition he set up a pavilion and enquiry office in an extension of the textual space of his paper. Some however have been less than appreciative of Newnes' achievements:

Newnes became aware that the new schooling was creating a class of potential readers – people who had been taught to decipher print without learning much else, and for whom the existing newspapers, with their long articles, long paragraphs, and all-round demands on the intelligence and imagination, were quite unsuited. To give them what he felt they wanted, he started Tit-Bits. (Ensor, 1968: 311)

Stead – Pioneering the Popular Campaign

As economic forces were taking a larger role in the development of journalism, it was no coincidence that what became known as the New Journalism became crystallized in the practices of the London evening papers in their search for new readers. Competition in London had intensified as cheaper evening newspapers, such as the *Pall Mall Gazette* and the *St James's Gazette*, reduced their prices from two pence to a penny in 1882, and it was in these papers, most notably the former, that the newer styles of journalism were introduced as a further commercial ploy to distinguish them from their more sedate morning relations. The genius of the *Pall Mall Gazette* (launched in 1865 by Greenwood) had been to bring the scope and variety of the more popular periodical reviews of magazines into daily journalism. It has been observed that 'Greenwood brought lightness, polish and intellectual alertness into daily journalism at a time when the morning papers had become heavy and tradition-bound' (Herd, 1952: 226).

The driving force behind this kind of journalism, which sought social commitment through a wider readership and aimed for an influence on matters of public concern, was the non-conformist and politically radical W.T. Stead. As early as 1880, writing on the Liberal Party's political programme, he had stressed both the 'political education' of the electorate and the 'prophetic character of the journalists' vocation' (Baylen, 1972: 373). He was a pioneer of investigative journalism being pursued for moral ends and saw the editor, as expressed in his article 'Government by Journalism', as 'the uncrowned king of an educated democracy' (1886). For him, journalism had to simply aim to change the world. Some commentators have located him within a longer tradition of radical journalism:

> *Stead's mercurial, hellfire temperament was that of the great pamphleteers. In his boldness and versatility, in his passionate belief in the constructive power of the pen, in so many of his opinions, even in his championship of women, he resembled Daniel Defoe and Jonathan Swift. (Boston, 1990: 101)*

It was as editor of the *Pall Mall Gazette* from 1883 to 1889 that he reached the pinnacle of his national prominence. During his tenure he brought cross-headings to the paper, together with popular developments such as scoops and a flair for self-publicity which drew attention to his newspaper, the development of investigative, campaigning journalism in the pursuit of socially progressive causes and the use of emotive and colourful writing. The cross-head was a presentational development that he copied from American newspaper practice. In contrast to the dense columns of the morning newspapers, the *Pall Mall Gazette* could be henceforth scanned at speed. He included the illustrations and line drawings that would further break up the monotony of the traditional printed page. He also employed specialist commentators to popularize knowledge of contemporary affairs and in his 'Character Sketch' he blended the interview, word picture and personality analysis. The social implications of these changes were clear, making ' … the page accessible to less resolute reading at the end of the day and possibly by the family at home' (Brake, 1988: 19).

The development of the interview was again an American import, but Stead deployed it with aplomb in broadening the popular reach of his journalism. One major coup was his interview with General Gordon in January 1884 before he embarked for the Sudan. As if to underline the growing importance of women to this newly personalized style of journalism, Stead employed Hulda Friederich as the chief interviewer for his paper.

His most famous exposé was the 'Maiden Tribute of Modern Babylon' story, which exposed Victorian hypocrisy on child prostitution in a series of articles from 6 July 1885. This synthesized all the ambition contained within Stead's journalism and campaigning fervour. It was a sensation, boosting sales to 100,000, and its notoriety led him to be imprisoned for three months for the alleged procurement of the 13-year-old girl, Lisa Armstrong, who was used as the bait in the sting which exposed the realities of under-age sexual exploitation in his undercover investigation. Stead's goal was both a moral and a political one. His passionate opposition to the wrongs of society was in keeping with much of the tradition of the 'old corruption' (Hollis, 1970), as it seemed to imply that there was nothing fundamentally wrong with the status quo that could not be resolved by the actions of good men and women. The 'old corruption' analysis tends to foreground individual failings and neglect deeper systemic issues, and critics such as Hollis maintain that it lacks any sustained political conviction. Onto his confidence in the reforming potential of the Victorian governing classes Stead grafted a moral purpose and wrapped this within a well-developed commercial pragmatism. He was a forerunner of a more personalized variety of what we might call today a 'journalism of attachment' from a deeply religious perspective. There are those however who are more cautious about his sensationalizing of sexual mores and its implications for journalism:

> *'Sex' had long been a journalistic staple. Stead not only brought it into a 'respectable' middle-class paper. He made it central to journalism as political intervention. (Beetham, 1996: 125)*

At the time, there were also some critics who were concerned about its substance. In a journal article in 1887, Arnold named the new phenomenon which was becoming such a prominent issue in public debate the 'New Journalism':

> *We have had opportunities of observing a new journalism which a clever and energetic man has lately invented. It has much to recommend it; it is full of ability, novelty, variety, sensation, sympathy, generous instincts; its one great fault is that it is feather-brained. (1887: 638–9)*

The success of Stead's paper encouraged a proliferation of penny newspapers in London, all of which attempted to exploit the market for the sort of journalism he had pioneered, and their success in turn undermined the circulation of the *Pall Mall Gazette.* This suffered a further blow when much of its revenue was lost because advertisers were anxious about being associated with the scandalous reputation it had acquired. However, his significance for modern journalism goes beyond the technical details of his paper's innovations and the moral mission which informed his work. His 'government by journalism' (Stead, 1886) meant that the civic responsibilities of the journalist and increasingly of the editor were forced to the forefront of the agenda. Stead was particularly prominent in this, using his imprisonment as a campaigning weapon to have the issues raised by the 'Maiden Tribute' story aired in public meetings up and down the country and to bring well-known figures to contribute to the debate he had started. The editor in the most melodramatic way had become the news.

The Extension of the New Journalism

The New Journalism was a combination of already existing features but these had been made more commercially attractive for a wider readership. In vehement opposition to the crusading conviction of Stead, Arnold believed that his New Journalism was the very antithesis of a medium which stimulated and elevated the masses (Baylen, 1972: 367) and was committed instead to the idea that it was commercially driven to find the basest tastes and opinions of the largest possible readership. In the way that the moment of its definition provided a fresh impetus to both the self-rationalization and the resulting critiques of journalism, it could be argued that the New Journalism was a discursive moment in the history of journalism. The clearest expression of its motivations were from Stead himself, spectacularly championing his own cause from prison and claiming the function of government by journalism as 'anybody paying a penny could cast a "vote" for a particular paper' (Stead, 1886: 655). Yet others saw the New Journalism as the natural extension of the traditions of the Fourth Estate:

> ... the newspaper press is the only strong means of keeping in check that prodigious evil, the decomposition of political probity ... its natural position of complete independency. (Greenwood, 1890: 118)

Much of the concern encapsulated in Arnold's article represented a kind of middle-class 'moral panic' that this sort of populist writing would incite the newly extended electorate, and this continued to reverberate into the new century. It was claimed that a shift in emphasis in the newspapers had meant that 'Instead of being the instructors of the people, many of our newspapers have become mere ministers to the passions of the people' (Adams, 1903: 584), while Perkin has commented retrospectively that it consisted of:

A knack of clever writing, great enterprise in bringing together the kind of infor-
mation which amuses or interests the public, tact in catching and following the first
symptoms of changes of opinion, a skilful pandering to popular prejudice. (1981: 51)

Stead was the champion of what Wiener sees as a longer process of the Americanization of the British press between 1830 and 1914 (Wiener, 1996: 61). Gossip, display advertising, sports news, human interest, fast stories transmitted by telegraph, cheap and increasingly visual newspapers, summary leads and front page news were all introduced to England in the 1890s. Many cheaper weekly publications, especially the Sunday papers, had adopted some of these features from the 1840s onwards in England but Stead had brought them to a daily readership. Stead, as well as being an innovator associated with the New Journalism, was an exception within the growing trend of the commercialized discourse of journalism as it widened its scope to broader and more profitable markets to the exclusion of social aims. Hampton (2004) has expressed this change in the emphasis and goal of journalism in terms of a shift from an 'educational ideal' to a 'representative' one, whereby newspapers stopped, in the main, trying to educate their readers and preferred instead to pander to what they considered were their already existing tastes. It was a shift from a didactic (i.e. explicitly setting out an educational agenda for readers) to a consumerist emphasis within journalism. Passion, moral indignation and political conviction were ousted by the more pragmatic requirements of a commercialized industry in order to maintain the interest and support of regular readers on behalf of the advertisers who provided the finance essential to its success. The dividing point at which he stood is well captured in the following:

The duty of journalism in the first half of the nineteenth century ... was not to
discover the truth. The emphasis was on the polemical power of the writer's pen.
Opinion and commentary were the essence of good journalism – except in the
recording of parliamentary activity where accuracy was considered vital ... By
the end of the century, technology and commercial need had elevated accuracy
and reliability, as well as the ability to meet the daily news deadlines, to the
heart of [the] profession of journalism. (Williams, 1998: 54–55)

It was this tension between the altruistic and commercial ambitions of journalism which was to shape the continuity of discourses around journalism to the present. By the end of the 1880s, Stead's idealistic vision for the New Journalism was obsolete. His missionary zeal was not in keeping with the more commercially successful miscellanies of his rivals. The business acumen of Newnes and later Harmsworth and Pearson allowed them to generate huge financial resources from broad-based magazine and periodical publishing, which they then invested in the development of daily newspapers that were able to integrate technological and stylistic innovations with the staples of popular print culture (Conboy, 2002) in order to make possible a daily journalism with the highest possible popular, and therefore commercial, appeal. Competition meant that success in the popular market began to converge around one commercialized and dominant form of newspaper.

Drawing in the Popular Audience

The *Star* extended this trend towards populism. Edited by T.P. O'Connor from 1888 until 1890, it was a halfpenny evening paper which was radical in both its politics and its layout and, as such, represented a continuation of the accelerating trends of the New Journalism but presented these in a more commercially acceptable form. O'Connor espoused a brighter method of writing, speed and human interest and also expressed a desire to demonstrate that: ' ... the journal is a weapon in the conflict of ideas ... '. In addition he was aware of journalism's need to gain the attention of the reader in a world of accelerating distractions:

> *We live in an age of hurry and of multitudinous newspapers ... To get your ideas across through the hurried eyes into the whirling brains that are employed in the reading of a newspaper there must be no mistake about your meaning: to use a somewhat familiar phrase, you must strike your reader right between the eyes.*
> *(O'Connor, 1889: 434)*

Its radicalism, following the style of the popular Sunday newspapers, and especially *Reynolds' Newspaper*, was leavened with human interest on a daily basis. Its layout broke up information much in the style of *Answers* and *Tit-Bits*, but with a news-oriented content that distinguished it from these papers. Its innovations included the Stop Press and lower case type for its cross-heads and lesser headlines. Its essential novelty, according to Williams, was that from the date of its publication the New Journalism began to look like what it was (Williams, 1961: 221).

The style of the New Journalism encapsulated the changing relationship between reader and newspaper. There was more sport, crime and entertainment and less politics, all in a livelier style and laid out more clearly in an attempt to be more broadly accessible and therefore more profitable. There was also a commercial imperative to cultivate a consistent editorial identity that was expressed as a more individual 'voice' within this new breed of popular paper. Familiarity bred profit. Salmon interprets the way in which the 'discourse of journalism should so insistently declare its personalized character' (200: 29) as inevitable at this point in the commercialization of journalism as a rhetorical strategy standing in for its lack of any authentic relationship with its readers. A political irony here with implications which continue to resonate within popular journalism today is that as readers were increasingly addressed in a more personal tone about matters which touched the everyday in their newspapers, they were correspondingly being marginalized from politics in those same newspapers (Hampton, 2001: 227). Above all, journalism in the daily press began to accommodate a more complete range of human experience as part of the spectrum of journalism's output, including the trivial and the sensational, confirmation that 'it is the sound principle to which we shall all come at last in literature and journalism, that everything that can be talked about can also be written about' (O'Connor, 1889: 430).

Creating a Mass Daily Publication: Harmsworth's *Daily Mail*

The *Daily Mail* was launched as 'THE BUSY MAN'S DAILY JOURNAL' and was an immediate commercial success, backed by the fortune Harmsworth had amassed in periodical publication and an appreciation of the importance of the link between advertising, capital investment and circulation. It was presented not as a cheap newspaper but as a bargain, well worth the small outlay: 'A Penny Newspaper for One Halfpenny'. It was traditional in that it carried advertisements but no news on its front page. In terms of its layout, headings and subheadings allowed for the gist of a piece to be taken in at speed. It contained no long articles as each piece was broken down into short sections with a great variety of coverage and lots for idealized woman readers who had been hitherto been a neglected part of the daily newspaper's audience. The daily women's column soon became a whole page and soon after they were targeted specifically and regularly in the Daily Magazine section.

Chalaby (2000: 33) argues the case for Northcliffe's position as the creator of a newly commercial form of journalism based on his combination of managerial and editorial skills. He certainly provided more news than rival publications, famously setting out his priorities in the following terms: 'It is hard news which captures readers ... and it is features which hold them' (English, 1996: 6). He insisted that his reporters wrote in a lively and engaging fashion no matter what the topic in order to differentiate his newspapers from the dull routine transmissions coming from the news agencies. There was news of sensations and disasters and crime reporting, all of which were successfully grafted onto his daily newspapers from the tradition of the Sunday press. Despite its emphasis on news there was, in fact, less politics than in any other daily paper. This has been reported as characteristic of his overall approach to the balance of content within his papers: 'We must not let politics dominate the paper ... [t]reat politics as you treat all other news – on its merits. It has no 'divine right' on newspaper space' (Clarke, 1931: 127), arguing that, through this emphasis on variety and topicality, newspapers should 'touch life at as many points as possible' (Fyfe, 1930: 270).

Yet his *Daily Mail* did not sensationalize by the standards of the day, certainly in comparison with the most popular Sunday newspapers, and moved to positions it was confident would gain the support of his lower middle-class readership. It reached its first million in daily sales by 1900 in large part stimulated by an exaggerated patriotic chauvinism that was termed 'jingoism', in particular relating to the Boer War (Hughes, 1986) which had by this point become a common feature of the New Journalism (Wiener, 1988b: 56). Such jingoism fulfilled all the overt attraction of banal nationalism for a mass audience (Billig, 1995) and Harmsworth turned the mediation of that national community into commercial gold. Under him, the ownership of newspapers had become a crucial element in the development of journalism (Chalaby, 2000: 29) and whereas the content had always been of central importance he now orientated the appeal of his paper predominantly towards the advertisers through its mass circulation, charging them rates based on every 1,000 copies sold, and in doing so he turned a mass audience into a source of institutional and personal wealth as well as of political power (Smith, 1973: 27). The genius of Harmsworth (Lord Northcliffe after 1907) lay in his ability to harness consumption, circulation and profit rather than any journalistic experimentation, confirming that:

> *Whereas the 'New Journalism' had been a radical alternative to the more conservative newspapers, Northcliffe created a popular journalism which was less interested in political and social action per se than as the means to increase circulation. (Goodbody, 1985: 23)*

Harmsworth's First Imitator: The *Daily Express*

Harmsworth's approach, hugely successful as it was on its own, was also to have an effect on the shape and content of journalism across the twentieth century because the very scale of his success left other proprietors little choice but to adapt the content of their newspapers to match or improve upon the pattern he had set, in order to achieve the profits which he had established as being of paramount importance to the commercial viability of any newspaper.

On 26 April 1900 the *Daily Express* was launched as a rival to the *Daily Mail* to exploit the new mass market for popular daily journalism which Harmsworth had opened. The paper itself innovated with regular news on the first page from 1901, a feature which had first been seen in 1892 in the *Morning* (Wiener, 1996) as part of this evening newspaper's distinctive shift from the respectable attraction of daily morning newspapers to the commercial classes and much more of a move towards market appeal and daily sales on the street.

Adapting the Language of the Popular Press

The language of this journalism was as important a site of change as its visual appeal and organizational practices. Matheson has identified one of the most important shifts of the early twentieth century in the way a totally new version of journalistic language came into being and was shared to a large extent across the range from quality to popular newspapers. This involved much more editorial intervention to make copy fit the format of a paper and saw the development of house-styles which attempted to fashion a much more unified approach to using a combination of language, the standardization of layout and even the range of opinions expressed in order to create the impression of a uniform identity throughout a paper. The role of a sub-editor was pivotal in shaping this new language in order to fit the copy into a format which allowed a newspaper to be read on the move, and tailoring it to fit the space available within the pictorial and advertising space (Matheson, 2000: 565). Smith also considers the language of this period's journalism as having undergone a fundamental change. The 'story' became the basic molecular element of journalistic reality, and the distinctions of categories of news into hard and soft became reconfigured as part of its discourse (Smith, 1978: 168). By 1900 daily journalism had become an area of increasing specialization and professionalization, with subeditors and managers of clearly delineated departments, with advertising playing a more central role and more scope for the political ambitions of powerful owners. Some journalists, particularly on large national newspapers, were now becoming well paid, increasing the status if not the reputation of journalism. The journalism of this period enabled a textual inscribing of many of the major characteristics of this era in a radically restructured format:

> *The entrepreneurial component of editing and publishing, the professionalization of journalists and journalism, and the transition from the wealthy, educated, leisured reader to the working, literate reader of the middle classes are inscribed in the changing cultural formations of the periodical and newspaper press throughout the period. (Brake, 1988: 10)*

Conclusion

Some commentators, such as Leavis (1932: 182–183), have argued that the popularization of early twentieth-century mass journalism had a negative cultural effect. She claimed that the papers of Newnes, Harmsworth and Pearson created a cultural division that had not existed before. There had certainly been no evidence of mass lower-class readerships in the fare of the daily newspapers before them, since this readership had remained marginalized within a lower public sphere of weekly newspapers and occasional magazines, broadsides and pamphlets. The most considerable achievement of the New Journalism was to make this reading public more tangible and – in commercially targeting the lower classes for the first time in daily newspaper form – it indicated the growing reality of the economic attractiveness of the lower classes as simultaneously a mass readership and a mass market for advertising. Certainly, it brought a further de-politicization of the working person's journalism as it sought out beneficial advertising connections that were unlikely to be associated with any form of radicalism. The political and generic implications of mass journalism have been well articulated by Tulloch:

> *To assemble mass readerships, the new press had to adopt the formula of the popular Sunday press and the burgeoning magazines. Mass readerships are essentially a coalition of different tastes, interests and political positions. Newspapers had to be created that had 'something for everyone'. The process pushed newpapers towards a consensus politics that aimed to maximize the audience. (Tulloch, 2000: 142)*

The changes ushered in by the New Journalism began to make their presence felt across the whole field of journalism. The kind of headlines Stead had borrowed from

American journalism and used in the *Pall Mall Gazette* had become integrated into the layout of *The Times* by 1887, along with an extensive use of sub-headings, and soon this integration of many of the features which had begun with Newnes and Stead had become the subject of a commentary across the press, such as in this example from *The Queen* of 1900:

> *This is an inquisitive age: all daily papers from the august* Times *downwards have now their daily column of personal news, and few are the magazines which do not publish monthly some report of an interview with this or that celebrity. So keen is the general thirst for information touching the private life of every individual. The telegraph wire and the penny post, the periodical press and the special reporter have, during the last half-century, provided the curious with new and extraordinary means of gratifying their relish for personal detail. (White, 1970: 78)*

All subsequent developments within the journalism of the twentieth century and into the next have been structured by the establishment of mass-popular journalism as the dominant and defining model. Movement along the spectrum and within it, as it adds new technological dimensions, is determined by a complex negotiation with that simple observation. Modern journalism after 1896 has been a balancing act between the demands of a commercialized journalism industry and the interest and even interests of the people, either as citizens or, more often, as consumers.

FURTHER READING

Caterall, P., Seymour-Ure, C. and Smith, A. (eds) (2000) *Northcliffe's Legacy*. Basingstoke: Macmillan. This provides a range of commentary and critique on this most influential of newspaper men in the early twentieth century.

Chalaby, J. (1998) *The Invention of Journalism*. Basingstoke: Macmillan.

Hampton, M. (2004) *Visions of the Press in Britain, 1850–1950*. Urbana and Chicago: University of Illinois Press. This provides an overview of the ways in which views of journalism as well as the practice of journalism itself changed over a period of a hundred years – invaluable in considering the ways in which functions and definitions of journalism have changed over time.

Jackson, K. (2001) *George Newnes and the New Journalism in Britain, 1880–1910. Culture and Profit*. Aldershot: Ashgate. This gives a detailed account of the changes in mass print culture ushered in by this seminal figure, who had an enormous influence on popular journalism at the turn of the century.

Wiener, J. (ed.) (1988) *Papers For the Millions: The New Journalism in Britain, 1850–1914*. New York: Greenwood. This provides a definitive exploration of the integration of the 'New Journalism' into Britain at the end of the nineteenth century and how it was to shape much of the century which followed.

2

The Impact of Broadcasting and the Public Sphere

Introduction

Starting from the creation of the BBC this chapter will look at the key developments and themes relating to public service broadcasting in both its state-sponsored and its commercial varieties, and how these have contributed to shifting emphases in journalism. Two centuries after the first acknowledgement that periodical publications might serve the public as a sphere of discussion with those in authority as chronicled by Habermas (1992) broadcasting technologies were politically channelled into a second manifestation of the public sphere which was to have a profound effect upon the understanding of journalism within British culture.

Just like the first public sphere, the journalism of broadcast public service has not been without criticism of its lack of inclusivity or its innate conservatism, yet despite these reservations it has managed to radically alter perceptions of journalism's function and the extent to which this can be related to and distinguished from other media products. This second public sphere has been shaped by the hierarchical restrictions of central government just as the periodical press of the early eighteenth century had been, but it has also had as interesting an impact on the evolution of a democratic engagement with the public as its older relation. This chapter will introduce discussions of the interplay between technology and journalism as a public service. It will explore the impact of the arrival of radio into the world of a print monopoly and consider the reaction of the press to broadcasting within its own tradition of 'educational' and 'representational' ideals (Hampton, 2004) together with the increasing influence of a third 'entertainment' ideal. It will also examine the ways in which the early conventions of radio influenced the form and content of broadcast journalism – conventions which have had a lasting effect on the public's expectations of impartiality and balance in broadcasting in general. This examination will include the BBC's attempt to construct a national popular audience, in part to justify its public funding, and the ways in which the tone of that popular address has shifted from paternal to populist over a century. It will then move on to consider the impact of television journalism from its introduction to the commercialized variant in the form of ITN from 1955, and the cumulative effect of commercial pressures on the journalism of public service broadcasting as it strove to articulate the interests and opinions of the people.

The Potential of Radio

The first new technology of the twentieth century to have an influence on journalism was radio. It was to add a completely new reach and status to journalism's repertoire and it was to do this, in the first instance in Britain at least, protected from the economic pressures for profitability that had come to define the activities of most other areas of journalism and, furthermore, as an attempt to provide a politically independent public service. The tone and reach of radio journalism were to have consequences for the more established forms of print journalism and would later be influential in the subsequent development of a distinct British television journalism tradition.

The vital decisions which were to mark the social and economic identity of broadcast journalism as a public service for most of the twentieth century were taken in a few short steps. In November 1922, the British Broadcasting Company was formed, along the lines of a public utility such as a gas, water or electricity company and with John Reith as its General Manager. It was made up from the range of companies who were then selling radio sets licensed by the Post Office and who had been granted a monopoly to avoid what was assumed would otherwise be a descent into competitive chaos. Protection from foreign competition was granted as a commercial reward for putting up the initial financial investment, and in addition a proportion of the revenue from the licences was returned to the company. It was, in the words of one historian, 'a curious hybrid of commercial interest and government responsibility' (Street, 2002: 28). The potential importance of broadcast journalism to the health of democracy and to the ability of the public to participate in political decision making was understood from the start and has continued to be signalled by the number of government reports that have subsequently been commissioned, from the Sykes Committee of 1923 to Ofcom in 2007. Emanating from this identification of the democratic imperative at the heart of this variety of broadcast journalism, the development of the concept of public service broadcasting has both shaped other forms of journalism and enabled broadcast journalism to differentiate itself as a communication form throughout the twentieth century. To achieve this, regulation has played an essential part in the maintenance of broadcast journalism's role as a purveyor of information deemed to be of importance to the national population and in sustaining democratic participation, unlike the press which has been able to structure itself with minimal state intervention into what was, in effect, a purely commercial relationship with its audience.

In 1923 the Sykes Committee rejected advertising as a possible form of revenue for the company, fearing that it would lead to what was perceived as the anarchy of American broadcasting, and it was in the pages of its report that the concept of broadcasting as a form of 'public service' was coined (Crisell, 1997: 21). Yet in its early years, journalism was by no means a central part of the BBC's output. The Newspaper Proprietors' Association pre-emptively pressured government into restricting radio news broadcasts to one 30-minute bulletin per day without features or interviews, as they feared that radio news would prove 'more fleet than

Fleet Street' (Crisell, 1997: 15) and compromise the circulations of their own products. There was to be no news until after seven o'clock in the evening and no news from any other source than the main news agencies (Reuters, the Press Association, the Exchange Telegraph and Central News). The BBC's journalism was therefore simply a second-hand re-working of the agencies' information, and in order to emphasize this fact, it had to announce the provenance of its content at the opening of each of its bulletins. It was dry stuff indeed, much more medium than message. Yet despite the primitive nature of radio's early journalism, newspapers refused to carry listings of any of its programmes for fear that they might detract from their own fare. This led to the appearance of the *Radio Times* as early as 1923 to counter this stance.

Navigating Political Challenges

Something of the political background to the emergence of radio journalism can be deduced from the fact that the Representation of the People Act of 1918 had given universal voting rights based on residence to those aged over 21 and over 30 in the case of women. This meant that from that point onwards it was essential for the government to pay much more attention to the widest possible public opinion in order to bolster its own democratic credibility. Reith was therefore being entrusted with the task of producing a politically acceptable role for radio journalism in making a distinctive contribution to this broadened democracy in his negotiations with newspaper owners, Post Office officials and politicians. His ability to juggle these competing demands within the new medium was first tested during the General Strike that took place between 3 and 12 May 1926. The strike was called by the Trades Union Congress in support of coal miners who were resisting attempts by the owners of coal mines to impose wages and conditions on their employees. The TUC called on key workers such as transport workers, steel workers, printers and dockers to come out in support of the miners. The General Strike finished after negotiations between the government and the TUC ensured that discussions between the mine owners and the miners should resume, although the miners' strike continued until much later in the year. During the ten days of the strike all national newspapers were closed by industrial action. With restrictions on its broadcasting of news on the national strike lifted, the British Broadcasting Company was the sole national forum for the dissemination of news apart from the *British Gazette* – a temporary government propaganda publication. It broadcast five daily bulletins and tried to provide an authoritative and balanced range of reports, as well as attempting to demonstrate to its listeners and to the government that it could remain independent. Its approach satisfied neither the trades unions nor government absolutely, but the service provided the listening public with news in what would otherwise have been an information blackout during a national crisis. Reith was thus the mastermind of an approach which sought to both inform and to create at least an impression of consensus in the midst of a national emergency.

Aiming for a National Consensus

From this point radio journalism could claim to have established an operational position around which national opinion could form, thereby playing a part in the construction of a reinvigorated sense of national community. It has been pointed out, however, that this construction of consensus was far less impartial than it claimed to be, as it filtered out the social causes of the massive gulf between the government and working people which had triggered the General Strike in the first place (Scannell and Cardiff, 1991: 33). The political and cultural consequences of this approach to balance remain evident in the traditions and practices of today's broadcast journalism, as it still addresses a national-specific audience, underplays any analysis of social issues insofar as these are represented as being driven by events rather than processes, and remains prohibited from editorializing.

Radio journalism increased its credibility after the General Strike because the carefully constructed tone of sobriety within Reith's approach could be contrasted against the extremes of opinionated newspapers (such as the *Daily Herald* on the left and the *Daily Mail* and the *Daily Express* on the right of the political spectrum) with which both public and politicians were familiar. Its location outside the direct influence of advertising and the financial imperative to make a profit, combined with both a subscription paid via a licence fee from the general public as consumers and its constitutional commitment to provide a balanced approach to political issues – all created an impression of a medium of consensus which could serve as a guide to citizens in their decision making. The increasingly profit-driven, commercial press was more transparently a business than a balanced report on important current affairs and was not – after Prime Minister Lloyd George's purchase of the *Daily Chronicle* in 1918 in order to further consolidate his party's influence, and the well-publicized political machinations of newspaper owners such as Beaverbrook and Northcliffe – sufficiently above the suspicion that it could be bought and programmed by those with the money and influence to do so. The hopes for radio journalism as it arrived on the political scene of the 1920s could not have been higher:

> *A sense of civic responsibility and a wider knowledge of public affairs might be encouraged through common access to the discourses of public life, through the balanced presentation of the facts and the issues at stake in current political debates and policies. These interlocking processes were to be the desired effects of a conception of broadcasting as an instrument of democratic enlightenment, as a means of promoting social unity through the creation of a broader range of shared interests, tastes and social knowledge than had previously been the portion of the vast majority of the population. (Scannell and Cardiff, 1991: 13)*

The recommendations of the Crawford Committee of 1926 led to the founding, by Royal Charter, of the British Broadcasting Corporation in 1927 with John Reith continuing as its head. Broadcasting in Britain, unlike its counterpart in the USA and its print rivals at home, was released from the pressure to make a profit as it was envisaged that a licence fee would provide adequate finance. It began a prolonged struggle with government to produce a definition in practice of a public service medium, run on behalf of a public and free from sectional political or financial influence but with a different form of pressure – to negotiate and maintain its independence from state sponsors. This is a struggle which persists to the present day and one – as in so much that is of relevance to journalism – which requires an understanding of historical context for a full comprehension of the current issues and debates.

Fear and Morality

From the start Reith had an extremely moral view of the role that radio broadcasting in general, and not simply its news service, should play in developing a broader sense of the national community as an enlightened and informed public (Reith, 1924). It was therefore designed with the explicit intention of contributing to the shaping of society as a whole (Williams, 1990). Although not construed as a predominantly journalistic medium, the triple goals of the BBC in general – to educate, inform and entertain – were entirely suitable for a workable vision of British journalism in its broadcast form.

While the anxieties of the newspaper owners with regard to this broadcast rival were predominantly economic, those of politicians were more grounded in concerns over the potential of a more immediate transmission of political reporting. The content and style of broadcasting were determined to a large extent by a fear of radio's potential to brainwash listeners. Such fears were to appear justified throughout the twenties and thirties as the totalitarian regimes springing up in Germany, Italy and the Soviet Union employed broadcasting to shape the politics of the era, and subsequent fears of the negative cultural effects of mass communication such as 'brainwashing' then became commonplace among cultural commentators. In fact, radio journalism was constructed around a set of longer-term anxieties, particularly those concerning the political potential of the populace which were reminiscent of the fears which had accompanied the development of political reporting in print in previous centuries as encouraging the power of the uncontrollable mob (Conboy, 2002: 23–42). What public service broadcast journalism needed to achieve was a balance between these older anxieties and the scope of the new technology, between the economic implications of public ownership and the weight of government expectations that it should retain a balance which was all too often lacking in the newspaper press.

Creating Journalism for the Listening Audience

The BBC's performance during the General Strike may have persuaded the government that radio journalism could be trusted to develop its own news, albeit still heavily dependent on the same sources which supplied the newspapers with much of their material, yet the development of alternative networks for newsgathering was slow. It was broadcasting five hours of news per week by the end of the 1920s and had tentatively started to develop an independent network of reporters and sources, but it did not found its own dedicated news department until 1934. In 1930 the BBC won an important victory in its move towards autonomy by constructing a specifically aural approach to the reporting of news. It gained the right to alter Reuters' material so that it could be rewritten in a way which was better suited to a voice reading rather than an internal ear reading.

To counter the growing sensationalism of the newspaper press in the 1930s and its increasing dependence on circulation boosting stunts and competitions, the BBC set out to reinforce its own notions of taste, tact and propriety. One consequence of this was to present a voice on air that used the accent of the Home Counties' upper middle classes, which sat somewhat at odds with its remit to provide an inclusive public service. If radio had made the metaphorical voice of print journalism literally audible, it was doing the same for social class.

Questions of access and accountability became extended to the audience in ways which had hitherto only been implicit through circulation figures and profitability in print journalism. In establishing its credentials as a public service broadcaster, keen to include the opinions of an audience paying a compulsory licence fee, the BBC introduced the Listener Research Unit in 1936. In the same year, the Ullswater Committee recommended the ground rules for proportional broadcasting time during election campaigns for the major parties, again indicating the politically inclusive and balanced role which radio journalism was intended to play in allowing access to politics to the wider electorate.

War Shapes a National Channel of Communication

The Second World War was to prove a defining period for the development of the prestige of the BBC institutionally, both at home and abroad. Its journalism in particular became emblematic as a model of democratic discourse to counter the flow of broadcast totalitarianism. The newspapers, handicapped during the war by a shortage of paper and in a period of rationing, the advertising budgets they had become so dependent on were seriously diminished. Yet the BBC's journalism did more than simply compensate for the spaces left by newspapers: it evolved into something much more assured in its mission to inform.

The news, for example, started to be constructed in a way which was more consistently directed towards patterns of speech. Attempts were also made to be more inclusive of the social varieties of English and to dispel the impression that a Received Pronunciation accent was either more authoritative or acceptable than regional variants. In becoming more sensitive to accusations that it was nothing more national than the voice of the southern English middle classes, the BBC's deployment of Wilfred Pickles, a Yorkshireman with a strong regional accent, was an emphatic if short-lived signal of its ambition to be more inclusive in selecting newsreaders from as representative a range of backgrounds as possible. A longer-lived experiment was with Pickles's *We Speak for Ourselves* from 1940 to 42, which travelled the country collecting the stories of ordinary people from factory workers to housewives.

The insistence on an accurate and balanced reporting of the war for radio listeners was underlined as the only viable strategy by R.T. Clark of the News Department: 'It seems to me that the only way to strengthen the morale of the people whose morale is worth strengthening is to tell them the truth, and nothing but the truth, even if the truth is horrible' (Briggs, 1961: 656). The growing maturity and variety within radio journalism, displayed from its bulletins to its actuality began to gain for it a level of broad credibility which it had not enjoyed before the war. Furthermore, as it was the provider of news to as much as half of the population at nine o'clock each evening, 'it gave the individual an unprecedented sense of herself as part of the larger community' (Crisell, 1997: 62).

Growth in Content and Scope

During the war years the most significant change was the BBC's size, as it grew from 4,000 staff in 1939 to 6,000 by the beginning of 1940, and by November of that year to nearly 11,000, with journalism being the biggest beneficiary by far of this upturn (Curran and Seaton, 2003: 129). The importance of its journalism was paramount, as the focus shifted after the defeated invasion at Dunkirk in 1940 to providing credible information about the state of hostilities to the Home Front. Unsurprisingly, Mass Observation reported that radio had become the most important medium of information, already surpassing most of the press as a reliable source by 1941 (1949: 41). The daily news programme *War Report* from 6 June 1944 (D-Day) onwards garnered regular audiences of 10 to 15 million (Briggs, 1970: 662).

Postwar, the BBC was able to display a new-found confidence not just in its ability to represent accurately the events of the nation and the world beyond its shores but, in addition, in its aiming to provide access to much of the inner workings of the national community and their opinions and tastes:

> The BBC tries to show to its listeners the different currents of thought, the full and democratic flow of ideas, and the diverse opinions, that go to make up the voice of the British people. (Jacob, 1947: 16)

Many wartime developments in radio journalism were integrated into its peacetime routines. Postwar, most news was still sourced from agency material although there was a growing trend towards foreign and specialist correspondents. Its coverage of politics also progressed into a more sustained format with *Today in Westminster* which ran from 1949.

The BBC had also developed a particular brand of imperial public service broadcasting from 1932 in its Empire Service and this was incorporated in 1939 into the Overseas European Services. The overseas reputation of the BBC after the war was enhanced to the extent that it could continue from 1948 as the more formalized

BBC External Services. From 1965 this was consolidated into the BBC World Service which was from 1993 integrated into BBC Worldwide. It has provided a unique global variant of public service broadcasting which may have had its roots in imperial communication but has subsequently been shaped into something altogether more subtle, and in developing a different set of news values to those of domestic service it has achieved a consistently high level of credibility on the world stage (Wallis and Baran, 1990: 51).

The Advent of Commercial Radio Journalism

There has been little to challenge the BBC's dominance of public service journalism from the commercial radio sector. In 1970 the Conservative government favoured extending the commercial radio network, especially at a local level, and subsequently from 1973 new commercial radio stations were allowed to provide news bulletins. However, a fifty year developmental lag had left few areas to colonize or exploit commercially and therefore radio journalism in its commercial form was restricted to a kind of journalism which could be wrapped around programmes, typically drive-time bulletins that could make money for advertisers, with less impact on the overall shape of radio journalism than the BBC's journalism had had. This meant that despite the fact that by 1995 there were 160 commercial radio stations to BBC's 38 local stations, there was little innovation or challenge to compete with the BBC's radio journalism range. One notable exception was LBC News Radio which from 1973 provided London with an all news and information service, becoming specifically renowned for the quality of its current affairs programming, particularly in its phone-ins on topical matters. In general terms commercial radio journalism has concentrated on softer issues, preferring to keep a distance from 'broadcasterly' modes of reporting and staying closer to audience-focused discussions (Starkey and Crisell, 2009: 19). Yet even in those areas where commercial radio had made some sort of progress the BBC has been quick to develop its own branded alternatives. A good example here is Radio 5 Live's sport and news which from 28 March 1994 provided regular half-hourly bulletins but supplemented these with a broad range of coverage in order to put a popular spin on a full range of issues that related to public interest in a non-specialist vein (Hendy, 1994: 15–16).

Digital Innovation in Radio Journalism Audience Construction

However, despite the dominance demonstrated by the range, variety and quality of BBC radio journalism, the journalism provision of Independent Radio News in recent years has demonstrated how digital technology is enabling a commercial news provider to provide much more specific niches within the public sphere. IRN provides news bulletins, packages and text copy for most of the commercial radio stations in the UK. No organization has the expertise or the financial might to challenge the BBC's large-scale radio journalism provision, but IRN is exploring how far it can tailor news bulletins via a small team of journalists towards particular lifestyle markets. IRN provides four-hourly bulletin services, remodelled for their clarity of appeal to specific target groups – a three-minute, mid-market, BBC Radio-2-style service; a 90-second, faster-paced and upbeat tabloid-style service; and two other bespoke bulletin services for Kiss FM and Magic FM. Niblock and Machin (2007) have studied how this can be made possible by combining digital broadcast technologies and increasingly sophisticated consumer-monitoring through audience behaviour data, providing a 'gatekeeper' role which is not located in one specific individual or group but in a synthesis of the journalist, the advertiser and the consumer. This then demonstrates how a contemporary engagement with broadcast technologies can shift the boundaries of what had become established as the traditional audience for radio:

> *An important notion arising from this study is to what extent the concept of 'public' has become reconfigured as a target 'market' in commercial journalism. (Niblock and Machin, 2007: 188)*

Television Journalism: A Slow Start

In the wake of radio broadcasting, the next technologically led shift in the content and style of journalism was one that began with television journalism but whose implications immediately started to have an effect on all news media. From the 1920s onwards Movietone had provided newsreels to the cinema industry before the advent of television in an example of the continuing tradition of the blending of news and entertainment in journalism, but cinematic news was to be gradually eased out of the journalism market by the arrival of television. Television broadcasting was to provide an unfulfilled promise of a different emphasis to public service broadcasting until the intervention of commercial innovations triggered a genuine engagement by the BBC with the full potential of this new technology for journalism.

On 2 November 1936 the BBC started a television service that was limited to an area of 100 miles around Alexandra Palace in North London. Gaumont and British Movietone newsreels provided the news for the BBC as they had been doing for the cinema, rather than the BBC providing its own televised journalism, since its television menu was concentrated more on a diet of light entertainment and outside broadcasts, most notably the coronation procession of George VI in May 1937. It was only after 1946 that the BBC began to make wider use of the medium for journalism. Despite the head start which it had had in terms of broadcast journalism experience, and also despite the speed of developments in communications technology during the war, the conservatism of the BBC's version of television journalism was rooted in its isolation from any national competitor and its adherence to a particularly narrow view of the potential role of the medium for journalism.

Anxieties about the compatibility of the new medium with the corporation's rigorous standards were expressed by the BBC's first Controller of Television, Maurice Gorham, who raised concerns about the need for television news to 'subordinate the primary functions of news to the needs of visual presentation' (Wyndham Goldie, 1977: 41), and he considered that a large part of his responsibility was to maintain a vigilance in matching visual material to the corporation's traditional standards of trust and impartiality. In these early years, as an illustration of this cautious approach, the idea of a news presenter on camera was considered a threat to the corporation's obligation to observe impartiality, so in order to achieve a compromise within the new medium an anonymous male voice read the bulletins over a sequence of illustrations such as charts, still photographs and captions (Scannell, 1996: 14).

The Broadcasting Monopoly Cracks

The Beveridge Report, published in January 1951, provided the first critical overview of the structure and provision of the BBC, concentrating on the issue of its monopoly and stressing the public service contribution of broadcasting to the democratic process:

> *Generally, we should like to see broadcasting used more and more as a means of assisting the democracy to understand the issues upon which it is required to decide at elections (1951: 265).*

It was highly critical of the London-bias of the BBC's journalism, an observation which was to influence debate on the regional structure of future broadcasting developments. However, its general conclusion was to recommend the continuation of the BBC's monopoly provision. Despite this endorsement of the corporation, it was a dissident report from Selwyn Lloyd which was to prove the driving force for Conservative counter-proposals when they regained office in October of that year, because the Conservative party was concerned, according to Wyndham-Goldie, that the BBC had managed to establish 'a radical attitude in political matters' and that it was 'biased against Conservatism' (1977: 105). Selwyn Lloyd's report argued for a commercial reshaping of broadcasting which would include both a regionalization of broadcasting and the decentralization of the BBC. There was none more vociferous in their condemnation of this development that Reith, who in giving his evidence to the Committee claimed that in his view commercial broadcasting was akin to 'dog racing, smallpox and the bubonic plague' (Crisell, 1997: 86).

The Television Bill of March 1954 introduced commercial television to Britain and included an Independent Television Authority to supervise the required balance, accuracy and impartiality which, it was felt, would continue to inform the structure and public service component of its journalism. The group of regionally based companies which made up ITV, all contributed to the Independent Television News which provided a national news service. ITN's first news broadcast on 22 September 1955 was differentiated from that of the BBC by its reliance on several popular and commercial American television strategies. In addition to its commercial dynamism, as ITN was dedicated solely to the gathering and presentation of news, it made a formidable rival to the BBC as a journalism outlet. ITN's mission was 'to make significant news more interesting, more comprehensive and more acceptable' (Crisell, 1997: 92). Some of the differences in approach were immediate. As contrasted with the BBC's output, it was quicker to exploit a scoop than its more cautious competitor. It pioneered vox pop interviews in support of stories in the news and brought a level of aggression in interviewing not seen on the BBC. This style of enquiry was to reconfigure the relationship between the State and broadcast journalism in ways which Reith could never have imagined, as it ushered in a new era, making politicians more accountable to the public via journalism and making politics more entertaining for the viewer. In its political coverage, ITN used fresh and articulate interviewers such as Robin Day and Chris Chataway, who rejected a deference to politicians as the standard approach and took a professional pride in asking probing and sometimes downright blunt questions. As if to underline the populist thrust of ITN's presentational style, Chataway was already a celebrity, having been a world record-breaking, 5,000 metre champion as recently as 1954; Day was soon to be voted the TV Personality of the Year by the Guild of TV Producers in 1957; and many of the editorial staff on the set were recruited from the popular end of Fleet Street. Day himself recalled 'ITN set new standards of rigour, enterprise and pace for television news, making the BBC version look stiff and stuffy, which it was. Ludicrous taboos were swept away by the post-1955 wind of change' (Day, 1989: 82). By 1956–7 the influence of this style of critical interviewing of politicians had become the norm (Seymour-Ure, 1991: 168). From the beginning, broadcasters wrote their own news to project their personality and input, and it is claimed that:

> *Their voices lacked the clerical blandness of many BBC announcers. They were permitted touches of humour and even of disrespect. (Hood, 1967: 106)*

It marked the beginning of a popularization of broadcast journalism both in its content and the audience it was aimed at. ITV was to become one of the drivers of a cultural move from deference – a popularizing dynamic of social change which assisted the erosion of class hierarchies of taste and distinction.

ITN news changed the terms of the debate on public service journalism entirely after 1955, generating the innovations which had lifted television into its own as a journalistic medium. The BBC's news was simply not as good, as exciting or as well presented as the new commercial variant. In particular, the introduction of television, which was independent from government by reason of its commercial funding, was to restructure the awkward collaboration between journalism and the State which had existed while the BBC held a monopoly in its public service provision. As a regionally based set of companies, ITV also boosted the quality of news in the regions. It was not just in its news bulletins that the difference was evident. From 1956 *This Week* was produced by Associated Rediffusion in an attempt to provide a similar sort of populist approach to current affairs; documentaries from another regional company, Granada, such as *Searchlight*, followed in 1958; and then *World in Action* in 1963 – all designed to challenge what was perceived as the middle-class orientation of the BBC's fare. Yet the quality of ITN's journalism and its influence in shaking the BBC out of its complacency would not have come about if it had not been for the intervention of a robust regulation of the quality of its public service news provision. The Independent Television Authority insisted on ITV's sticking to its commitment to quality and the length of news provision in the early days of ITN, despite the cost and also despite the initial unwillingness of the owners of the various regional companies which made up ITV to make this commitment on their own initiative.

The BBC Responds to Competition

The BBC was forced to respond to this new aesthetic of television journalism in order to retain its credibility as a public service in a newly competitive and inevitably populist environment. From 1959 Hugh Greene, as Head of News at the BBC, precipitated a reciprocal move to a more personalized and lively style. In order to effect this, old programmes were analysed and refashioned. Reporters began to write their own commentary and speak it over the pictures broadcast. More drive and enthusiasm – and above all a greater respect for the medium of television in all its visual aspects – were to be insisted upon. In fact, the popularization project within BBC journalism had developed such a momentum that Briggs (1995: 156) claims that editor in chief of BBC Television News from 1959, Stuart Hood, was of the view that its News Division should be 'as good as the *Daily Mirror*', which was at that time the most successful newspaper in the world, a tabloid with a circulation of over 4.5 million, which was larger than the audience for BBC television news. The BBC also began to respond within current affairs programming, extending its specific claim to distinctiveness in public service journalism. In 1955 Grace Wyndham Goldie took *Panorama* and changed it into a heavyweight contributor to political debate, thereby enhancing the journalistic agenda of television. Briggs underlines its contribution in the following terms:

> During the years after Suez, it became a major weekly event in itself, whatever might be happening on any continent. People stayed at home to see it: public figures, British and foreign, sought to appear on it. (1995: 164)

Other successful innovations included *Tonight*, which was introduced by the BBC on 18 February 1957 at 6.05 p.m. as a 40-minute news magazine that displayed a much more varied diet of entertainment, politics and even music. It was to provide an extremely influential model for early evening current affairs programmes.

Radio journalism responded to the competition of lively current affairs programmes on television by launching on 28 October 1957 what was to become its flagship for quality political journalism – the *Today* programme. This was to be the earliest successful example of a current affairs magazine broadcast at breakfast time.

It began as a general interest programme but soon became transformed into the hard news-dominated format familiar to contemporary audiences. It provides an interesting case of a programme moving away from softer, apolitical features towards being a harder-edged political show (Donovan, 1997) by creating a blend of current affairs, live interviews with politicians on the affairs of the moment, and in-depth political reporting. Its success provided a pattern for subsequent political reporting on the BBC, and the programme is now widely considered to set the nation's political agenda (Starkey and Crisell, 2009: 28).

ITN Ups the Stakes

The Pilkington Report of 1962 was to recommend changes in broadcasting policy which would have an impact on the quality of journalism on both the BBC and ITV. The most immediate beneficiary was the BBC, which was awarded a third channel in preference to ITV, a decision which enabled it to provide a popular late-night menu for its mainstream audience at the same time as developing the sort of in-depth late-night news review style which was to culminate in *Newsnight* in 1980 with its robust quizzing of politicians on the issues of the day. However, for commercial television the 1963 Television Act which followed on from Pilkington was to provide a much more robust role for the regulatory body, the Independent Television Authority, in order to ensure mainstream scheduling for current affairs programmes which dealt with live social issues (notably *This Week* and *World in Action*) as a journalism of 'social justice'. A two-way flow between state-sponsored and commercially funded variants therefore continued to shape the output of the two providers of television journalism.

ITN was again able to provide the initiative when it changed its successful format for main late-evening news in order to placate the ITA, which had insisted that the ITV companies should not only provide the finance for high quality news but also broadcast it at a time which would maximize viewing figures. After much internal debate within ITN because of concerns that it was risking the success of its short populist news format, *News at Ten* was launched on 3 July 1967. Until that point news bulletins had been short on both channels, varying in length in the early years from 12 to 15 minutes until the arrival of the 30-minute *News at Ten*, which for the first time on British television allowed for the more in-depth treatment of a series of carefully crafted and produced journalism packages. The BBC was forced to follow the lead and extend its own coverage to match. As in 1955 on ITN's launch, it was once again a 'symbolic moment' in television journalism (Seymour-Ure, 1991: 141).

Drawing on an American model, it employed two newscasters to develop pace and variety within the bulletin, with the newscasters playing off each other journalistically and stylistically and thus extending the projection of personality on screen. Such a two-man presentation team was new to British television, and this was also distinctive from other bulletins in a higher dependence on its own reporter-led packages and the blending of populist and serious. Interviews were used more frequently to develop and contextualize stories and there was a greater reliance on the visual presentation techniques and footage that had hitherto been associated with documentaries. The 30-minute slot enabled the ITN news to be both more populist – dealing with issues aimed at attracting and pleasing large audiences – as well as more detailed at the same time. The success of such news formats led to increased broadcasting hours for public service television journalism, with lunchtime news bulletins from 1972 and extended early evening news programmes from 1976 for both ITN and the BBC.

Thatcher and the Onslaught on Public Service Broadcasting

After such a period of consensus around the provision of public service broadcast journalism, which had spanned the best part of sixty years, the 1980s were to witness an attack on the BBC as a publicly funded service as well as those who produced politically engaged commercial television journalism. Suspicions among senior politicians of the political potential of broadcast journalism are nothing new and in fact these have contributed considerably to the shaping of its environment, but this period witnessed the most sustained and ideological assault that it has ever experienced (O'Malley, 1994; 2001). The BBC in particular had come to be regarded by the Conservatives in general, and Thatcher and her coterie in particular, as 'an irritatingly arrogant, cosily protected establishment dinosaur': they consequently had earmarked it for eradication in their radical right-wing revolution (Curran and Seaton, 2003: 208).

This hostility towards public service journalism in its BBC incarnation was manifested in three ways: first, via direct attacks on its journalism; second, by the placement of chairmen who were sympathetic to the Conservative government; and third, through the more incremental process of policy changes. There were clashes with the Conservative government over the BBC's attempts to provide analysis of the Falklands conflict in 1982 which saw Argentina and the UK at war over the sovereignty of these islands in the South Atlantic. Both *Panorama* and *Newsnight* were branded as traitorous and the Conservative-supporting tabloid newspaper, the *Sun*, cheered from the sidelines (Chippendale and Horrie, 1992: 123). This hostility was also directed towards ITV on account of their *Death on the Rock* investigation in 1988 and towards both broadcasters in the ban on Irish extremists on ITV and BBC between 1988–1994. This ban meant that the words of political representatives of the Republican and Loyalist groups in Northern Ireland could only be reported on television or radio if they were read by an actor.

The appointment of Chairmen of Governors who sympathized with Thatcher's perspectives on the BBC, in particular, gave the government a direct influence over the BBC, first in Stuart Young in 1983 and then in Marmaduke Hussey in 1986. Hussey in particular was used to manoeuvre out Alasdair Milne, the distinguished former BBC producer who had risen to become its Director General and had overseen most of the political arguments with the Conservatives in the early 1980s. Milne was replaced in 1987 by Michael Checkland, a Thatcher-supporting former accountant, as if to emphasize what was then becoming the central issue at the BBC.

This placing of political allies was augmented by Conservative pressures on broadcast journalism's regulatory bodies which culminated in the deregulatory Broadcasting Acts of 1990 and 1996. From the regulatory point of view, the Peacock Report of 1985 was set up with a brief to look into the possibility of introducing advertising onto the BBC. What it ended up recommending was a deregulation of commercial broadcasting which was subsequently to inform the 1990 Broadcasting Act. As a direct consequence of this legislation, the ITV companies would be awarded to a highest bidder not as previously, but after first satisfying the regulatory body of their commitment to a public service ethos. Cash and competition, not the quality of public provision, had become the decisive factors. The link between ITV and Channel 4 was severed and the Independent Broadcasting Authority became a 'light touch' Independent Television Commission which would not be as interventionist in matters of quality or resourcing. The volume of regional journalism continued to be prescribed but there was no recommendation as to the budgets which should be directed to this output, with obviously consequences for the quality and range of journalism produced.

As a result of these decisions, the 1990s saw a general decline in the amount of money invested in television journalism outside news (i.e. current affairs) and the elevation of market choice and value for money above concerns for the quality of provision. Yet it also produced the paradoxical outcome that the reforms handicapped the commercial providers of journalism, especially as their advertising market shrank, while they enhanced the position of a BBC invigorated by a brief to align itself in many of its operations in a more commercially aggressive manner.

John Birt and the BBC's Push for Populism

The direction of public service broadcasting, perhaps because it does not belong to the public directly, has often been determined by strong-minded individuals whose personal vision has chimed with the prevailing ideological and technological climate. One such person was John Birt. It would be fair to say that no individual since Reith has had such a direct impact on the shape and content of the BBC's journalism as Birt. He had produced *Weekend World* (1972–1988) for London Weekend Television and had also risen to be Head of Current Affairs at the same company. Birt had been interested not only in developing a brand of political journalism, interviews and agenda-setting for the Monday newspapers, but also and most especially in the intellectual preparation of its journalism, deploying a hard-hitting and cerebral presenter, Brian Walden, to this effect. It was a formula soon to become known as the Birtian 'method'. While at LWT in 1975 he penned what was to become the definition of his philosophy on television journalism:

> There is a bias in television journalism, but it is not a bias against any particular party or point of view – it is a bias against understanding. (Times, 28 February 1975)

He proposed longer items, more context and a populist approach to draw people who would not normally be interested in politics into the big themes of the day. The solution he proposed for the BBC was for a unified news and current affairs department with subject teams as the organizing principle for the station's output, with a mission to provide both information and analysis. In 1987 he was drafted in as Deputy Director General, to lend his production and editorial experience to the journalistically inexperienced Director General Michael Checkland, who had been appointed by the Conservative administration. In this role he took over responsibility for the recruitment and training of journalists in the newly integrated News and Current Affairs Directorate and from 1990, under his tutelage, bi-media journalism became the driving force for efficiencies of personnel and finance. From 1992 to 2000 he was Director General. In response to the challenges of commercial competition and hostility from Conservative politicians towards the very concept of the BBC as a public broadcaster, Birt's 'Issue Journalism' was introduced in an attempt to create a more in-depth variant of popular mainstream television news with a Reithian-sounding 'mission' to educate the viewer. It sought to provide less stories but with more perspective. This was to be counter-balanced by an attempt to provide great accessibility in current affairs but has since been interpreted as a drift towards more entertainment-driven values in the BBC's journalism. Birt's contribution to the news and current affairs agenda was profoundly influenced by the perceived necessity of providing the BBC with a distinctive brand of journalism in an increasingly congested market and legitimating its privileged position within public service broadcasting by offering a more popularized range of journalism.

Born (2005: 57) claims that the main emphasis of John Birt in coordinating the BBC's news and current affairs departments from 1987 was 'the need to give news stories a methodically researched, analytical context in order to provide more journalistic depth and superior understanding'. This has not been without its detractors. Birt sought to counter what he saw as the generic shortcomings of television journalism, its alleged 'bias against understanding', by expanding the time available to the news issues of the day, but was criticized for a style of reporting which was more centrally managed and more overtly didactic in its 'mission to explain'. There was also an increased popularization of political presentation, with presenters such as Andrew Marr breaking new ground in providing pithy and witty accounts of the day in Westminster with at least as much emphasis on coining an entertaining phrase as providing informational content.

Attempts at Renewal

In 1992 the BBC's own policy document *Extending Choice* started discussions about the renewal of the Charter planned for 1996 and stressed its continuing vision of public service journalism:

What then, are the defining characteristics of the BBC's public purpose?

Firstly, the BBC should aim to provide the comprehensive, in-depth and impartial news and information coverage across a range of broadcasting outlets that is needed to support a fair and informed national debate. (Franklin, 2001: 103)

Beyond the renewal of its charter and the creative interpretation of public service for a new age, the BBC's 2002 digital television initiative was a well-orchestrated and well-timed move into digital provision, and it underpinned the success of its website at home and abroad as one of the most visited and well-regarded of national broadcast sites. Nevertheless, it was a vision toughened by an appreciation of its place in an increasingly competitive market environment that was mostly hostile to state-sponsored public broadcasting. In response to technological and economic challenges, it has launched news channels such as BBC News 24, BBC Online and BBC Worldwide, with the latter proving one of the BBC's most successful income-generating and fully commercial ventures. The drive to compete, as Ursell (2001: 188–189) has pointed out in her analysis, is just as apparent in the publicly funded BBC as it is in any of its commercial rivals.

As is often the case with public service journalism, however, it was a political and not a commercial issue which was to jolt the BBC into a reconsideration of both its status and its relationship to the State. In the wake of the Gilligan Affair of 2003, Hutton (2004) found that the government had not acted to 'sex-up' intelligence regarding Iraq's alleged weapons of mass destruction, as BBC journalist Andrew Gilligan had claimed, and that it was the BBC which should be considering its journalistic practices. The Chairman and Director both resigned. The Neil Review (2004: 6) ordered into its practices listed five traditional principles which should underpin the corporation's journalism, almost as a twenty-first century recapitulation of public service broadcasting. These were:

- Truth and accuracy.
- Serving the public interest.
- Impartiality and diversity of opinion.
- Independence.
- Accountability.

Recommendations included warnings on the use of anonymous sources and the retention of notes pertaining to interviews, especially with unnamed sources, and counselled that BBC journalists should not write regular articles expressing an opinion on current affairs for either newspapers or magazines (Neil, 2004: 17) in case the impartiality and commitment of the BBC not to editorialize might then appear to have been compromised.

The Contribution of Channel Four

The most significant contribution to the development of public service journalism after the introduction of ITN news in 1955 was the arrival of Channel 4 News in 1982.

The Annan Committee had published its report in 1977 which in turn had led to the creation of Channel 4 (and particularly *Channel 4 News* as an in-depth provider of a politically and economically dominated, high-quality public service daily news programme during prime time). All broadcasting reports up to the Annan Report had contributed to a growing consensus around the notion of public service broad-casting. Annan continued this pattern but took a more pluralistic view according to which broadcasters should provide for the fullest possible range of social groups. *Channel 4 News* was designed to draw on a radical synergy between commercial and publicly funded television journalism and was committed from the start to a propor-tion of 50 per cent international news and an approach that could be characterized as 'broadsheet'. To deliver this blend it had an hour-long peaktime slot between seven and eight o'clock in the evening, and as a commercially funded, free to view, analyti-cal in-depth news programme, there was nothing comparable anywhere else in the world. It was funded by advertising but its time was to be sold by ITV in order to avoid direct competition. Its founding Chief Executive outlined its ambition:

> *We did not want stories of individual crime, or of minor natural disaster. We did not want coverage of the daily diaries of the Royal family.* Channel 4 News *would deal with politics and the economy. It would bring coverage of the City, and of industry. It was to report on developments in science and technology, and in the arts. It was to cover the politics of other countries and to supplement that reporting with the output and insights of foreign television programmes.* (Isaacs, 1989: 127)

It quickly developed a loyal audience of around a million a day throughout the 1980s, although by 1993 it was decided that it must raise its own advertising. *Channel 4 also* developed current affairs programming as part of its public service journalism. *Dispatches* was launched as a counterpart current affairs programme to *Panorama* on BBC and *World in Action* and *This Week* on ITV. Channel 4 has maintained this commitment even as the BBC and ITV have struggled to resist the temptation to programme more populist fare. Bolstered by Channel 4's journalism, public service broadcast journalism of all varieties was able to provide a consumer-based range well into the nineties and did not succumb to what were to become inevitable pres-sures from the late 1990s onwards to chase viewing figures as the ultimate arbiter of success – in preference to maintaining a distinctive and probing content.

Documentary and Current Affairs

Real experimentation and change were introduced in the mixed format current affairs programmes of both broadcasting regimes. As these changes began to make their way into the public consciousness so too did the status of news and indeed television journalism, in general, continue to improve throughout the 1950s and 1960s. The combination of innovation and commitment in particular to investigative journalism as part of its public service remit gave investigative journalism a new status (de Burgh, 2000: 26), thereby defining it for a generation. Television became respected in its dealing with current affairs, acting as a critical gaze for the public into politics and even politicians' pronouncements in ways more accessible than ever before. During the 1970s the presence of serious investigative and current affairs journalism on all three channels meant that audiences were kept informed of developments at home and abroad, and these often proved extremely popular. Holland records that *This Week*, for example, was regularly in the top 20, with audiences of up to ten million (Holland, 2006: 52). The Guildford Four and Birmingham Six cases which had seen men imprisoned for alleged IRA bombing campaigns in these cities in 1974 were re-opened and declared miscarriages of justice in 1989 and 1991 respectively on the basis of work produced by journalists on ITV current affairs programmes. However, in the late 1980s and the early 1990s the deregulatory momentum of the Conservative government started to take its toll on the sustained quality of this style of journalism.

Celebrity Investigative Journalism

The drawback to documentary investigative journalism is that in an era driven by the bottom line of profit, it is expensive, politically volatile for news corporations, and not hugely popular unless it can be combined with some entertainment value. This has led to a range of recent hybrid experimentations as the conventional cutting-edge documentary in a traditional style is marginalized or even transcended. The structural and institutional changes that followed the 1990 Broadcasting Act – insisting on the marketization of production facilities and the subsequent loss of studios considered too expensive for individual broadcasting companies to maintain – has had a detrimental effect on working practices, resulting in increased casual labour and short-term contracts which have all impacted negatively on current affairs journalism. One compromise solution has been to combine investigation with a more prominent personalization and even sensationalization of the subject matter. Holland cites Adam Holloway's *No Fixed Abode*, produced by Granada in 1992, as a landmark:

> *The role of the journalist has thus expanded. The introduction of the personality of the journalist and their own commitment to a story has added a different type of authority. The fascination generated by the emotional pull of these programmes means that they respond to the 'market' demand for bigger audiences, as well as to the demand for greater transparency in the journalist's role. (1998: 90)*

Since then investigative television journalism has included Roger Cook's sensationalist and confrontational heavy-man investigative show and the rise of alternative comedians as radical journalists as in the case of Mark Thomas and the celebrity-driven Donal MacIntyre. All have contributed towards the trend for entertainer–journalists, and display a foregrounding of the investigative journalist over the subject matter and the personality over the content. This has brought a more personalized approach to contemporary issues, although such a personalization of issues *per se* does not rule out quality journalism. Macdonald has vindicated its deployment, if it manages to '… provoke the range of questions that need to be opened for debate if we are to have a vibrant democracy' and in doing so challenges '… unquestioning and complacent beliefs in the communicative success of rationality and abstraction' (2000: 264–265).

Donal MacIntyre's series of investigative reports, *MacIntyre Undercover* (November 1999), could be taken for instance as either an example of a new form of market-orientated, celebrity-driven journalism or as a reinvigorated approach to establishing fresh channels of enquiry to reveal uncomfortable truths – or as an astute blend of the two as some suspected of Stead a century before. MacIntyre's programmes dealt with issues such as football hooligans, the world of glamour modelling and the abuse of people in a care home, and have since brought arrests, resignations and closures. They were a wider media sensation because of his role as undercover reporter and *post facto* star. They also reveal a great deal about the current configuration of journalism within the broader media landscape. Another remarkable recent example of this hybridity was the programme *Living With Michael Jackson* with Martin Bashir which in early 2003 became one of the most talked about television events of the new millennium, dealing as it did with serious issues and exploring reflexively the nature of contemporary celebrity – a cross between the celebrity interview, a documentary and ultimately a news scoop. Bashir himself, his motivations and techniques, in the best contemporary fashion became a central part of the story.

Apart from these exceptions, the worst consequence of the trend to make celebrity-driven and brief format investigative programmes is summed up by the lack of any current affairs provision on ITV and the decline of the BBC's flagship *Panorama*, now truncated to a half-hour slot and topped and tailed by a celebrity presenter, Jeremy Vine.

There have been notable occasions when the assumption that audiences will tolerate this systematic dilution of standards of public service provision has been overturned. Often they have voted by remote control as viewing figures have plummeted! *News at Ten* was moved to 11 p.m., outside peak viewing, and an earlier slot for *Tonight with Trevor McDonald* was used to cover its current affairs obligations. Barnett and Seymour quote one producer as saying that this constituted an 'utterly cynical form of journalism' (1999a).

A further extension of this celebrification of investigative current affairs was exemplified in a recent BBC documentary *Famous, Rich and Homeless* (2009), in which celebrities posed as homeless people and were filmed as they confronted the most obvious horrors of this life on behalf of the viewer, who is caught between empathy for homeless people in general and a voyeuristic curiosity about what this experience can tell us about these celebrities' personalities under pressure. It is much more a celebrity *Big Brother* on the streets than a serious and issue-based documentary. Maybe real people are becoming too difficult a subject for the BBC's documentary makers.

Conclusion

Public Service Broadcasting in both the BBC and via the commercial output in the UK has produced a distinctive form of journalism. This has moved from the paternalist to the populist under pressures that are cultural (in a country moving to a less deferential attitude to authority), political (in response to hostility to the principle of publicly funded journalism) and commercial (in the face of competing technologies). Whatever its current shortcomings, there is no doubt that it still manages to provide a credible supplement to the output of newspapers and other news media. The BBC remains one of the most authoritative sources of journalism in the world and one upon which much secondary commentary and debate is based, increasingly so in its online provision in fact.

Certainly there are concerns raised by the inability of the 2003 Communication Act to redefine public service broadcasting for the new century (Petley, 2006: 42–45) while it asserts that undefined public service broadcasting should be accessible as well as authoritative in presenting accounts of the contemporary world. Ultimately it falls to the BBC to fill the gap left by commercial broadcasting in its headlong drive for audiences and revenue (O'Hagan and Jennings, 2003: 38). The licence fee and its public service provision of a universal service have survived the onslaught of Thatcherite neo-liberalism in the form of deregulation and the crowding of the market by new technologies which have offered a plethora of alternative channels. Indeed, in the present economic climate, it appears to be one of the few solutions to the continued provision of public service journalism. In a commercial environment, news is expensive to produce and currently, in the advertising downturn, publicly sponsored journalism paid for by a universal levy such as the licence fee allows for the maintenance of quality.

The BBC can still claim that the licence fee enables it to provide a huge range of output which it can transfer across technologically diverse platforms in order to provide an exceptional return for what is a minimal individual outlay.

FURTHER READING

(All of Briggs' work on broadcasting should be considered essential source reading.)

Barnett, S., Gaber, I. and Seymour, E. (2000) *From Callaghan to Kosovo: Changing Trends in British Television News 1975–1999*. Harlow: Westminster University Press. This is a contemporary and polemical account of changes in television news over the late twentieth century.

Briggs, A. (1961) *The History of Broadcasting in the United Kingdom (Vol. I): The Birth of Broadcasting*. Oxford: Oxford University Press.

Briggs, A. (1965) *The History of Broadcasting in the United Kingdom* (*Vol. II*): *The Golden Age of the Wireless.* Oxford: Oxford University Press.

Briggs, A. (1970) *The History of Broadcasting in the United Kingdom* (*Vol. III*): *The War of Words.* Oxford: Oxford University Press.

Briggs, A. (1979) *The History of Broadcasting in the United Kingdom* (*Vol. IV*): *Sound and Vision.* Oxford: Oxford University Press.

Briggs, A. (1995) *The History of Broadcasting in the United Kingdom* (*Vol. V*): *Competition.* Oxford: Oxford University Press.

Crisell, A. (1997) *An Introductory History of British Broadcasting.* London: Routledge. This is a fine overview of the specific contribution of radio broadcasting to debates on journalism and public service.

Curran, J. and Seaton, J. (1993) *Power Without Responsibility.* London: Routledge. The chapters by Jean Seaton provide an excellent complement to some of the ground covered by Briggs from a more politically engaged perspective.

Hendy, D. (2007) *Radio Four: Life on Air.* Oxford: Oxford University Press. Although not exclusively about the journalism output of that broadcast institution this certainly provides an excellent analysis of the contribution it has made to the Reithian public service principles that underpin its journalism.

3

Patterns of Ownership and Control

Introduction

The ownership and control of news media can have a direct and sometimes indirect influence on the quality and substance of the journalism they provide. This influence can be exerted via the direct imposition of the will of an owner on a newspaper or a television provider or it can come via the equally powerful influence of a leading politician or government of the day. Such influence can emanate from corporate anxieties about profit-making or from concerns voiced on behalf of the public about the quality of public communication. Across the history of twentieth-century journalism, we can observe several examples of the struggle between commercial and state attitudes towards the quality of journalism and the access which people have to it. These concerns have led to debates on regulation which have had a particular effect on broadcast journalism, as well as to threats of imposing legislation on the press in order for it to behave as a responsible constituent within the public sphere.

Sales, an audience share and advertising revenue have all been powerful influences on the content of every form of journalism throughout the twentieth century. This political economy of journalism has had an effect not just on the quality of journalism but also on the range of perspectives which can be offered within an environment which is so driven by commercial pressures that most varieties of journalism are not only sponsored by advertising but also literally shaped by it. Even publicly-funded variants must compete in its shadows.

The question of personal control through the years from Alfred Harmsworth to Rupert Murdoch as opposed to institutional control needs to be considered, although the debate cannot be restricted to the private ownership of the press as the case of the foundational influence of Reith at the BBC illustrates. This chapter will chart the developments in ownership within news media organizations from the press barons to media moguls and conglomerates, considering the impact of these changing patterns on both print and broadcast journalism. It will also consider debates on the role of regulation as a very British, compromise solution to providing an element of balance in the control of journalism, from the Sykes Report of 1923 to the setting up of Ofcom in 2003. Furthermore, it will look at the policing of the borders of self-control within the press from the 1949 Press Commission and the formation of the Press Council in 1953 to its replacement by the Press Complaints Commission in the early 1990s.

Commercial Imperatives: Advertising and Audiences

Freed from the burden of taxation from 1855 onwards, periodicals and newspapers increasingly targeted readerships on behalf of advertisers who were willing to pay for their attention. This influence grew to the point of the Harmsworth revolution in 1896. It was here that advertising and ownership converged to the extent that newspaper ownership had become a crucial element in the development of journalism (Chalaby, 2000: 34). It was the placing and size of hugely lucrative display advertising for brands, department stores and fashions which, in the case of the *Daily Mail*, necessitated the boxed and truncated style of newspaper presentation which was to dominate the twentieth century. Henceforth journalism would sink or swim depending on the attractiveness of its product, not only to its actual readers but also to a market designed around a stereotype of this audience and constructed with advertisers of particular products in mind. The one major exception to this model for a while was the BBC, which had the more altruistic goal of serving and educating the public in exchange for a guaranteed income from licence fees. However, this began to change as soon as the corporation was placed under a quasi-commercial pressure in its competition with ITV from 1955, which meant that while the BBC was not dependent on advertising revenue and the associated viewing figures it was still forced to justify its guaranteed income in the context of a set of commercial companies which were.

The Direct Influence of Ownership

In addition to the influence of advertising and competitiveness in the marketplace for audience attention, the influence of ownership has been a key factor in the direction, shape and philosophy of journalism. Again, this is nothing new. John Walter II, as owner of *The Times*, invested in the printing technology offered by the steam-driven König-Bauer presses which from 1814 were to enable his newspaper to become the leading organ of mid-Victorian Britain. Edmund Levy was also astute enough to launch the *Daily Telegraph* immediately after the abolition of a stamp duty on newspapers in 1855, a paper which was able to seize the attention of a middle class who wanted a more entertaining daily newspaper to contrast with what had become the dry severity of *The Times*. And in 1865 Greenwood was the first owner to really perfect a suitable adaptation of the innovations of the American New Journalism for an evening metropolitan audience with his *Pall Mall Gazette*.

Journalism, Business and the Press Barons

There had been newspaper chains before the twentieth century and these had grown in size and complexity as a means of rationalizing economies, to better exploit more efficient transporting and printing throughout the late Victorian period. Within these trends towards economies of scale, it made commercial sense to acquire a range of newspapers. The men who did this became known as the press barons because of their independent wealth, their political influence and the unconstrained power they wielded over their newspapers. These press barons became notorious in both popular and political critiques as the dominant model of newspaper ownership in the early twentieth century.

By that point, journalism had definitely become big business. The costs of starting a newspaper in London demanded considerable financial and advertising support. These have been estimated as increasing from £25,000 in 1850, to £100,000 in 1870, and to £500,000 by 1900 (Lee, 1976: 76–103). This long-term trend was less than fully welcomed, provoking complaints that 'journalism has sunk, or is at least in danger of sinking, from a liberal professional to a branch of business' (Escott, 1917: 368). The leading proprietors who were referred to as 'press barons' – notably Lords Northcliffe, Beaverbrook and Rothermere – presided over a period which continued the trends towards concentration, competition and entertainment in print media. By 1910 Northcliffe, Cadbury and Pearson were producing newspapers which accounted for one third of the national daily morning market and 80 per cent of the national daily evening market (Smith, 1979: 163). Rather at odds with received opinion, Curran demonstrates that instead of personifying a radical interlude in the history of print journalism the press barons, in fact, continued to develop the medium in precisely the same ways as had preceded it and were to follow it (Curran and Seaton, 2003). He observes though that one function of representing them as an exception, as a breakdown in normal service, is that this allows the history of journalism to be narrated as consisting of a golden age preceding the barons and a liberalized era of professionalized independence following them. However, neither narrative is helpful in understanding journalism's past or, indeed, present. All the press barons attempted to use their publishing power to propagandize to large readerships and assumed that they exercised an absolute measure of power over the opinions of both ordinary readers and leading politicians, but Boyce concludes that this was a major reason for their ultimate failure to achieve lasting influence: 'Northcliffe failed in his supreme ambition because he sought to mould rather than exploit, the world of high politics' (Boyce, 1986: 103). This confirms the logic of the processes at work within journalism since 1855; journalism had become less the predominantly political activity of previous generations and had moved increasingly towards being a commercial proposition at heart, a consummation of the process Lee summarizes whereby 'economic forces would gradually dominate political ones' (1978: 117). This did not however prevent Rothermere and Beaverbrook in particular from continually attempting to reinforce their political ambitions through their business.

Accounting for the behaviour and influence of newspaper proprietors from the standpoint of a one-time national editor with a good grasp of history, Greenslade has concluded:

> ... as privately owned commercial enterprises and, having developed from personal political platforms, most newspapers were not democratic institutions. There was no public service ethic embedded within them, demanding impartiality or neutrality. Owners might pay lip service to such an ethic in order to assert their own independence from the state or other vested interests. They might even claim that they had a public purpose as part of their sales policy, a pretence to attract readers. For their part, editors might shout loudly about having complete independence from their owners: they and they alone, made decisions about what went into their papers. But it was all a masquerade. Ownership conferred rights on proprietors to do as they wished. (2003: 11)

Northcliffe, Beaverbrook and Rothermere: Impact and Consequences

Northcliffe demonstrated an understanding of the range of the potential for a market penetration of every social class in establishing the *Daily Mail* and the *Daily Mirror* and by eventually acquiring *The Times* in 1908. Chalaby has observed that:

> He was not the only press proprietor to control different types of newspapers, of course, but he was the most successful in creating and maintaining newspapers for every branch of the reading public. (Chalaby, 2000: 42)

Northcliffe may have launched jingoism into the modern era during the *Daily Mail*'s coverage of the Boer War (Hughes, 1986) and he may also have conspired to bring down Asquith's government in 1916 and continued, encouraged by this success, to assert his influence on the administration of Lloyd George even after being invited to join the government as Head of the British War Mission to the USA in 1917, but in general terms the press barons elevated commerce and entertainment above politics as the prime motivations of journalism. Having established an economic independence, their politics were much less dependent on the parties and the establishment than ever before.

Max Aitken – soon to be knighted and to take up the more familiar title of Lord Beaverbrook from 1911 – had moved to Britain from his native Canada in 1910 as a wealthy entrepreneur, extending his business interests while winning a seat in Parliament in the same year. He began to acquire a range of newspaper titles and eventually managed to gain a controlling share of the ailing *Daily Express* from 1916, at which point he gave up his parliamentary seat. To complement this daily presence, he founded the *Sunday Express* in 1918. His ambition to use his newspapers to advance particular political causes was encouraged by his direct involvement in government in both World War I (as First Minister of Information) and World War II (as Minister of Supply and later Minister of War Production). He took a particularly strong line on Empire Trade between 1929–31, campaigning for protectionist tariffs to privilege trade between countries of the British Empire and unveiling the helmeted crusader as the emblem of his newspapers' imperial commitment. With the *Daily Express* and later the *Sunday Express*, Beaverbrook continued to purvey his Empire politics and combined their existing middle-class aspirational tone with an old-fashioned right-wing populism. He also used his editorial control to maintain a strong advocacy of appeasement towards Hitler, promising as late as 1938 that there would be no war with Germany in that or any other year. He was – with his belligerent, idiosyncratic politics and authoritarian interference in the running of his newspapers – perfect material for satire, which is what he became when Evelyn Waugh famously portrayed him as Lord Cooper in his novel *Scoop*.

After Northcliffe's death in 1922 his brother, Lord Rothermere, inherited control of Associated Newspapers and continued with a very similar authoritarian and interventionist approach to newspaper ownership. The Zinoviev letter, which purported to demonstrate collusion between the Soviet Union and the British Labour Party – a forgery with no substance in fact – was published in his *Daily Mail* four days before the elections in 1924 to discredit the Labour Party, accompanied by headlines reinforcing the implications of this letter, such as 'Civil War Plot by Socialists' Masters' (*Daily Mail*, 25 October 1924) and 'Vote British, not Bolshie' (*Daily Mirror*, 29 October 1924). Such aggressive attempts at political intervention by proprietors in the pages of their newspapers proved one of the decisive factors in the government decision in the 1920s to set up the BBC as a public service without hectoring proprietors or the commercial demands of advertisers.

Rothermere also joined Beaverbrook in the Empire Crusade of the early 1930s, which pitched both the *Express* and the *Mail* against the Conservative government of Stanley Baldwin and led to one of the most famous expressions of political frustration with newspaper journalism of the twentieth century when Baldwin accused them of exercising 'Power without responsibility, the prerogative of the harlot down the ages'.

The Limits of Personal Influence

In addition to such expressions of personal political opinion, there was also a more subtle impact on the content and range of the newspapers. The imperative for the commercial success of mass market newspapers tended to dictate an acquiescence in the general opinion of their readers, meaning that it was ultimately this readership's conservatism which was more a shaper of news values than owner eccentricity or a political hobby-horse:

> *In reality, their main impact lay in the way in which their papers selectively represented the world. This tended to strengthen the mainly conservative prejudices of their readers, and reinforce opposition, particularly within the middle class, to progressive change. (Curran and Seaton, 2003: 47)*

Despite this rather reactive dynamism, the aggressive self-promotion of the press barons still caused the debates about press freedom and influence to enter a different dimension. Because of the increased profitability of popular newspapers and the greater sophistication of these newspapers' exploitation of advertising revenue, Northcliffe and Beaverbrook appeared capable of wielding a direct influence on politics. At this point the claims of newspaper proprietors that their personal economic freedom was synonymous with general political freedom had become commonplace and politicians were loath to challenge their rights on this point. As a consequence, the representative ideal became the foundation for the defence of a market or libertarian view of the press that was congenial to the press barons' own personal interests (Hampton, 2004: 167). They were, in other words, able to claim that their own economic interests were synonymous with the more generalized freedom of the press and even the interests of their readers. It is a set of claims which still has resonance in many of today's newspapers and emanates from owners as well as editors.

Yet there were contemporaries who perceived the influence of the press barons as all-pervasive through their products:

> There has never been, in this or any other country, so tremendous an engine for stamping the public thought with the bias of a single mind as that controlled by Lord Rothermere today ... Leaders have ceased to have importance in this journalism of stunts and apoplectic seizures; but the news columns have been saturated with the prejudices and policies which the Harmsworths sought to impose on the public mind ... But in the case of the systematic manipulation of the news, the suppression of facts that seem to support the purpose in view, the public have no such corrective at command. They do not, being for the most part simple and ignorant people, suspect the enormous fiction of which they are the sport. They accept what they read in good faith, and innocently suppose that they have themselves conceived the opinions which have been insinuated into their minds by the daily trip of the Rothermere press. (Gardiner, 1923: 567–568).

There was certainly a cause for concern here as the vast holdings of the press barons allowed them to further consolidate their press empires and therefore to control the range and content of the press. After 1922, four men – Lords Beaverbrook, Rothermere, Camrose and Kemsley – dominated the national scene. By 1937, it has been estimated that they owned nearly one in every two national and local newspapers, as well as one in every three Sunday papers that were sold (Curran and Seaton, 2003: 40). This sort of acquisitiveness was not uniform however. In contrast to the press barons who grew their national ownership, Lord Kemsley saw four newspapers close (the *Sunday Graphic, Empire News, Sunday Chronicle* and *Sunday Dispatch*) but concentrated his efforts on the highly successful and increasingly prestigious *Sunday Times*.

Nevertheless, their attempts to become dominant players in the formation of public opinion were constrained by the complexity of what actually formed people's political views. Britain's newspaper readers did not back fascism in the 1930s, Labour was not destroyed as a political force, and the political preferences of the right-wing press did not manage to secure a Conservative victory in 1945. The problems of running a commercially successful newspaper which was driven by politics rather than a commercially pragmatic engagement with the views of readers were demonstrated by the Duke of Northumberland who, backed by Conservative party supporters, had bought the Tory *Morning Post*. By 1937 no purchaser could be found and it simply went out of business. The *Daily Herald*, from a left perspective, had also suffered economically because of its direct political positioning until Odhams brought it into their portfolio in 1929; it managed, for a short period in the 1930s, to reach the pinnacle of commercial success while still continuing to be directed editorially by Labour Party and TUC policies.

Reconfiguration of the Popular Market

Even at the time of the launch of the *Daily Mail* and for some years beyond this point, the press still resembled the early Victorian press in many ways (Koss, 1981: 431), and the revolutionary impact of Harmsworth's intervention in the field of daily journalism would have to wait until the 1930s to truly demonstrate its impact (Murdock and Golding, 1978: 130). A few powerful groups began to dominate the field of production, bringing a monopolization which led to a narrowing of the range and appeal of journalism. Patterns of ownership were also increasingly linked to a style of journalism which was shaped to match an increasingly competitive and homogenized mass market. Circulation increases could only be achieved by newspapers concentrating on a popular formula which narrowed the scope for alternatives. Sales therefore increased as the alternatives to mass appeal came under the pressure to adapt or be squeezed out of business. In addition, understanding the place of advertising was becoming a more precise and sophisticated activity within journalism. Commercial pressures to make circulation calculations and readership profiles more accurate led to the foundation of the Audit Bureau of Circulation in 1931, which was the culmination of the influence of the American import of market research in the 1920s.

The circulation wars triggered in the popular market of the 1920s and 1930s saw 30 newspapers close between 1921 and 1936, although the total sales of newspapers actually doubled (Curran and Seaton, 2003: 39–41). Circulation wars had started in 1928 with the *Daily Mail*'s insurance scheme. This was replaced up until the late 1930s by free gifts for subscribers. Such promotions forced up costs which were then covered by an increased advertising revenue, but these led to a reduction in editorial expenditure – leading to a decline in public affairs news in much of the popular press of this period and a narrowing of the political range, with the exception of the *Daily Herald* which still had a third of its content based on public affairs (Curran and Seaton, 2003: 44). This rise in costs discouraged new entrants into the newspaper market unless they were prepared to conform with commercially-driven imperatives.

The *Daily Herald* had started its life as a daily newspaper with a joint ownership by the TUC and the Labour Party and a mission to provide an alternative view of the world for its readers. The union leader and later Labour Minister, Ernest Bevin, was quoted as expressing the view in 1919 that:

*Labour's press must be a real educational factor, provoking thought and stimu-
lating ideas. In addition it must not be full of the caprices of princes, the lubrici-
ties of courts and the sensationalism produced by display of the sordid. All these
things are but passing phases and are the products of an evil system which is
rotten at the base. (Richards, 1997: 10)*

Despite the commercialization of the *Daily Herald*, after it was sold to Odhams in
1929 and relaunched the following year, it remained a successful alternative to right-
wing publications and their patterns of control in its maintenance of an editorial
partnership with the politics of the TUC.

During the 1930s it was the relaunch of the *Daily Herald* which – in shifting partially from its identity as a campaigning socialist newspaper – was able to attempt a
reformulation of mass-commercial appeal and with its layout, advertising and commercial gimmicks grabbed the lead in the field by attaining a readership of over two
million by 1937. The *Daily Express*, galvanized by this, restructured its own layout
and appeal to outdo the *Herald* and had sales of 2.39 million at the same point. The
Mail became the loser in this as it failed to match the popular appeal of either of these
newspapers and fell back to 1.58 million.

This period also saw alternative strategies to the routine practices of big-business control and a right-wing political dominance in newspapers. The Communist Party launched
the *Sunday Worker* in 1925 which was then developed into the *Daily Worker* in 1930,
which depended to a large degree on reader support to maintain a directly political
newspaper. In a similar attempt at reader control of the political direction of a newspaper, *Reynolds' News/Sunday Citizen* was bought by the Co-Operative Party in 1929. But
the strangest of all partnerships was a hybrid of greater complexity and pragmatism than
even the commercialized *Daily Herald*. The *Daily Mirror* – without a majority shareholder
and cut adrift from Rothermere's empire and then relaunched as a left-of-centre commercial newspaper in 1934 – was directed at a largely apolitical working class first (as its
director Cecil King admitted) as an exercise in journalistic cynicism (Cudlipp, 1953: 104),
but this matured into a genuine engagement with its readers. Even by the start of the
Second World War it was demonstrating the success of its relaunched appeal to the non-
political working-class reader, a constituency that had not been fully captured by any
particular paper up until this point. The *Manchester Guardian* took the decision to form
a unique style of governance when it became owned by the Scott Trust in 1936 which
guaranteed both its editorial independence and its continued liberal stance.

Postwar: Between Barons and Moguls

Seymour-Ure (1991) considers that there was an intermission between the early
press barons and the later media moguls, during which time he observes certain
consolidating tendencies within families and news media groups presided over by
what he terms 'crown princes' who inherited a family ownership before economic
consolidation led to the rise of a conglomerate style of multi-media ownership. For

instance, when Lord Camrose died in 1954 ownership of the *Telegraph* passed to his son Michael Berry (later Lord Hartwell), who maintained control from 1954 to 1986 when it was sold to the Canadian, Conrad Black, who was much more the model of a global media mogul. Seymour-Ure concludes:

> *The trend of ownership across the post-war years had four interlinked parts: independent ownerships declined; the provincial groups carried on; there were manoeuvrings among the major chains; and – the greatest upheaval – Kemsley left the market altogether and was replaced by a new player, the international Thomson organization. (1991: 52)*

After paper rationing and the decline in advertising which had hampered the press in the years during the Second World War and beyond, newspaper journalism needed to cope with a very changed commercial landscape. This was one which was increasingly affected by the commercial rivalries of the pre-war years and by the rise of radio as a rival to the audience for newspapers and from the mid-fifties by the advent of commercial television journalism as a rival magnet to newspapers for advertising. A continuing intensification of the competition for circulation, advertising and profit was creating a certain sort of journalism with clear political implications. It culminated in what McManus (1994) has criticized as 'market-driven journalism'. This saw newspapers at the left of centre and following the liberal tradition forced out and an increasing levelling of journalism towards a market-orientated consensus which appealed to advertisers and the economic interests of owners. On the abolition of newsprint rationing in 1956 there came a newly competitive wave for newspapers, once again fully exposed to the requirements of the advertisers. These required either a quantity or quality of readers and left little space for the smaller-circulation, left-leaning newspapers, meaning that the *News Chronicle* (1960), the *Daily Herald* (1964) and the *Sunday Citizen* (1967) were all forced out of business within a short period. Consequently, the editorial consensus had been shifted to the right of the political spectrum not just by the political preferences of the majority of the surviving newspapers but also on account of the commercial process itself which was attracted to more politically conservative perspectives. Curran and Seaton explain it in these terms:

> *The market was not a mechanism which impartially represented consumer demand, and harmonized editorial and public opinion. On the contrary, it gave added impetus to the right-wing drift of the post-war press in a way that exceeded the rightward shift of public opinion because the market mechanism was itself skewed to the right. (Curran and Seaton, 2003: 106)*

Thomson: A New Vision of Control

The first properly modern media mogul was Thomson. He represented the prime exemplar of 'concentration, conglomeration and internationalization' (Seymour-Ure,

1991: 121). He had started with a chain of small-town Canadian newspapers and radio stations and then bought the *Scotsman* in 1954, the Kemsley chain of local newspapers, and the *Sunday Times* in 1959. He became a book publisher, developed the small ad business in *Yellow Pages* (an American invention) and diversified further into package holidays to become the biggest tour operator by 1989. Despite his media beginnings he moved steadily, if not stealthily, to become more of a non-media business player. Once he had acquired *The Times* in 1966 he made Rees-Mogg the editor, who set about modernizing the paper with the introduction of by-lines, a restructuring and rationalizing of the constituent sections of the paper and – in keeping with the owner's interests – by introducing a business supplement and a Saturday review.

Charles Wintour has passed the following observation on the consequences of Thomson's drive for commercial success in newspaper publishing, indicating the new dynamic within news media ownership which he established and claiming that he had:

> *raised the status of the editor and the editorial department, yet at the same time diminished newspapers into a product ... The Thomson papers are not used as a vehicle for personal propaganda but they are strongly consumer-oriented and therefore tend to be bland. (1972: 189)*

Thomson was not simply a wealthy foreign exile seeking to establish himself within British society and politics through his acquisition of newspapers. His ambitions were based on a more modern vision of global corporate power in which British newspapers acted as convenient and profitable stepping stones.

The Political Effects of Corporate Consensus

Beyond individual ownership, it was the corporatization of newspapers which represented a new phase of control, a trend which was characterized in 1968 by the change in title of the Newspaper Proprietors' Association to the Newspaper Publishers' Association, indicating the shift in emphasis within newspapers from the fact of ownership to their place within a publishing business. The Press Commission recognized this pattern of change in its 1977 report when it claimed:

> *Rather than saying that the press has other business interests, it would be truer to argue that the press has become a subsidiary of other interests. (Royal Commission on the Press, 1977: 149)*

Big business was more and more likely to find its own interests directly or indirectly amplified in the newspapers it owned, together with the more conservative values which underpinned them. This was by no means restricted to the popular press, even at the elite/quality end of the market, journalism was being forced to pay its way as part of larger corporate concerns:

The increasing conformity of the British quality press, in style and substance, is an example of this fundamental tendency of oligopolistic competition to serve the centre of the market at the expense of minority tastes. (Hirsch and Gordon, 1975: 45)

By the mid-1970s newspaper ownership was being increasingly located within the commercial enterprises of a few of the moguls' corporate operations:

- Beaverbrook Newspapers: 15.8 per cent of daily and Sunday papers.
- Associated Newspapers: 7.2 per cent.
- Reed International: 29.6 per cent.
- News International: 18.7 per cent.
- Thomson Organization: 7.3 per cent. (Press Council Annual Report, 1974: 116–119)

Murdock and Golding consider that these ownership practices have had a restrictive effect on the range of opinion, ultimately narrowing the political consensus with its consequent threat to democratic debate:

We would ... suggest that the central band of views and opinions which emerge as dominant in this process draw on a view of political and social process which is more subtly contentious than it appears. In emphasising consensual and dominant values, it reaffirms a highly specific ideology to which no counter is easily available. (1978: 148)

Murdoch: The Ultimate Mogul

Of all the proprietors of media organizations in the twentieth century, none has managed to acquire such a level of global penetration as Rupert Murdoch. Already a successful newspaper proprietor in his native Australia he came to Britain in the 1960s to take over several British newspapers, before becoming an American citizen in 1985 in order to further pursue his commercial interests in that country. His ability to cross-subsidize his media concerns has meant that, particularly in Britain – with both satellite television as well as newspapers at both ends of the market, both daily and weekly – he has built a position of strength from which to influence most developments in contemporary British journalism. The great difference between barons and the most potent of the modern moguls lies in the new global reach of modern corporate power, and Murdoch's role in this process of globalization is stressed in the following assessment:

The great myth about modern proprietors is that their power is less than it used to be. The fiefdoms of Beaverbrook, Northcliffe and Hearst, often invoked as the zenith of proprietorial omnipotence, were in fact smaller by every criteria than the enormous, geographically diffuse, multi-lingual empires of the latest newspaper tycoons. The profits and total circulations of the old-school proprietors were invariably lower, their papers thinner, the scope of their influence and news-gathering machines more local; none dominated so many world markets simultaneously as does Murdoch in Britain, the far east and Australia. [sic] *(Coleridge, 1994: 2)*

His first move was to purchase the *News of the World* in 1969 at which point – as if to indicate that the personal influence of an owner in the editorial processes of a newspaper had not diminished in this new phase of corporate control – Murdoch told the editor Somerfield: 'I didn't come all this way not to interfere' (Hollingsworth, 1986:18). Later that year he bought the *Sun* and immediately began to restructure its editorial character and journalistic style to exploit the growing permissiveness of the age, with its iconic Page 3 Girl and a blend of light-hearted and entertainment-led journalism designed to capture the youth market. In Shawcross's biography of Murdoch he is clearly depicted in terms of the broad set of values he has brought to his publications including the *Sun*: republicanism; stalwart support for American values of global free-market capitalism; anti-liberal; and especially anti-gay and anti-feminist. A shift to the right of the political spectrum was to take a little longer but it was no less dramatic when it came about in the 1979 election with his *Sun* newspaper (Shawcross, 1992: 209–210).

The editorial shift of his key newspapers matched a political change of direction personally – from a social libertarianism to a militant economic libertarianism – indicating that even within contemporary patterns of media management it is important not to exclude the possibility of a raw exercise of social and political power through ownership of mass media (McKnight, 2003: 357). This personalized role was picked up in the sardonic comments of playwright Dennis Potter (who had named his cancer 'Rupert') on the *South Bank Show* in 1994:

There is no one person more responsible for the pollution of what was already a fairly polluted press. The pollution of the British press is an important part of the pollution of British political life.

Sympathetic editorial appointments are also key to his brand of proprietorial control at arms' length, first with Lamb on the *Sun* from 1969 and then with MacKenzie from 1981 until 1994, who was to preside over the newspaper's glory days (Chippendale and Horrie, 1992).

This blend of personal intervention and conglomerate expansion continued in 1981 when Murdoch acquired both *The Times* and the *Sunday Times. The Times* in the mid-nineteenth century had virtually seen itself as an estate of the realm, and the esteem it had acquired was perpetuated by Northcliffe, who, having bought it in 1908, thought seriously of bequeathing it to the British Museum not to embalm it with the mummies but to secure its independence. In precisely that spirit it was bought by Colonel Astor on Northcliffe's death in 1922, specifically to secure it from party politicians such as Lloyd George (Seymour-Ure, 1991: 265). The paper still prided itself on being the most authoritative 'journal of record' and to this end continued to carry detailed law reports, parliamentary coverage and various official announcements that were not easily justifiable by the news values of the day but which proclaimed the importance of the institutions concerned to the social order, including the monarchy. To this end *The Times* continued to publish the daily Court Circular on its Court Page (Seymour-Ure, 1991: 266). Its editorial claims to independence were ratified by a board of directors that included such luminaries as the Governor of the Bank of England and the President of the Royal Society, until Murdoch almost immediately dismissed Harold Evans from the editorship and moved him across to the *Sunday Times* despite the existence of this board.

According to Young (1984), it took less than two years for the *Sunday Times* to become 'a hard line paper of the Right' on foreign policy and industrial relations. Under Murdoch's proprietorship it became a Thatcherite organ, partly as a pragmatic response to the rise of a set of political convictions of which he approved and which had become the dominant ideas within British political circles, but more directly on account of the appointment of Andrew Neil as its editor in 1983:

> *Neil was a Thatcherite before Thatcher, an avid free marketer fervently preaching the cause of deregulation, privatisation and supply-side economics. As a meritocratic Conservative he disliked inherited privilege ... (Greenslade, 2003: 387)*

Neil's appointment was part of a general shake-up in the editorial hierarchy of the *Sunday Times* in which section editors from the pre-Murdoch era were to be gradually weeded out (Curran and Seaton, 2003: 83). Neil could demonstrate an understanding and empathy with Murdoch's project:

> *Rupert expects his papers to stand broadly for what he believes: a combination of right-wing Republicanism from America mixed with undiluted Thatcherism from Britain ... the resulting potage is a radical-right dose of free market economics, the social agenda of the Christian moral majority and hardline conservative views on subjects like drugs, abortion, law and order and defence. (Neil, 1996: 165)*

Murdoch's most controversial cross-media manoeuvre was the way in which he was able to launch his Sky TV satellite television station, in apparent contravention of the existing monopoly law, when in 1989 Margaret Thatcher's Conservative government allowed a loophole in its Broadcasting Bill to permit him to continue his nascent satellite television enterprise, as well as to own 35 per cent of the British national press (Barnett and Gaber, 2001: 68). This episode was the most conclusive demonstration of the operational style of the mogul as opposed to the direct and immediate style of the baron, as the mogul is interested in establishing more general political support to deliver future regulatory favours (Tunstall, 1996: 88). Murdoch has consistently used his newspapers as 'cash cows' for other commercial projects and this was nowhere more effectively illustrated than in his dealings with the satellite market. Profits from his newspapers allowed him to run an early version of Sky TV at a loss, thus avoiding the attention of the Monopolies Commission to become the dominant player in the field and, as it was often proclaimed in his newspapers, a more viable alternative to the general television provision than that which was offered by the BBC. Barnett and Gaber summarize the tone and content of journalism which Murdoch achieved through this process:

> *The shift towards more consensual and consumerist politics makes it less likely that individual owners will wish to involve themselves in personal crusades, at least on issues of fundamental political ideology (although crusades on more narrowly defined moral or consumer issues have probably become more frequent – for example on legalization of cannabis, reduction in petrol prices or abolition of bank charges. Political support becomes a more pragmatic issue, a combination of personalities, business interests and feedback from readers. (2001: 65)*

Maxwell: Bombast and Bankruptcy

In contrast perhaps to Thomson and Murdoch, Robert Maxwell continued the tradition of Beaverbrook and Astor to the extent that he had migrated to Britain in order to build his business and become an influential social and political operator. Having started with the purchase in 1951 of the then minor publishing house, Pergammon Press, he moved onwards and upwards, first becoming a Labour MP for Buckingham in 1964 and then acquiring Mirror Group Newspapers which included both the *Daily Mirror* and *Sunday Mirror* as well as the *Daily Record* and *Sunday Mail* in Scotland. The purchase of the *Mirror* titles in particular was intriguing as he had remained a self-proclaimed socialist with a pro-Labour affinity despite his business success. His bombastic interference with the *Mirror*'s editorial – sometimes commandeering the front page or the leader column for his own views, or inserting pictures of himself involved in some self-promotional stunt, or exerting his constant direct intervention over the head of the editor – certainly placed him well within the older traditions of the press barons and also earned the *Daily Mirror* the nickname of the *Daily Maxwell* (Greenslade, 2003: 397). His business affairs and general reputation were less than salubrious, and *Private Eye* lampooned him as 'the bouncing Czech' on account of these, in a reference both to his financial unreliability and his national origins. A former editor of his *Daily Mirror* dubbed him 'a mixture of buffoon and bandit' (Greenslade, 2003: 396). He launched an ambitious transnational newspaper, *The European*, in 1990, but in an increasingly fractious financial atmosphere surrounding both his personal and business finances he was found dead, floating in the sea off his yacht, in late 1991.

Proprietors and Editors: Shifts in Power

As the pattern of ownership developed over the century, so too did the relationships between editors and proprietors. Directly or indirectly, however, these conformed increasingly to the pattern outlined by Arthur Christiansen who had edited the *Daily Express* from 1933 to 1957 as an early model of the editor-manager:

I was a journalist, not a political animal; my proprietor was a journalist and a political animal. The policies were Lord Beaverbrook's job, the presentation mine. (Christiansen, 1961: 144)

There were exceptions, depending on the structure of the newspaper in question. At the popular end of the market the *Daily Mirror*, from its 1934 relaunch, had vested enormous autonomy in its editors from Bartholomew through to Cudlipp. One could also still find examples of an earlier model of the sovereign-editor (Tunstall, 1996: 101) surviving on some of the elite newspapers. C.P. Scott had edited the *Manchester Guardian* from 1872 to 1929 and was the significant mover in enabling that newspaper to become protected from much of the naked opportunism of other newspaper take-overs by setting up the paper as a trust in 1936, an institutional solution which has survived to the present day. Willian Rees-Mogg as editor of *The Times* (1976–1981) and David Astor as the owner-editor of the *Observer* (1948–1975) also belonged to this tradition of sovereignty, with varying styles of autonomy reflecting the status of the newspapers as institutions. In the 1960s and 1970s the myth of the 'sovereign editor' had persisted yet this had been replaced by the 1980s and 1990s with a newly potent reality – the 'entrepreneurial editor' (Tunstall, 1996: 79).

Despite all of his acquisitions and changes in personnel, Murdoch's most revolutionary intervention in the management of his newspapers dates from the shift in production to Wapping in 1986 which forced changes which reverberated across the entire British news media. The subsequent weakening of trades unions saw a corresponding increase in the power of a new generation of aggressively entrepreneurial editors who were acting out the editorial identities of their proprietors. Sir David English (1971–1992) who oversaw the resurgence of the *Daily Mail* as the populist scourge of the left (and the centre for that matter) was one of the pioneers of this trend. Paul Dacre, having observed his modus operandi as deputy editor for many years, continued the trend. Neil (1983–1994) and MacKenzie (1981–1994) were typical examples of the Murdoch-approved editor in their aggressively street-wise '"common man" personal style' (Tunstall, 1996: 125).

Black took over Telegraph Group in 1987 when he bought the *Telegraph* titles from the last of the Berry family, and his editor Max Hastings confirmed both his expectations of a powerful media mogul and his own expectations of the pragmatism of newspaper editorship when he explained his understanding of their professional relationship on the *Daily Telegraph*: 'Well it doesn't bother me, because I've always been a capitalist myself... I've never really believed in the notion of editorial independence I would never imagine saying to Conrad, "You have no right to ask me to do this. I must observe my independence", because Conrad is, as it seems to me, richly entitled to take a view when he owns the paper.' (Bevins, 1990: 13-14). He was succeeded by another authoritarian editor in 1996 – Charles Moore.

Despite the close co-operation of editors with proprietors, it is clear that the wishes of the proprietor will still hold sway. To complement this direct form of control, other ways of ensuring the unanimity of editorial policy were to be found in the careful selection of key personnel or in the allocation of resources to preferred areas of a newspaper's coverage. Maxwell, Black, Murdoch and Matthews, in control of Express Newspapers, have all been known to supplement that more subtle sense of interference with a more robust set of strategies which have ranged from encouraging self-censorship among chief editorial staff to the literal rewriting of editorials.

Political Concerns About Press Content

There have been enough concerns over the content and behaviour of the press in the twentieth century to warrant political threats to legislate but these have usually been faced down by calls to defend the hallowed 'freedom of the press', a rhetoric that few politicians would take on despite its flimsy constitutional basis or historical grounding in fact. Newspaper owners would prefer to argue either for general laws to be made more pertinent to press practices or for owners and editors to monitor their own activities on behalf of the public. Indeed there have been times where both of these have been proposed as solutions to the perceived excesses of newspaper journalism in the twentieth century.

Bingham (2007: 80) comments on the longer-term concerns with regard to the intrusive reporting of newspapers across the century which had brought in legislation or the threat of legislation before the crisis of the 1980s which had led to the Calcutt Review. The perception that newspapers were using the divorce courts as an excuse for the printing of salacious and unnecessarily prurient stories in the 1920s led to the 1926 Judicial Proceeding (Regulation of Reports) Act (Savage, 1998: 511–528), and the sensationalism of the press was a cause for concern in the lead up to the founding of the Press Council in 1953: the curbing of sensationalism was, in fact, considered by many to be one of its chief remits (Murray, 1972). Yet all of this counted for little, given that the ultimate arbiter of any newspaper's power appeared to be accepted as 'the market'. Would people buy what these papers printed? There were severe limitations on what could be done to alter the ways in which newspapers operated, given the enormous economic power and political connections of many of their owners and the rhetoric of the traditions of press freedom which they selectively brandished whenever threatened.

The first indication that nothing was really going to change in the post-war era came with the conclusion of the Press Commission in 1949. This had been widely regarded as having been set up to deal with the various concerns which had accumulated throughout the 1930s, including circulation wars, journalism's refusal to engage with the real social and political ills of the era, and what was widely considered as the untrammelled influence of owners over the content of newspapers. Part of the momentum behind its discussions was provided by the professionally motivated National Union of Journalists. The agreement to set up a Royal Commission was part of a wave of popular sentiment which had been harnessed by the *Daily Mirror* so successfully and by the Labour Party that had emanated from the Beveridge Report of 1942: this was convinced that Britain needed to become a fairer and more just, even a more egalitarian society. Yet the Press Commission concluded rather timidly that overall market accountability could provide a full enough range of political debate and opinion to inform a properly functioning democracy, and that intervention in the market by legislation would be a cure worse than the disease (Seymour-Ure, 1991: 262). From the Commission's Report came recommendations on the education of journalists which, it was hoped, would raise standards in the profession. Also included was the establishment of the Press Council, which began its work in 1953 with a brief to supervise recruitment and to monitor monopolistic trends and the processing of complaints. Yet its 25 members had all been drawn from the industry under scrutiny. A further Royal Commission in 1961–62 had the financial state of the press and the concentration of ownership as its chief remits and in 1974–1977 the structure and performance of the press were debated by another Royal Commission as well as the issue of individual privacy balanced against press freedoms. The latter was to become the most contentious of all issues for print journalism for the rest of the century. However none of these commissions provided any concrete outcomes to redress the inevitable structural consequences of the increasing monopolistic control of the press.

Another extremely important civic attempt to monitor broadcasting and press issues has been the Campaign for Press and Broadcasting Freedom, which was founded in 1979 to champion broad media and democratic freedoms and campaign against the vested commercial interests of media groups; this was on behalf of the ordinary audience who were concerned at the erosion of the democratic potential and the lack of diversity in the news media. This campaign has acted as a particularly articulate contributor to debates on media policy and loses no opportunity to stress that market forces by themselves will not lead to a diversity of opinion and expression and that governments have to ensure a regulatory framework in both the press and broadcasting to achieve a proper democratic accountability (Doyle, 2003: 93). In recent years, its work has been complemented by Media Wise (launched as Press Wise in 1993) whose aim is to bring together victims of 'media abuse', concerned journalists, politicians and media lawyers in order to campaign for an increased accountability within the news media. Its campaigning includes the publication of authoritative reports on current issues of concern within journalism practice and the organization of conferences where such issues can be debated with the express aim of increasing the public accountability of journalism.

Press Complaints Commission

Despite the clubbish consensus emerging from the Royal Commissions which salvaged politicians' and liberal journalism's consciences to an extent, it was inevitable that the sort of traditional market-driven excesses which had, in part, led to the setting up of these commissions would eventually lead to more severe pressure to legislate. The most serious threat to intervene in the autonomy of newspapers to do very much as they pleased came during the 1980s and 1990s in the investigations which concluded in the Calcutt reports and the compromise of the Press Complaints Commission.

In the late 1980s the British tabloid press reached a crisis in its relationship with politicians and the public. Prejudiced and inaccurate reporting, speculative stories about the private lives of prominent figures and aggressive long-lens photography provoked a storm of criticism. (Bingham, 2007: 79)

The Press Council – set up in 1953 and funded by the Newspaper Society very much as an insider institution – was abolished by the Calcutt Inquiry in 1990. The PCC succeeded it from January 1991. In May 1993, it responded to criticism by proposing changes that included the installation of a majority of non-press members.

Frost's account (2004: 106) of the first ten years of the PCC's adjudications does not make for encouraging reading, with only 3.8 per cent reaching adjudication and a mere 1.6 per cent of complaints upheld from the almost 23,000 submitted. The oft-cited and extremely disingenuous defence of the Commission itself of its own practices usually runs along the lines that adjudication is a last resort and much good work is done short of the adjudication process and that the figures do not reflect the constant dialogue between the PCC and editors and between journalists framing their activities by reference to the Code. In an apparent acknowledgement that it appeared to outsiders as a process run by an industry covering a minimal number of bases to avoid further governmental scrutiny, and with very little regard for the public it purports to serve, Gerald Kaufman as Chair of the National Heritage Select Committee was reported to have commented on Lord Wakeham, Chairman of the P.C.C. as being 'like a eunuch trying to do the best in the circumstances' (*Guardian*, Nov. 8, 1996: 7).

Snoddy has indicated just how important this form of self-regulation actually is to the future health of all journalism:

In the end, talking about and encouraging high standards and ethics in newspapers – tabloids as well as broadsheets – is not some sort of self-indulgence for amateur moral philosophers or journalists with sensitive psyches: it is a very practical matter, involving customer relations, product improvement and profit ... Unless such issues are taken more seriously, future generations could be reading about many of today's newspapers in the history books, rather than actually reading the papers themselves. (1992: 203)

Self-regulation can only continue to slip, especially in the popular press and an increasingly popularized elite press, as long as increasingly fierce competition forces these newspapers to vie for readers on an ever more frenetic scale, as was exemplified recently when Andy Coulson, the editor of the *News of the World*, had to fall on his sword – resigning in the wake of revelations that his paper had tapped into the mobile phone conversations of members of the Royal household.

A more robust approach to these issues as matters of public importance, and not restricted to the self-interests of the newspapers themselves, has been demanded by other voices, notably Julian Petley, a member of the Campaign for Press and Broadcasting Freedom:

... the PCC specifically should replace serving with former editors on its adjudication panel, and accept third part complaints. Finally, newspapers should appoint a readers' ombudsman, independent of the editor, to deal with complaints and audit the overall standards of that paper. (Petley, 2003: 83)

State Regulation and Broadcast Journalism

There have been regular debates and committees reporting on broadcasting policy driven first by anxieties about its influence; second, by an appreciation of its role in the democratic process; and third, by a need to weigh up the balance against the raw market forces of the newspaper industry. We can summarize the main reports which have acted to safeguard the public service nature of broadcast journalism until the free market revisionism of the 1980s. Sykes (1923) established the principle of public service; Crawford (1926) confirmed that the BBC should be structured as a public organization to be run at a distance from central government; Ullswater (1936) confirmed the public service model as the cultural and political preference rather than any commercial variant; Beveridge (1951) outlined a preference for the continuation of the radio paradigm for television broadcasting, but its recommendations were ignored in favour of a minority report which the Conservatives used to fashion a Broadcasting Act in 1954 that introduced regionally-based commercial competition for the BBC's journalism but which nevertheless insisted on a strong regulation of the commercial stations' public service output; Pilkington (1962) confirmed for the BBC the superiority of a public service against the commercial public service model of ITV in awarding the third channel to the corporation in 1964, yet also enabled the Independent Television Authority to have greater power to insist upon a consistently high-quality prime time news and current affairs journalism on commercial television; finally Annan (1977) recommended a greater diversity of provision, and this led to the launch of Channel 4, with its news and documentaries supported initially by advertising revenue from ITV.

After over half a century of consensus around the imperative for a public service provision of broadcast journalism in prime time, from the 1980s, under the influence of one of the dominant ideologies of the era, free-market solutions to the issue of media policy, led to a liberalizing of the news media in favour of big business solutions while maintaining that this was a move from State control to a freedom of choice for individual consumers. The privatisation of public services and a competitive spur to those surviving public services became the orthodoxy of the period. This was particularly relevant to the BBC, which Margaret Thatcher took a personal as well as a political dislike to. To an extent this was nothing new. Harold Wilson as Labour Prime Minister (1964–70 and 1974–76) had attempted to exert leverage on the BBC to gain better coverage for his government (Franklin, 1994: 82) and was convinced it had a bias against him. However, what distinguished the Thatcherite onslaught was not only its vindictiveness but also and above all its meshing with the emergent ideological preference both in the United States under the presidency of Ronald Reagan (1981–1989) and in much of the Western world for neo-liberal market solutions to questions surrounding public policy. The licence fee was temporarily frozen thus forcing the BBC into the market – a shift which it has, nevertheless, managed with great success. These developments have meant that conglomeration, concentration and cross-ownership have come to be seen by many commentators as greater threats to a diverse and democratically accountable news media than any direct state intervention had ever been.

Ostensibly, the Peacock Report of 1986 was to look into the financing of broadcasting in the satellite era. In effect, it led to two subsequent Broadcasting Acts which transformed the media landscape into one which allowed more marketized control over broadcast journalism than ever before. The Independent Television Commission was one innovation of the 1990 Broadcasting Act and this was charged with bringing a 'lighter touch' to its regulation. While the Act protected the BBC as the 'cornerstone of public service' it also gave purpose and direction to market-oriented solutions which were already incipient within the media ecology, but in itself it did not initiate changes (Ursell, 2001: 180).

Next, the deregulatory Broadcasting Act (1996) established frameworks for the development of digital broadcasting and further liberalized the rules on cross-ownership. It also established the Broadcasting Standards Commission which monitored and adjudicated on issues of taste and decency as well as unfair treatment and the infringement of privacy by broadcasters. The Act provided for six digital multiplexes, each of which would be capable of carrying six channels, and in so doing signalled a shift towards more narrowcasting and away from broadcasting, as each of the outlets was expected to define itself amidst more competitive pressure; single-issue channels would inevitably lead to a diminishing sense of a shared experience or common context for the reception of news, with clear implications for citizenship. The 1996 Broadcasting Act's restriction of ownership to a 20 per cent upper ceiling on newspapers only disqualified a proprietor from cross-owning terrestrial TV and/ or commercial radio licences or vice versa. Local newspaper proprietors from now on could own regional terrestrial television licences but the 20 per cent upper limit restricted further cross-ownership. A flurry of takeovers ensured that within a year there were merely three major ITV players – Carlton, Granada, and United News and Media – plus the Scottish Media Group, and these have since been consolidated still further to be controlled by just three firms: Granada Media, Carlton Communications and the Scottish Media Group (Doyle, 2003: 48).

The Communications White Paper published in December 2000 proposed removing the 15 per cent limit on the slice of commercial television that any single company could own, paving the way for the emergence of one super provider and thus reducing competition and variety in the provision of news on commercially-funded television. It also proposed the creation of a super-regulator in Ofcom. Ironically perhaps, given that this emanated from a Labour administration, the ensuing Conservative criticism regretted the Paper's inability to define the role of public service broadcasting. Ofcom was set up by the Communications Act of 2003 (see www.opsi.gov.uk/acts) to oversee an increasingly merged media environment where distinguishing between radio, television, online and newspaper journalism was increasingly being seen as a redundant exercise.

Overt State Control

Controlling of journalism has also meant using overt state control at many points over the century, ranging from suppression and censorship to more subtle forms of consensual self-censorship by journalists themselves. D-notices – effectively allowing a committee of politicians and the military to declare certain details of national defence as being off limit to publication in newspapers – were introduced for the first time in 1911 and these have to an overwhelming extent been adhered to ever since whenever they have been invoked. D-notices were replaced by DA-notices in 1993 after both the evaporation of the Soviet threat and the rise in anxieties about terrorism. These represent a more consensual product of negotiation between the military and senior journalists who request but do not enforce secrecy by themselves. There remains no appeal against the judgements of the government of the day on official secrecy.

An equally subtle form of state intervention arose during World War One when Reuters was secretly brought under government control, as this was gauged as proving more effective in controlling the flow of news to the press than censoring the output of newspapers more directly (Putnis, 2008: 141). This solution meant that the press would effectively serve the State in time of war without falling under direct government control. Wartime – either at home or abroad – is always a defining moment for government relations with journalism. Inevitably it means a restriction on what can be reported, and increases interference by politicians and the military in pre-publication decisions. By and large the censorship which operated throughout the First World War was a self-imposed and voluntary contribution to the war effort by the leading proprietors and editors whose only reservations lay in the intrusions of the Press Bureau into the exercise of their patriotic duties (Lovelace, 1978: 309–319).

The most flagrant act of political intervention early in the last century came in 1918 when Lloyd George bought the *Morning Chronicle* in order to assure press support for his Liberal Party. It was partly in response to this sort of threat that the BBC was organized with a specific concern to avoid a direct interference by the government of the day in its affairs.

Williams (1998: 132–138) outlines that one of the main objectives of the Ministry of Information from 1939 was less concerned with outright propaganda in the form of news control, since the Press Association and Reuters occupied the same building in Fleet Street. This meant that it was a relatively straightforward task to ensure control of the information flow, and that more energy could be focused on ensuring that the journalism produced could communicate a sense of social unity in the war effort.

During World War Two both the *Daily Worker* and the *Week* (both communist-owned) were closed down on 21 January 1941, despite their tiny circulations of 1 per cent of the national readership (Curran and Seaton, 2003: 57), but this was part of a broader antipathy to criticism emanating from the left of the newspaper spectrum from the government and was demonstrated in hostility towards the *Daily Herald* and the *Daily Mirror, Reynolds' News* and the *Sunday Pictorial*. All of these were critical of what they perceived to be the unnecessary loss of lives on the war front, as well as a lack of movement on the security of citizens and longer-term social reform on the home front. Churchill wanted the *Daily Mirror* closed down as well but the majority of national newspaper owners and editors saw where this sort of illiberalism could lead and therefore opposed him, sensing that this 'freedom of the press' was something which distinguished Britain from the countries it was fighting! As the war drew to an end, the BBC introduced a 14-day rule as a form of self-restraint to prevent itself becoming embroiled in the political controversy of a live political debate in parliament. This meant that it would not report on the matters discussed in parliament during the previous fortnight.

There has been notable state intervention in broadcasting on specific occasions, specifically in the case of Northern Ireland which played a huge role in the face-offs between broadcasters and both BBC and ITV during the 1980s. *Real Lives – At the Edge of the Union* was shown on the BBC in 1985 to the massive annoyance of the Conservative government, who claimed it was allowing terrorists the 'oxygen of publicity'. There was an attempt to ban the programme and after a strike by the NUJ at the BBC on 7 August, it was broadcast two months later with a few alterations. The commercial sector also became involved in political controversy. In 1988 *Death on the Rock* from ITV's Thames Television was broadcast as scheduled but to huge political criticism. It substantiated earlier claims that British Special Forces had been involved in the targeted assassination of suspected IRA members in Gibraltar. This kind of political criticism laid the foundations for the broadcasting ban that followed from 1988 to 1994 which forbade the direct broadcasting of the words of paramilitary/political organizations and meant that actors had to be used to voice-over pictures of the speakers themselves. This characteristic hostility to the independence of broadcasting institutions which chose to go against government preferences on matters of internal security also contributed to the penning of a new Official Secrets Act in 1989. Both programmes demonstrated the sort of opposition which broadcast journalism can face in Britain when it happens to disagree with the government of the day.

It is clear that journalism has played an important part historically in maintaining national unity and support for the military during periods of warfare (Knightley, 1982; Taylor, 2003). In the modern era, when the legitimacy of war is often highly contested within the British public, it is essential that journalism continues to provide as consensual a view of any conflict as possible, and various governments have taken steps to ensure that overt censorship does not become apparent (Schlesinger, 1992: 296). It is much more problematic to consider the public accountability of journalism during conflicts which have less than total national approval. The 1982 Falklands' War was a case in point. McNair (2003a: 205) has identified this conflict as a turning point in military operations where the management of news and opinion was at least as important as the success of the actual military operation. One advantage for the government was that the islands were some 8,000 miles away from Britain and so what was in effect an experiment in the selection and management of news could be conducted. Journalists who were suspected of harbouring opinions less than supportive of the military operation were excluded from the pool of those who were approved to travel with the taskforce.

Lexical arguments between the Thatcher government and the BBC on the use of 'the' or 'our' troops, pushed debates about patriotism and treachery to new and very public levels of intensity and were trumped by the *Sun*'s coinage of the expression 'OUR BOYS', which entered the language at this time. Indeed the language of war reporting was to become a very significant aspect of the partiality of journalism from this point onwards. In the Iraq conflicts many commentators and analysts have queried the unwritten consent written into coverage. Not only has there been a manipulation of information but there has also been a new style of language created for the contemporary military conflict (Collins and Glover, 2002; Hodge and Kress, 1993; Keeble, 2005a; Temple, 2008: 143). Even in more general terms there is an overarching preference by the national media to preference the interests of their particular national/political community (Billig, 1995). Inevitably perhaps, as news cannot be narrated from nowhere, it builds in a bias towards what is already at least softly-politicized coverage in favour of what is perceived as a national political consensus.

There is little overt political censorship in peacetime in the British news media but there are altogether more subtle ways in which information can be crafted for or withheld from the public. The Official Secrets Act is the most immediate and arbitrary instrument for the suppression of information which the government considers vital to the national interest, while the 30-year rule sets up a shelf life on the suppression of material which could embarrass or threaten the state.

News management is a further, subtle means of political control over both the content of journalism and the access which journalists have to political information (Eldridge et al., 1997: 23). Within extremely busy agendas, journalists can often find it all too convenient to settle for a carefully crafted political communication. From the 1980s campaigning pressure groups, charities, minority political parties and quangos have all learnt the lessons about the orchestration of public communication via journalism after the success of the Saatchis in providing Margaret Thatcher with a winning set of media strategies.

Conclusion

The personalities in control of the institutions of journalism have become less prominent over the century in terms of their public parading of their status and power, and with regard to direct intervention. This is explained by the growing corporatization of journalism within broader media portfolios. There are both overt and more subtle forms of control which have been exerted over the content of journalism. Whether these have taken the form of censorship in wartime, consensus politics or adhering to the prevailing economic orthodoxy, journalism has tended increasingly not to rock the boat. In general, we must conclude that over the last thirty years the balance has swung in the direction of neo-liberal solutions with direct consequences for journalism. McChesney has written that there is nothing inherent in the technology which has determined a shift to conglomerate control and the rule of the market across all media decision making, including in the provision of public service journalism. Owners have opted to adopt this set of ideological and commercial imperatives because this makes it easier to make profits from their products. The journalism and culture produced by the global media system are highly conducive to the neoliberal political economic order (McChesney, 2003: 38).

The effect of conglomeration as a trend within journalism production is that the journalism becomes less important than the profits, as it is simply one part of a diverse and relatively incoherent set of holdings across various business sectors. Given the already reduced political spectrum offered via the ownership of newspapers by wealthy individuals and organizations this further erodes the range of public choice. From 1990 each successive Broadcasting Act has encouraged such a narrowing to accelerate. The White Paper of 2000 claimed somewhat disingenuously that '[f]ostering competition is the first step to promoting plurality in the media' (2000: 36). But, of course, as Doyle points out, competition and pluralism are not the same thing (2003: 131).

Freedom of choice in a profit-driven market may not best serve the needs of journalism within an entertainment market. This signals that there is clearly a continuing requirement for the role of regulation as a last resort to protect pluralism because when 'misallocations of market power occur in media, the result is the corrosion of our civic life' (Hargreaves, 2001: 5).

FURTHER READING

Coleridge, N. (1994). *Paper Tigers: The Latest, Greatest Newspaper Tycoons and How They Won the World.* London: Mandarin. This is an account of the personal foibles of the news media owners, and assesses the extent to which their personalities shaped their institutional output.

Cottle, S. (ed.) (2003) *Media, Organization and Production.* London: SAGE. This takes a systematic look at the interactions of the technologies and organization of news media organizations on their output, in a refreshing counterbalance to analyses which focus purely on the textual output of journalism divorced from these important institutional frameworks.

Seymour-Ure, C. (1996) *The British Press and Broadcasting Since 1945.* Oxford: Blackwell. This is a good narrative overview of developments in the second half of the twentieth century.

Tunstall, J. (1996) *Newspaper Power: The New National Press in Britain.* Oxford: Clarendon. This is an essential update on the changes emanating from late-century developments in the ownership and management of newspapers within the prevailing political economy of those years, which are of continuing relevance to the contemporary scene.

4

Women as Consumers and Producers of Journalism

Introduction

One of the driving imperatives of the New Journalism of the late nineteenth century had been the incorporation of women readers within the daily press. This had had the aim of delivering those female readers to the advertisers of domestic and fashion products which provided most of the most financially lucrative display advertising in the newspapers. At the same time, an increasingly successful and influential advocacy journalism educated women in terms of their political rights and social potential. One of the lasting legacies of the juxtaposition of these two developments was that women began to slowly claim a place for themselves as journalists within the mainstream.

However, this is not a straightforward tale of women's emancipation within journalism either as an audience or as producers. Women had been energetic contributors to early print culture in England during much of the seventeenth century, yet had often been implicitly excluded from discussions within the early public sphere on account of its essentially male construction. Despite this, women did participate as part of an alternative and competing public sphere through their own print practices (Halascz, 1997), and even women of lower and middle rank contested this public sphere of male letters. They had acted as writers, printers, managers and prominent members of the Stationers' Company until various economic and social shifts began to consign them to a restricted public role as the eighteenth century progressed and the Company began to contribute to a generalized male dominance in print culture. New controls of the press favoured the capital of groups of established printers and men of property, thus isolating individual women printers. McDowell (1998: 5) argues that women had been pivotal to print and literary culture until they became socially and politically marginalized by transformations in the demarcation of sex-roles in the eighteenth century.

Women's contribution to and reception of journalism remain live and problematic aspects of journalism in general. Debates will be considered in this chapter on the limitations of women's contribution to journalism from within a 'velvet ghetto' (Creedon, 1989), the increase in 'soft news' and lifestyle journalism as one limited career path for women, the alleged sexualization of popular culture and accusations of the tokenistic deployment of female newsreaders as 'news candy'; it and will allow readers to assess where we are at the moment both in terms of the representation and the employment of women in journalism.

Women: Hidden from the Mainstream

Women in journalism are narrated, as is so often the case, as 'hidden from history' (Rowbotham, 1996), often doubly so as journalism tends to present itself as either being about men, for men, and by men or only of relevance to women when dealing with domestic and gender-restricted issues in women's magazines. This chapter will attempt to do something to redress that balance by indicating that women have always contributed more than has been apparent in traditional histories of journalism, despite the fact that they have at worst been erased from history sometimes quite literally, as in Pebody's *English Journalism and the Men Who Have Made It* (1882), or at best marginalized within mainstream narratives. This is ironic considering the extent to which the dominant trend of journalism from the late nineteenth century whence much of the impetus for modern journalism comes has been to include styles of writing and illustration that are of greater interest to an idealized woman reader. Including women in the history of journalism constitutes part of what Adburgham (1972: 9) has called 'rescue work'.

Nineteenth-Century Women Journalists

During the first half of the nineteenth century, women continued in their capacity as contributors and writers on magazines targeted at the fashionable, leisured female reader, as they had done for most of the eighteenth century, but were excluded from the masculine world of full-time journalism on newspapers. Sebba writes of the steady opening of journalism to women in the nineteenth century: 'Becoming a journalist in Victorian times was one of the very few routes open to intelligent women with some education to rise beyond humble origins or out of a failed marriage' (1994: 3). However, the inclusion of women in the increasingly professionalized arena of newspaper journalism was extremely problematic for the whole notion of mid-Victorian professionalization as:

> The nineteenth-century creation of professions – whether journalism, medicine or engineering – was always predicated upon the exclusion of women and others deemed unsuitable for the job. The presence of women in journalism threatened its status as a profession. (Beetham, 1996: 43)

Writing for magazines allowed women to work from home anonymously, efficiently and respectably, remaining confined to their designated domestic space while enabling them to earn an irregular income and contribute to the household economy through the fruits of their education even though they 'often wrote in "drag"' (Easley, 2000: 154) for Victorian periodicals and increasingly for newspapers. Prolific women journalists of the time included Christian Johnstone, who worked as editor of *Tait's Edinburgh Magazine*, Harriet Martineau, who provided topical commentary particularly in leading articles for the *Daily News* from 1855 to 1862, and Margaret Oliphant, who worked on a wide range of influential and male-orientated magazines and reviews including the prestigious Edinburgh-based *Blackwood's*.

In 1848 Eliza Lynn Linton became the first full-time female Fleet Street journalist on the payroll of the *Morning Chronicle*, most notably as a Paris correspondent. She was not employed in the casual, freelance way which had become common for women journalists at the time, having gained respect for her reporting, and therefore did not need to hide behind the convention of anonymity. Lady Florence Dixie was another pioneer in women's journalism, first providing reports on life and politics in South Africa from 1881 to 1882 for the *Morning Post* and then, on her return to England, contributing articles on a range of topical issues from Irish Nationalism to the Women's Suffrage movement. With the New Journalism of the 1880s and its increased emphasis on personal tone, interviews and the emotionalism of sensation – targeted increasingly at a female readership – women journalists were more in demand than ever. Flora Shaw was notable for her efforts as a trail-blazer for the New Journalism on the *Pall Mall Gazette* from 1887 onwards, particularly for her reports from Gibraltar before she moved to work on the *Manchester Guardian*. Hulda Friederichs was another journalist who provided many of the interviews on that same paper which Stead deployed as a key marker of this new style of popular journalism. Emilie Peacocke provides an illustration of an emergent route into daily newspapers at that time by starting on her father's *Northern Echo* in 1898 (since such family contacts were essential for women in this period if they were to create an opening) and then moving to the *Daily Express* as a reporter in 1904 until she become editor of the women's page of the *Sunday Express* from 1918 onwards (Chambers et al., 2004: 25).

Advocacy Journalism

The trajectory of women's increasing involvement in mainstream journalism was matched by the momentum building around women's discussion of their political and social rights. As late as the 1840s, despite the fact that women had edited radical, unstamped newspapers in the 1830s – such as Eliza Sharples on the *Isis* of 1832 – women were still being systematically excluded from the discourse of radical politics. The Chartists' demand for 'universal' voting rights in the mid-century, for instance, continued to mean votes for men alone. Nonetheless, women pioneered the return of a form of public writing which recalled the earlier era of women's journalism from the mid-seventeenth century by including a radical social critique for a wider audience. White (1970: 47) sees this era heralded by the appearance in 1846 of *The Female's Friend*, a magazine which dedicated itself to 'elevating the character and condition of women'.

From the 1860s, magazines and periodicals dedicated to issues on women's rights flourished generally across the United States and Western Europe. As part of this growing trend in England we can see the *Englishwoman's Journal* which was edited by Bessie Rayner Parkes from 1858. This was followed by *The Lady's Review* in 1860 which was the latest attempt to incorporate into a women's magazine a discussion of the social changes affecting women. It was not however a commercial success and folded within the year. The *Alexandra Magazine* (1864–65, continuing as the *Englishwoman's Review* until 1910) and the *Victoria Magazine* (1863–80) both made a serious contribution to the cause of women's emancipation and suffrage. The *English Woman's Journal* (1858–64), edited by Jessie Boucherett, which pronounced polemically in favour of women's rights, was influential but had a limited circulation. The *Woman's Suffrage Journal*, edited by Lydia E. Becker from 1870 to 1890, was one of the longest surviving and most prominent attempts to secure a specifically radical form of women's journalism that campaigned on women's issues. They all suffered, like the more broadly defined radical press of the early nineteenth century, from the irreconcilable tension between the necessity for commercial success in the increasingly commodified field of journalism and the desire to promote radical alternatives to contemporary problems. Yet they did succeed in setting the terms of the debate around women's rights which were to become influential in mainstream political debate and their coverage in journalism as a whole.

In 1903 Emmeline Pankhurst founded and led the militant movement that was called the Women's Social and Political Union of women suffragettes (WSPU). She also published the feminist journal *Votes for Women* (1907–18) which achieved a circulation of 40,000 despite or because of its radicalism. It was adamant that the voting issue was simply one element in a wider pattern of economic and sexual exploitation of women.

There were also attempts to introduce more broadly politicized interventions into the sphere of women's journalism. These included from August 1907 the Women's Trade Union League paper which was aimed at a proletarian readership and edited by Mary Macarthur, *The Woman Worker*, and from 1914 the *Women's Dreadnought* which was launched as the suffragettes' official organ.

Advocacy journalism on behalf of the suffragette cause belongs to a special category of journalism in that it was not primarily intended to be profitable and was more to be judged according to its ability to involve women in the process of political self-determination. DiCenzo (2000) claims that the suffrage press in Britain was central to the advancement of women's access to the public sphere. In this context, its success can be assessed against the fact that it drew women into patterns of communicative production and organization like at no point since the seventeenth century, and contributed directly to women being able to argue for their cause: through this there was building pressure on the political establishment to effect the franchise being extended for women over 30 in 1919 and those over 21 in 1928 (Tusan, 2005).

The Return of the Suppressed

Within the mainstream, women had been identified by the New Journalism as commercially essential to wide-scale success, since it was they who took most of the significant decisions within the domestic economy and were becoming more affluent as social and economic changes meant that it had become more common for women to be working outside the home in paid employment. The New Journalism took on many of the attributes that had been associated with women's journalism in magazines for over a century and made these attractive to a wider and more general readership through the inclusion of more personal detail and human interest in its news. In his accusation that the New Journalism was 'feather-brained', Arnold's (1887) criticism of the New Journalism was not only based upon cultural elitism, it was also implicitly critical of its engagement with these hitherto feminized characteristics. Beetham has also pointed out that: ' ... the opposition of "reasonable" against "featherbrained" implicitly mobilized the vocabulary of gendered identity' (1996: 119). The New Journalism also drew on the visual character of the magazine which Beetham (1996: 126) characterized as a further 'feminisation', since femininity had been located in and defined by appearance to an extent that masculinity had not. Furthermore, it borrowed the conversational tone of the magazine and incorporated this more than newspaper journalism had previously done in its reporting. This was made explicit by Harmsworth, who identified 'woman appeal' as being crucial to his *Daily Mail* (Friederichs, 1911: 55), especially once it had begun to devote Page 7 to women's stories, fashion and domestic issues.

This incorporation of a 'feminized' discourse and representational modes was not designed to empower women, as it merely allowed a profit to be better extracted from their custom, yet increasingly feminized modes of representation in journalism encouraged more women into the job. Women journalists were becoming more visible as their by-lines increased in newspapers and magazines, and consequently journalism began to appear more often as a potential employment option for women, although their role was too often restricted by the sort of gender stereotyping illustrated by Arnold Bennett who, while he was editor of *Woman*, wrote a small book called *Journalism for Women* (1898) in which he made his opinion quite plain:

> *In Fleet Street there are not two sexes, but two species – journalists and women journalists, and we treat the species very differently. Women are not expected to suffer the same discipline, nor are they judged by the same standards. In Fleet Street femininity is an absolution, not an accident. (Adburgham, 1972: 272)*

Harmsworth himself, embittered after the failure of his *Daily Mirror* in 1903 as a daily newspaper written by and for women, may also have helped nourish the conviction in Britain that females were biologically unsuitable for mainstream journalism (Delano, 2003: 274).

Despite this apparent hostility, women were prominent enough in journalism for the Society of Women Journalists to be founded in 1895, and by 1898 the issue of women in journalism had become pressing enough for *The Woman at Home* to run a symposium entitled 'Is Journalism A Good Profession For Women?'

Women Become a Key Market

Building on the intimacy of tone of the New Journalism (Campbell, 2000; Salmon, 2000), a community in print based on increasing reader identification was to become key to the expanding market for all types of journalism in the twentieth century. This was most obviously expressed in women's magazines and particularly on their problem pages which served as a barometer for changing social and cultural trends. Yet there was little overt political debate in these magazines despite the rise of the suffrage movement. They chose to follow rather than lead public opinion – a rather conservative option but consistent with the approach of most commercial journalism which was acutely aware of the pragmatism required for success within mass markets. It was to take several decades of grafting and combating prejudice before the cross-over of women journalists into the daily press was to begin in earnest.

In certain specialist areas, with senior editorial support, there could be exceptions but this could not detract from the overall invisibility of women journalists. Most of the elite press in Britain through the 1950s ignored women altogether. The only women's pages in national newspapers were in the popular market and these tended to be dominated by fashion and society gossip. Katharine Whitehorn, who started her career at this time, has observed:

> Grander papers didn't have women's pages at all; women journalists in the main paper were supposed to write in exactly the same way as men, and there weren't many of them ... The very phrase 'women's journalism' was a term of disparagement. (Whitehorn, 1997: 1)

The popular press incorporated features of woman's magazines earlier than their broadsheet cousins. In 1954, Marjorie Proops started work on the *Daily Mirror* as a columnist with a celebrity brief. Many of her topics were drawn from concerns expressed in letters to her 'Dear Marje' advice column, which ran in the weekly magazine *Weekly Mirror* from 1959 and for which she would gain recognition as a household name. Through the social experimentation of the 1960s, she began to shift the emphasis increasingly to tackle serious issues such as co-habitation before marriage, the use of contraceptives and drug addiction. This was so successful that she was invited to transfer this formula on a daily basis to the *Daily Mirror* in 1971. The agony aunt column subsequently became an influential commentary on the changing mores of British women in daily newspapers, as they had long been a part of the women's magazine agenda. Certain of the most powerful of newspaper columnists were women such as Jean Rook on the *Daily Express* and Lynda Lee-Potter on the *Daily Mail*, both of whom from 1972 onwards made powerful contributions to the 'public idiom' of their newspapers in their interviews and opinion columns – defining the place and role of a women's voice in a middle-brow national identity.

As a notable exception to Whitehorn's rule, Mary Stott as women's editor of the *Guardian* (1957–1971) pioneered feature writing that was a step away from the agony aunts and problem pages of magazines and the popular press in attempting to widen the resonance and reach of journalism aimed at women. As the world began to open up for women she gave space to writing about balancing work and child-raising, depression and physical problems relating to women, and she also included letters from readers who were allowed to play their part in developing a new public sphere of women's discussion, most notably for ordinary women who could begin to glimpse the possibility of direct action and organization to effect change in their own lives and in the lives of other women (Chambers et al., 2004: 39).

Women's journalism has developed alongside lifestyle features more generally in the broadsheet press from the 1990s to include more that is of interest to increasingly affluent and socially engaged professional women readers. This may have resulted in a greater number of women journalists writing for contemporary newspapers but even here, as Heller has commented:

> *Historically, the role of the female newspaper writer has been to leaven the seri-*
> *ous (male) stuff of reportage and analysis with light dispatches – news from the*
> *realm of the domestic, the emotional, the personal. (1999: 10)*

In other areas of journalism, women remained remarkable by their invisibility. Julia Langdon was the first woman to be appointed as a political editor, on Maxwell's *Daily Mirror*, as late as 1984. Women political editors and editors have been seen on national newspapers, with Eve Pollard at both the *Sunday Mirror* and the *Sunday Express*, Patsy Chapman at the *News of the World*, Wendy Henry and Bridget Rowe at the *People*, and most recently Rebekah Wade who became, from January 2003, the first woman editor of a national popular daily newspaper when she took over at the *Sun* in what may have appeared to be a rather pyrrhic victory for women. Nonetheless, women continue to be under-represented at senior editorial levels in most forms of journalism apart from magazines.

Women's Radicalism Reborn

From 1972 onwards *Spare Rib* represented a radical invigoration of the tradition of the women's paper for a very different era as part of what has been termed the 'second wave of feminism'. It operated as a collective with several women who had already gained experience in the underground press on titles such as *Oz* and *Ink* (Cadman et al., 1981), including Rosie Boycott who then moved on to become editor of such mainstream publications as *Esquire* and the *Daily Express* and later both the *Independent* and the *Independent on Sunday*. They aimed to 'put feminism on the newsstands' by adopting a broad political agenda to target a mass readership of both feminists and those ripe for persuasion. It was also their intention to compete with the glossy magazines which meant that *Spare Rib* had to be very thoughtful about the 'politics of appearance' (Cadman et al., 1981: 77). Through its strategic approach it became a major contributor to debates about the changing politics of women's experience of the world. Continuing the traditions of feminist advocacy journalism at a local level, from 1975 the Bristol-based *Shrew* and the *Manchester Women's Paper*, influenced by the political ambition of *Spare Rib*, represented prominent attempts to attract readers of mainstream women's magazines, with the latter particularly adopting a style that was lively but 'discreetly feminist' (Cadman et al., 1981: 73).

Characteristic of *Spare Rib's* ambition to include the widest possible spectrum of debate on women's issues, it moved to incorporate black and lesbian issues into the mainstream of its collective and editorial concerns in the 1980s. Its continuing success led in 1985 to the launch of publications such as *Everywoman* and *Woman's Review*. Despite its contemporary impact and lasting influence it finally went out of business in 1993, in many ways a victim of its own success in bringing aspects of the feminist debate into the mainstream of social debate.

Women had been successful in promoting their own issues around sexual and gender politics from the 1960s and 1970s to the extent that their polemical writing had begun to have an impact within mainstream journalism. One of the most celebrated attempts to bring the politics of feminism to a daily newspaper with sympathy and not a little humour came from Jill Tweedie, in a column entitled 'Letters from a Faint-Hearted Feminist' on the *Guardian* from 1969 to 1988. Institutionally, however, women were not as successful in gaining specific recognition either professionally or in terms of trades union recognition as a constituency with their own agenda. By the 1990s the NUJ could claim that it had produced at least the glimmer of an awareness of gender issues by setting up an equality council, but it had not produced any figures on women's promotion prospects since 1984 (Dougary, 1994: 115 and 238). In response to the poor record of the National Union of Journalists in challenging the inherent sexism of journalism, the Women in Journalism group was set up during the mid-1990s. Sisters, indeed, were being forced to do it for themselves.

Women Journalists on the Radio

There could have been no more patriarchal point of departure for the BBC than the appointment of John Reith as its Director. A traditionalist and culturally conservative, his vision of the public service broadcaster was entirely masculine in its emphasis as he sought to create a paragon of enlightened and serious public communication. Women were not permitted to read the news, as it was judged that their voices did not have the necessary authority or resonance. This view persisted until the late 1960s:

> *Male voices, they said, in the end carried more authority. In the late 'sixties this was a widely held view. (MacGregor, 2002: 116)*

Despite this reluctance to engage with women as performers, it was a woman who was to play a significant role in the differentiation of broadcast journalism from the patterns of newspapers in the early days of the BBC. The broadcast delivery of journalism was problematic as it needed writing which was designed more for the ear, more for oral delivery, than those who had been trained on newspapers were accustomed to providing. This required a perspective from outside traditional and culturally conservative boundaries. So it fell to a woman, Hilda Matheson, to develop a style of writing that sounded more natural when read aloud. To create a structure in which this style could operate on a consistent basis, in 1928 she commissioned a report into the way the newly formed News Section should operate. It recommended that news agencies should provide their full wire service to the BBC and that bulletins should be structured with home news first; this was to be followed by overseas and sports news. The report has been described – because of its seminal impact – as simply the most important document on news values ever produced for the BBC (Hunter, 2000: 43).

Another early pioneer was a Manchester-based documentary maker, Olive Shapley, whose programmes broke new ground for radio both in their technique and their subject matter (Scannell and Cardiff, 1991: 345) by allowing the voices of ordinary working-class respondents to be heard at a time when the BBC was exclusively a middle-class enclave which was echoed in its insistence on the best of Received Pronunciation (Chambers et al., 2004: 30).

An early experiment with dedicated programming for women came with *Woman's Hour*, which ran for nine months from 1923, but this was dropped because its grouping of women as a cognate group, like children, was considered patronizing and also because few women had time to listen at this time of the day (Chambers et al., 2004: 30). *Women's Hour* was re-launched in 1946 and is currently the BBC's longest running radio programme, demonstrating a more positive aspect of women's experience on radio in its exclusively women-oriented journalism. Yet the very success of the programme has been used to argue against any expansion of this style of provision as was illustrated by comments from Roger Laughton, Head of BBC's Daytime Television:

> *We've got Women's Hour on the radio and I don't think that we need to recreate that on television. It's the same argument that applies to women's pages in newspapers. We shouldn't need them. I'd argue that we're in a post-revolutionary situation. Far more people are now affected by a feminine (as opposed to a woman's) viewpoint and this should be incorporated into the mainstream of TV. (Coward, 1987: 98)*

Even Channel 4 – contractually obliged to cater for minority and otherwise excluded voices – was lukewarm towards programmes made by and targeted specifically at a female audience. In its early years it did commission *20/20 Vision* and *Broadside* but these were dropped according to Baehr and Spindler-Brown (1987) because it was considered that women's interests were adequately represented by its more generalist provision.

There is still a marked tendency within radio journalism for a partitioning of jobs for women. Writing of her experience in radio, prominent broadcaster Sue MacGregor recalls:

> *Eighteen years and four general elections on from the time I first joined Today, there are still remarkably few women fronting current affairs programmes. As programme producers and editors women are now universally accepted ... [from Afghanistan] Kate Clark, Jacky Rowland, Susannah Price and Catherine Davis from the BBC World Sevice all distinguished themselves with daily accounts of*

the battle, and their names became almost as familiar as John Simpson's. But the number of women as front-line political interviewers is still lamentably low.

Perhaps it is partly a matter of style: interviews are expected to be more con-frontational these days, and confrontation is an approach with which men are generally more comfortable. (2002: 326–327)

Women and Television Journalism

Given the preponderance of female news presenters currently on our screens, it may well strike contemporary readers as strange that it took so long for women to be regarded as suitable for all types of television news presenting. This was, in part, a hangover from the patriarchal attitudes which had spread from radio into television journalism, but this could not by itself explain the time lag. ITN did not sweep women to a position of equality in television journalism in anything like the same way that it championed popular and iconoclastic approaches to other aspects of its production from its inception. There were, however, isolated experiments – for instance, Barbara Mandell was the first woman to read a lunchtime television news bulletin on ITN in 1955, while Nan Winton in 1960 was the first female newsreader on national news on the BBC for a brief time before being asked to step aside. It was only in 1975 that Angela Rippon became employed as the first permanent woman newsreader on the BBC, and after that three years passed before ITN bettered that by providing in Anna Ford the first regular evening presenter. Thumin argues that the slow pace of change from to a position where women were considered acceptable in news and current affairs was partly due to a general male domination of public affairs, but also claims that it was linked to fears about television as a journalistic medium.

As television's place in society became more secure and more central, its inher-ent dangers – frivolity, passivity, feminization – had to be overcome. It had to be masculinized in order to be tolerable as the hub of national life it was clearly becoming. (Thumin, 1998: 103)

Sebba confirms this role for women journalists within a masculinized journalism in an incisive analysis of the attraction of the report that brought television reporter Kate Adie to prominence during the 1980 Iranian Embassy siege:

As the Embassy shook with the sound of gunfire, Kate was to be seen crawling along the pavement yelling for a microphone. She recognises today that the disturbing element in this kind of reporting is that 'it is just like the movies'. Inevitably, viewers come to expect their news increasingly to be served up as entertainment and a woman television personality – especially a pretty one – witnessing the danger is particularly effective in lending to the excitement an additional frisson. (Sebba, 1994: 266)

In light of this, it seems ironic that the same journalist, Kate Adie, was accused of refer-ring to the current generation of television journalists as 'bimbos' at the Cheltenham Festival of Literature in October 2001. However, it is also interesting to note that while women foreign reporters on television and in print continue to break down the barriers, they are still working within a pattern originally established by Lady Florence Dixie in the Victorian era.

Surveys and Statistics

Journalism's treatment of women as producers and subjects normalizes how women are presented to broader society. This is important because it 'plays a central role in shaping our perceptions of gender relations, sometimes conferring – and some-times defining – public recognition to people purely on the basis of sexual difference' (Carter, 2005: 259).

There is nothing more revealing of the difficulties facing women in journalism than surveys which capture the unequal distribution of jobs between men and women in journalism. Statistical evidence up until the 1990s remained patchy but an unsur-prising story was emerging nevertheless. Strick (1957) calculated that the ratio of women to men in newspapers was 1:16 and in magazines 1:3, reinforcing the gen-dered divide between these two forms of journalism and confirming the reality that women were an insignificant minority until the expansion of the journalist popula-tion in the 1960s (Delano, 2003: 285) through the growth in employment opportu-nities in television, magazines and radio in the consumer boom time of those years. Progress on newspapers continued to be slow but by 1975 Roger Smith (1976: 243) estimated that there had been an increase in women reporter recruits to local news-papers from 23 per cent in 1970–71 to 36 per cent in 1975–76 and on the national titles from 9.6 per cent to 12.6 per cent, although Smith found only five women among 239 news subeditors working on those national newspapers that were ready to provide him with information.

Changing social mores and economic models had led by the 1960s and 1970s to an increase in the number of women journalists, who had quickly become aware – due in no small part to the impact of the polemic of the feminist press com-bined with their direct experience – that there were issues around equality of expec-tation and aspiration in what had been until then a male-dominated sphere. This in turn had also led to many statistical and behavioural surveys which attempted to peer inside a set of practices which had survived unremarked and unchallenged for centuries. There was consequently a boom in explorations and surveys of the cultures of newsrooms, news-gathering and editorial decision making. De Bruin (2000) cites the increasing number of surveys of gender-related issues in the jour-nalism workplace in the 1970s and 1980s, from case studies on the position of women in the media hierarchy to the role of women in the organizational production processes.

Academic Debate

Van Zoonen (1994) has indicated that the problems surrounding contemporary women's journalism do not simply reside in representation or in personnel but are embedded within the 'gendered structure of media production'. Some of this structural bias has to do with the male traditions of the work but in more invisible ways it has to do with the very patterns of what has become valued as good journalism within institutions, particularly with regard to hard news. Research has proved inconclusive as to the impact of women journalists on the content and practice of journalism itself. Scholars such as Liesbet Van Zoonen (1994) and Linda Christmas (1997) have concluded that a female influence in newsrooms has changed the values of news production and that this effect could be recognized in much news writing by women from the 1990s, demonstrating a weakening of the 'hegemonic masculinity' (Connell, 1978) that had previously governed news values (Delano, 2003: 275). On occasions, women could break this stereotypical stranglehold, for instance, via reports from the Balkan war zones by women correspondents such as Maggie O'Kane, Janine de Giovanni and Kim Willsher, which frequently focused on the plight of non-combatant victims and the effect of the war on individual participants rather than on battlefield tactics and weaponry. Sport, too, was an area of journalism in which male dominance began to be undermined (Delano, 2003: 275).

However, Creedon (1989) has argued that increasing numbers of women, even within mainstream journalism, have continued to be confined to 'velvet ghettos'. Stuart Allan (1999: 136) has blamed this on the embedded masculinist bias within traditions of 'objective' reporting. Even while some successful journalists such as Kate Adie have be quoted as saying 'things have changed radically in the last 15 years for women reporters', in terms of the powerful managers and decision makers within journalism, little has changed to the benefit of women. Research results from different Western countries according to Van Zoonen (1998: 45) have demonstrated the continuing minority position of women in traditional news journalism, while prominent journalist Amanda Platell (1999: 141) confirmed that newspaper journalism in particular was simply a practice of 'institutionalized sexism'.

New Girls: New Ghetto?

Although the increase in lifestyle journalism of the 1990s has enabled more women to work in a wider range of areas, much of the increased output from women has been influenced by the 'new girl writing', from Zoë Heller early in the decade, through Helen Fielding's *Bridget Jones's Diary*, to Kathryn Flett's raw account of her divorce in *Girl Overboard* (1997). Heller herself (1999: 10–11) has described this form of journalism in the following terms:

> Writing 'as a woman' always winds up being a tiresome act ... But the demand for women's columns – composed in a self-consciously female voice – is astonishingly

hardy. One of the old liberal arguments is that they were said to provide an anti-dote to the chauvinism of a paper's invariably male-centric editorial ... It is a textbook example of chauvinism at work. (1999: 16)

The success of this form of journalism and the eagerness of women to produce it have been explained (Chambers et al., 2004: 137) by the breakdown of the women's movement in the 1980s and the subsequent celebration of individualism and consumerism within which the apparent success of women in winning certain arguments about equal rights has meant the justification of an ironic stance towards gender issues which have become popularized as 'post-feminism'. Indeed, such a perspective on 'post-feminism' does shed a sceptical light on the increasing presence of women in certain forms of journalism, particularly in the high-profile world of television news reporting and presenting. This returns us to the anxieties which have haunted women's journalism since the arrival of the New Journalism. The politicization of the personal – such a sloganized feature of the feminist generation of the 1960s and 1970s – may well have had its progressive aspects, but it has also been exploited within contemporary commercialized journalism as a strategy to incorporate more populist and less politicized approaches, which was certainly not the ambition of feminist pioneers of this period. Women television news presenters, particularly when they are young and photogenic, as well as prominent female by-lined columnists, can be seen to add to the market appeal of journalism without doing much to alter a highly masculine set of news agendas.

Conclusion

Women's journalism is at a complex juncture where, despite the presence of greater numbers of practitioners, older concerns persist about the ways they are deployed professionally, particularly on television and in restrictions to advancement in certain areas of 'serious' journalism and in senior management roles in the industry. Chambers et al. conclude that:

It is therefore not helpful to refer to the postmodern shift to infotainment as a 'feminization' of news. None the less, this shift has gendered implications, both positive and negative, for women both as journalists and as readers and audiences of the news. It could be argued that as market-driven journalism intensifies, larger numbers of women journalists are being employed to produce more emotional, sensational and therapy-style news while men get on with the 'real' work of 'hard' news'. (2004: 230)

Despite apparent advances, women continue mainly in the glamorous ghettos of journalism as opposed to the serious areas of news journalism. Newspapers remain the most under-representative area of news media for women, with less than 23 per cent of the workforce, compared to the highpoint of 55 per cent on periodicals (Delano, 2003: 275).

We can surely generalize that point from print culture to journalism of all styles and formats. The commodification of journalism has seen a tendency to include more lifestyle-oriented features, including more personalized accounts of experiences from both male and female writers. This forms part of a blurring of hard and soft news which has been a constant in the process of what we might term the 'magazinification' of journalism. Overall women's journalism is a contentious, ambivalent and hugely interesting set of practices which continue to shape a diverse public sphere, but it is much more within the mainstream of journalism than previously, as a commodified settlement within the predominantly patriarchal discourses which still structure much of women's contribution to that mainstream.

The increasing 'feminization' of mainstream journalism has all the characteristics of a hegemonic compromise, allowing female voices into the discourse of journalism while doing so on the terms of the dominant male perspective, particularly when they have the potential to improve profitability. The danger for the dominant perspective and the optimistic perspective for women's journalism is that once inside – no matter how compromised they are by the existing structures – women are potentially able to rearrange the existing patterns and reshape this discourse, however slowly. Incorporation is not one-way traffic.

FURTHER READING

Beetham, M. (1996) *A Magazine of Her Own? Domesticity and Desire in the Women's Magazine, 1800–1914*. London: Routledge. This provides an excellent account of the development of a particularly attractive commercial form of journalism for women within its economic and political contexts.

Chambers, D., Steiner, L. and Fleming, C. (2004) *Women and Journalism*. London: Routledge. This gives a wide-ranging account of the history of women in journalism across various media as well as an analysis of where how these forms of journalism are coping with contemporary demands.

Mitchell, C. (2000) *Women and Radio: Airing Differences*. London: Routledge. A precise account of the issues raised by women in the medium of radio; which includes some useful commentary on their contribution to journalism.

Tusan, M. (2005) *Women Making News: Gender and Journalism in Modern Britain*. Urbana and Chicago: University of Illinois Press. This gives an analysis of the range and vitality of journals and newspapers which sought emancipation for women and later challenged for a greater acknowledgment of women politically and culturally.

White, C.L. (1970) *Women's Magazines, 1693–1968*. London: Michael Joseph. Though long out of print, this book provides what is probably still the best overview of the changes in magazines targeted at women over three centuries, and also provides a basic understanding of where these publications have emerged from and how they have been developed commercially.

5

Technology and Journalism

Introduction

To bemoan the impact of technology on journalism would seem a rather futile occupation given that journalism is itself the product of a particular combination of technology and public communication. In fact from Gutenberg's development of mechanical printing from 1450 onwards any form of this public communication has always been structured in response to technological innovation. This means that from any long-term perspective we cannot consider technology in itself to be a threat to journalism, but more a necessary part of the structural environment in which it functions. This chapter will assess the impact of technology on journalism over the twentieth century while bearing in mind the broader contexts of these changes. It will explore whether these communication technologies – in extending the material of journalism to greater numbers at greater speed and offering an increasing degree of interactivity – have produced a confusion of plenty rather than increased access to political and social information. Futhermore, it will assess the extent to which more recent technological developments such as the internet have meant an ongoing challenge to the established professional and cultural parameters of journalism.

Technology's Roles

Rather than seeing technology as having a unilateral influence on journalism, this chapter would prefer to see technology's role as a series of negotiations between hardware and the multiple political and social functions of a specific form of commercial public communication. Williams (1994: 12–13) articulates two poles of opinion on how technological developments have played a part in creating the cultural form of the media in general. According to the first, in his account of this argument, if television had not been invented, certain social and cultural events would not have happened. He terms this view *technological determinism*. The second view considers that television's significance lies in the uses to which it is put, structured as they are by cultural or social drives which lie outside the development of the technology itself, where technology is a symptom of change of another kind – a by-product of a social process which is otherwise determined. This is referred to as *symptomatic technology*.

On account of its predominantly social nature, journalism is generally considered less often from a purely deterministic perspective. Briggs and Burke (2002), for instance, propose that technology has played a more intermittent role in the shaping of all forms of communication, including journalism, by zig-zagging between innovation and the conditions of reception while emphasizing the social over purely technological determinants. Winston (1998) also advances a powerfully persuasive view of technology that prioritizes the political and cultural factors which enable various technologies to be either adapted or neglected, a point reinforced by Cottle, whose (1999) study concluded that the adoption of particular technologies is socially and culturally determined. Certainly the history of technology in the shaping of journalism would appear to bear out this emphasis, particularly because of its slow accretion of influences and the way in which journalism often incorporates technological developments some time after their invention and only then when this incorporation can be effected within the existing parameters of an already successful cultural and economic form. In order to corroborate this argument we may draw upon one prominent historian of journalism who has claimed that newspaper journalism, for example, adapted slowly and then only in terms of distribution and efficiency to the technological advances of the twentieth century until the decisive impact of computer technology in the 1970s (Smith, 1979). While this account might appear to underestimate the subtle impact on the content and tone of newspaper journalism of first radio and then television, well in advance of the introduction of computer technology, it does articulate something of the time-lag in the incorporation of other technological developments which needed to await a suitable economic-cultural moment for optimum integration into the established patterns of journalism. The way that photography became included in the daily press is a pertinent example of how journalism managed technological innovation on its own terms.

Photography and Journalism

Although it is impossible to give a precise date for the birth of photography, it had been increasing in public popularity for much of the nineteenth century. Daily newspapers however laid only the most modest and occasional claims to incorporate illustration into their pages for much of this period. As photography became established, newspapers had slowly taken to having artists engrave versions of photos to fit within the reprographic technologies preferred by newspapers at the time, despite the fact that from 1884 there was a perfectly successful method for reproducing the full tonal range of a photograph in print with half-tone blocks. It was left to magazines to show the way. As titles multiplied, thousands of photographs were used each week. The *Daily Graphic* in 1880 had claimed to be the first daily newspaper to regularly reproduce halftones directly from a photographic plate on a rotary printing machine without an intermediate sketch. Rotogravure illustration, which used cylinder etchings, was first used in England from 1895 to reproduce illustrations at high speed within the process of newspaper printing. This technology was fully exploited by the *Daily Mirror* when it was relaunched in 1904 as the first illustrated daily newspaper, and it spread within a decade to the eminently up-market *Times* which began to include halftone photographs from 1914 onwards.

Gradually, photographs became a significant indicator of the trend towards the popularization of the newspaper press, from the 1930s to the first all-colour daily newspaper, *Today*, in 1986. However, the majority of newspapers had only really started to take photographs seriously under pressure from the impact of the popularity of the first cinemas of the first decade of the twentieth century in a striking but far from isolated example of the influence of a different media entertainment form on journalism. Cinema newsreels were introduced in 1910 – *Pathé's Animated Gazette*, with images and text. The apparent reluctance to employ photography in daily newspapers any earlier probably had little to do with technological feasibility and more to do with 'an unstated prejudice that pictures were somehow for the less literate, and the gentlemen of the fourth estate were very careful to preserve their real or imagined status as highly literate purveyors of the written word' (Wright, 2003: 65).

Technology and Newspaper Language

Throughout the history of the newspaper, technology has impacted on its style and content. On occasions, it has been technologies of transport and communication which have had just as significant an influence on the shaping of newspaper language as innovations in the production process itself. The *Daily Mail* from 1896 is a good example of this. Harmsworth introduced more efficient technology to speed up and enable the massification of the production process, which in turn provided him with a scale of national distribution never previously seen, and provided more reliable streams of revenue from carefully targeted marketing. The increasing efficiencies of the railway network in connecting London with the largest towns and cities across the UK enhanced this reach of distribution. A broader cultural appeal was grafted onto these efficiencies of distribution. This allowed the newspaper to generate a volume of sales sufficient to cater to a lower middle-class readership at an affordable price and ensured a product that was written and laid out in a way which would appeal simultaneously to this new readership and to the advertisers who subsidized the paper. The new product incorporated much of the bite-size, carefully constructed boxes of information which had become so successful in magazine-style digests of news such as the pioneering *Tit-Bits* of Newnes (1881), selecting and shaping shorter and more disparate pieces of news from the massively increased flow of information produced by the telegraph and later by the telephone. This meant that the producers of newspaper content had changed as well as the product itself, to the extent that the journalists had ceased to be collectors and begun to be sifters of information (Smith, 1973: 93). In order to fit the information within the spaces between the plethora of advertisements, the mass-market newspaper separated information from the style of language in which it arrived at the newspaper and related it in a concise and unadorned style (Matheson, 2000: 565). This process of internal editing not only harnessed technological and presentational changes; it also meant that the new readership could be addressed in a single style and the tone of the news could be more efficiently articulated than ever before. The launch of the *Daily Mail*, therefore, was the key moment for the development on a mass daily basis of an organ which could effectively combine its appeal to a new readership with all the technologies of mass production and distribution.

This internally edited, truncated language was further formalized by the development of the inverted pyramid layout. This convention lays out a hard news story with the most important information – responding to the five 'W' questions of *Who? What? Why? Where? When?* – gathered together in the lead paragraph, and the remainder of the details included in a diminishing order of importance. This means that the editing can be done from the bottom up so as not to disturb the essentials of the story. Yet this was not a presentational style driven solely by a technological appropriation of the telegraph, which had been a reliable form of communication since the 1870s, but more typical of the impact of technology on newspapers throughout history as a combination of commercial and technical responses to the need for newspapers to improve the communicative quality of their product (Pöttker, 2003: 509). The telegraph affected the language of the newspaper but at a pace determined by the existing requirements of the newspaper itself. When it incorporated the re-structuring of language which the telegraph encouraged, this was very much on its own terms. The new presentational style emigrated quickly from America – where the first examples of this style of journalism had been seen in the 1880s and 1890s (Schudson, 1978: 61–87) – to the UK within the newly commercialized forces unleashed by Harmsworth's *Daily Mail* and Pearson's rival *Daily Express* from 1900 onwards. Targeting specific social classes of readers on behalf of advertisers, who could reasonably expect that their financial outlay was money well spent, required newspapers to shape the layout and content of their product to match the perceived lifestyles and interests of readers. The inverted pyramid, with its selective prioritizing of key facts in descending order of importance, therefore had genuine social impact given that this prioritizing was mapped onto what could reasonably be assumed about the interests and knowledge of the target readership.

The narrative chronological style characteristic of the late Victorian newspaper gave way to the new structure within a relatively short period (Pöttker, 2003: 503) which was swept in on a tide of radical reformulation produced by the mass dailies, to the extent that by the 1920s the inverted pyramid had become the only form of reporting taught to journalists (Errico et al., 1997: 8). In terms of its wider influence on news practices and forms, the telegraph established the imperative to get the story first, before one's competitors, and the related pursuit of timeliness which has continued to impel news coverage towards 'present-ation' – that is, closing the gap between the event and its telling, together with the goal of displaying events in 'real time' (Bell, 1996: 3–4).

Beyond the mechanistic changes to the language of the newspapers which this innovation brought, Carey (1987) has argued that it has, in addition, had a profound yet often unacknowledged ideological impact:

The telegraph also reworked the nature of written language and finally the nature of awareness itself ... telegraphic journalism divorced news from an ideological context that could explain and give significance to events ... By elevating objectivity and facticity into cardinal principles, the penny press abandoned explanation as a primary goal.

Broadcast Journalism: Effects and Consequences

The establishment of a carefully circumscribed and monitored set of communication styles through radio and later television broadcasting, although initially a challenge to newspapers, gradually enabled them to develop a set of styles quite at odds with those of broadcasting. Broadcast journalism was mandated as a purveyor of a public service to provide impartial and balanced approaches, especially to political news. Consequently, the newspapers were able, like never before, to develop individual 'voices' which best captured the views and language use of their readers and to deal more provocatively and in a partisan fashion with what were selected as the dominant political and cultural topics of the day.

Radio broadcasting provided an interaction of technological innovation with a series of beliefs about twentieth-century mass society (Smith, 1973: 22) which generated two main anxieties. First was the fear of the masses harboured by government and the cultural elites and the suspicion that popular passions and politics could be influenced by a medium as potentially pervasive as radio. Second there was the fear of a descent into a maelstrom of technological chaos which could feed into the first fear if the limited waveband available was not carefully controlled. This concern appeared to be legitimated by the course of radio in the USA, which in contrast had 219 registered radio stations by 1922 (Street, 2002: 24). The nature of these anxieties and the British government's response to them illustrate how radio was created in the form of 'a social technology' (Williams, 1994: 24).

Amid such concerns, it took a fair time before some of the potential of the application of the new technology of radio to journalism was appreciated. One radio journalist is worth singling out as having demonstrated how the medium could be deployed to enhance the authenticity of reports. Richard Dimbleby produced the closest thing in twentieth-century Britain to a journalistic dynasty. He was prominent enough as a journalist to be knighted for his contribution to broadcasting, was the father of two of the most celebrated contemporary names in current affairs, Jonathan and David, as well as being Managing Director of the *Richmond and Twickenham Times* from 1946 which was to grow into one of the most successful local newspaper chains. His enthusiasm for radio journalism was fired by his experience of the competitive intensity of American broadcasting, and he pioneered many of the features which we now take for granted, such as live interviews and pacy reports from foreign locations. He was driven by the conviction that 'News could be presented in a gripping manner, and, at the same time, remain authentic' (Dimbleby, 1975: 64). The most famous illustration of this belief was in 1936 with his renowned live report from a telephone box on the fire raging at Crystal Palace, which scooped the newspapers as they had already finished printing the next day's news. He was also to become the voice of major public occasions such as the Coronation of Elizabeth II in 1953 and the funeral of the assassinated American President, John F. Kennedy, in 1963.

Even though it took many years – well into World War Two, in fact – for the BBC to be able to build up its own network of correspondents, by the end of hostilities it was the most trusted news medium for the majority of the British population. As well as the declining public trust in many newspapers which had, for example, insisted until relatively late in the day that there would be no war, including those such as the *Daily Express* and the *Daily Mail* which had supported the fascists up until the mid-1930s, Engel (1996: 141) claims that the war was the turning point in boosting the credibility of radio journalism as people switched on their radios to hear the latest and most accurate news. Laconically, but with more than a pinch of truth, Tom Driberg had argued that the main role of the BBC in the war had been to teach people to stop believing newspapers – 'newspapers at any rate of the more garish sort' (Briggs, 1995: 69).

The rise in the reputation of radio journalism's reliability through the late 1930s and 1940s led to three shifts in the language of the newspapers. First, they had a justification to be more opinionated as a contrast to the prohibition of editorializing on the BBC and its statutory obligation to maintain a political balance. Second, they began an incremental shift towards patterns of popular speech and a more 'rounded' view of the social experience and aspirations of readers. Third, they developed a more punning, less informational style of headline, with a diminishing need for the literal style of radio and later television. All of these trends were more noticeable in the popular press first, but over the course of the next half-century all had become identifiable across the board as part of a general process of popularization (LeMahieu, 1988).

On the Cusp between Radio and Television

Although television had seen some experiments in reporting before the war, and despite the BBC's further development of the medium post-1946, the corporation had not been able to think beyond the confines of the aural approach to journalism developed by radio, with its news readers out of sight. Grace Wyndham Goldie – who worked as a producer for the corporation before becoming its Head of News and Current Affairs – described the predicament of journalists at the BBC with regard to television thus:

> ... *their speciality was the use of words; they had no knowledge of how to present either entertainment or information in vision, nor any experience of handling*

visual material. Moreover, most of them mistrusted the visual; they associated vision with the movies and the music hall and were afraid that the high purposes of the Corporation would be trivialised by the influence of those concerned with what could be transmitted in visual terms. (Crisell, 1997: 74)

Radio journalism had moved itself away from a text-based approach to news, one that had been largely imposed upon it by newspaper owners and government, yet the BBC was initially unable to fully grasp the imperative for television journalism to develop a visual approach appropriate to the medium. From 1946 to 1954 it was narrowly focused on words and suspicious of any personalization of the news, which meant that it refused to countenance presenters on-screen. In a bizarre re-enactment of the first radio news as simply an aural version of the Reuters reports written for newspapers, the evening television news was simply the radio news announced by an anonymous voice off-camera. Anonymity was inherited, almost as a reflex, from the radio broadcasting of news and was a short-lived attempt to make a new medium conform to the traditions which had emerged out of an older one. It was an attempt which was destined to fail. There was a short, ten-minute, televised newsreel five times a week, but this merely copied the cinema format of footage with a voiceover, thereby displaying both a lack of imagination towards the possibilities of the new medium as a purveyor of journalism at the same time as acknowledging the necessity of borrowing from other entertainment genres in its search for a suitable approach to visual journalism. The coronation in 1953 is widely considered to have been a watershed in television's fortunes as for the first time more watched this on television (20 million) than listened to it on radio (Briggs, 1979: 466–467). The event certainly enabled the medium to acquire some of the immediacy and communal involvement which radio had been able to generate around events of contemporary importance, yet it was from the BBC film department that more televisually appropriate approaches were to migrate into television news production. This culminated in the production of *Press Conference* in 1952 (incidentally pioneered by Wyndham Goldie herself) where politicians were asked questions about topics of the day by a group of print journalists; *News and Newsreel* from 5 July 1954; and *Special Enquiry*, which 'was aiming to forge a new style of television journalism, something peculiar to the medium of television, but as honest and incisive as British journalism at its best' (Scannell, 1979: 103).

There had been minimal stylistic adaptation to the potential of television journalism until 1955 when ITV introduced a commercially-funded, much more populist, accessible and less deferential style of news coverage that more fully exploited the entertainment potential of the medium and which, in doing this, borrowed much from American practices. The success of commercial television journalism required a strategic response for newspapers to remain competitive. This prompted the press to take risks and push back boundaries in a bid to retain the allegiance of young readers (Bingham, 2004: 14). Broadsheet Sunday newspapers also began to experiment with free colour magazines and expanded their feature coverage, starting with the *Sunday Times* in 1962. The mass popular press responded by aiming 'below television'

(Tunstall, 1996: 59) with gossip and behind-the-scenes material, as well as features, interviews and gossip on the stars, while the elite press began experiments with a range of specializations aimed at the new professional classes, particularly in the expanding public sector. Newspapers further exploited the new technological environment for their own purposes and developed an interesting co-dependence on television as it provided opportunities for previews and reviews of television programmes, and also – particularly but not exclusively in the popular press – a host of stories about the stars and commentary based on the storylines of popular television programmes. All of the newspapers began to employ media correspondents who maintained close links with this fertile territory for entertaining, profitable and easy news sources.

Under the influence of the more probing television reporting of politics, the 1960s became the great decade for investigative newspaper journalism. From 1963 the *Sunday Times* Insight Team set the pace, rising to its pinnacle of achievement in the 1970s as 'a role model for investigative journalism' (Doig, 1992: 46). At the popular end of the spectrum, 'Mirrorscope' was 'a game attempt to provide serious analysis in the rough and tumble of the tabloids' (Evans, 2002) and its 'Shock Issues' of the 1970s provided more sensationalized coverage of topical themes.

At the same time the trend towards naming individual journalists, particularly in specialist newspaper columns, gathered momentum. As newspapers began to supply more in the way of commentary, often depending on idiosyncratic opinion, this meant that individual journalists' writing could hardly continue to be published without a by-line. Furthermore, television increasingly needed articulate commentators on the sorts of specialist subjects now covered in the papers, which meant, in turn, that named journalists could enhance their reputation and that of their paper by appearing live on screen as expert contributors. The last bastion of anonymity was *The Times* which resisted until 1967. Another significant accelerant to the rise of the named specialist journalist was the figure of the newscaster, particularly on ITN from 1955 onwards, and star interviewers such as Chris Chataway and Robin Day – with Cliff Michelmore on the BBC from 1957 – whose personal styles made up much of the appeal of television. Seymour-Ure has commented on the wider implications of the decline of anonymity for journalism:

> *Anonymity, like the uniform of nurses or the police, highlights the role, not the person performing it. In journalism, it therefore bolstered the idea of objectivity in reporting the news. Its disappearance fitted an era in which electronic media were taking over the 'hot' news role and papers were selling the personal expertise of their staff at interpretation, comment, analysis, more than for traditional hard news. (1996: 155)*

As television enabled one form of celebrity to rise, namely that of the journalist, it also contributed to the opposite trend – the debunking of status, privilege and expertise by bringing elite politicians and other prominent public figures into everyone's living room for consideration and evaluation. Crisell argues that:

... television showed people in close-up, 'warts and all'. It revealed every manner-ism, uncertainty and hesitation. Mystique evaporated. The great and the good – aristocrats, statesmen, 'authorities' and experts – turned out to be people like the rest of us, their average physical blemishes and peculiarities implying average fallibility. (1997: 118)

General-interest illustrated weekly magazines like *Picture Post* were forced out of business in the late 1950s and were joined on the scrapheap by some national daily newspapers early in the sixties with the closure of the *News Chronicle* and *Daily Herald*. Such publications could simply not attract a sufficient amount of suitable advertising to fend off the competition from a highly popular television journalism which was rapidly becoming the generalist journalistic medium par excellence. However, as always in tech-nological changes within journalism, the picture is more integrative within the general news media environment rather than a straightforward case of a monopoly of influ-ence with television driving all its rivals for cover. Those print publications which sur-vived were able to adapt and integrate the lessons of television journalism's dynamism and popularity. Something of the subtlety of this interaction is caught by Murdock and Golding when they write on the contraction of newspaper sales post-Second World War:

Television is only a limited part of the explanation for this contraction. In its initial phase, commercial television generated much of its own revenue rather than stealing it from the newspapers, and early research into audiences showed that viewing actually stimulated readership of the populars, though it did have negative effects on the purchase of the qualities. In the longer term, however, television clearly did provide an alternative and increasingly attractive source of popular journalism and general entertainment. (1978: 133)

Where television did have a direct impact on other media was in its ejection of cin-ema out of the news business by the 1960s. This was simply because it was providing the latest news on a daily basis rather than as a digest of the previous week as cinema newsreels had done. This was part of a more general realignment within journalism across the media markets. By the early 1960s, television journalism had become the dominant popular medium, and the news/features balance in the press as a whole had shifted to accommodate television's demonstrable superiority in dealing with the news of the moment. In 1957, 30 per cent of people chose newspapers as their main news source, 46 per cent radio and 24 per cent television. By 1962, 52 per cent were treating television as their main news source, with only 31 per cent opting for newspapers and 17 per cent for radio (Crisell, 1997: 94).

The Shaping of Television Journalism

It has been claimed that TV's main effect was to change the way in which people used their papers, rather than to reduce their overall use (Seymour-Ure, 1991: 148). In contrast to the obvious partisanship of the press, television – because of its visual nature and its immediacy – seemed to promise a closer approximation to the truth. The broadcast media themselves also played their part in amplifying this belief. Elliott claims that they developed 'a peculiar fascination for the creed of factual objectivity' (1978: 184). In its visual reshaping of journalism, television moved increasingly towards formats which prioritized market appeal just as most print journalism from 1855 had been shaped by a similar sort of commercial pragmatism. It is a paradox of technological developments in twentieth-century journalism that the very forces which had initially enabled television journalism to provide a genuinely popular version of public knowledge, in a form which was lively and accessible to a wider social audience than ever, should end the century accused by many of contributing a great deal to the destabilization of the concept of good journalism. The very technological and popular gains, which appeared at one point capable of delivering more information, more speedily, to a larger audience than newspapers were able to access, have engendered styles of presentation which are criticized as incapable of delivering high-quality journalism. Such criticisms are often based on the assumption contained in John Whale's striking metaphor (1969) 'The Eye Half-Shut' that television is technologically impaired. The entertainment values which had done so much initially to contribute to the development of television journalism continued to encroach even in the sphere of its current affairs. It has been alleged that the most notable early victim of this tendency was *This Week* which was taken off the air in 1978 because, in the words of Mike Townson, the editor of its replacement *TV Eye*, it was too journalist-centred and had become 'boring'. Towson subsequently was one of the first to be credited with 'grafting tabloid style and values onto broadsheet journalism' (Holland, 1998: 85).

Technological changes set within the context of the political economy of a news media market have increasingly been incorporated as a series of changes in content and format which seek to retain more of a fragmenting audience. Whereas in the early days of radio tens of millions of listeners would gather in their homes for the evening news bulletin from a monopoly provider, journalism in the early twenty-first century needs to attract people leading much more diverse lives and exposed to a teeming array of media output. The profit motive which had always formed an essential part of journalism in all its forms has now become the predominant motivation and has turned journalism into something quite different from its previous incarnations (MacManus, 1994). Particularly in relation to television, this has led to a range of experimentation in the styles and formats of journalism which has attempted to maximize its competitiveness and has also led to a 'deeply rooted professional tension between its "televisual" and "journalistic" dimensions' (Dahlgren, 1995: 47).

The core of this debate lies in the fact that television has become more of an entertainment genre rather than an informational one, and that, as media markets converge – blurring the lines between information, education and entertainment – television journalism has been deployed as a complement to other entertainment on television in order to retain large viewing figures, but at the risk of compromising its quality. In 1967 colour's introduction added further fuel to critiques of television journalism as it conformed even more to a cine-version of popular reality. Neil Postman (1986: 87) concluded that entertainment had become 'the natural format for the representation of all experience' and that television was the culprit, integrated alongside and sometimes within the formats of informational journalism. Key to this is television's tendency to simplify through a standardized pace of reception and a desire to make an immediate impression with broad and instant comprehension (Ekström, 2002: 265). Postman (1986) has also argued polemically that the entertainment bias of the medium constricts news and current affairs into gaps between its entertainment programming and that this encroaches upon the integrity of its journalism. A dramatic illustration of this trend towards entertainment genres comes in the interpretative two-way relationship between anchor and correspondent – wherever possible full of first name familiarity, levity and witty banter concerning the piece being reported. To underline the show-business appeal of leading anchor-persons in the news, their status as general media celebrities is so great that they now have enormous cross-over potential in other broadcast formats. This indicates the progression of the status not of journalists *per se* but of journalists as media celebrities. Jeremy Paxman on *University Challenge*, Fiona Bruce on *Call My Bluff*, John Humphrys on *Mastermind*, Alastair Stewart as the host of *Police, Camera, Action*, Trevor McDonald's news spin-off *Tonight With Trevor McDonald*, a post credit-crunch *Property Watch* including BBC news presenter Kate Silverton, and Jeremy Paxman hosting a search for children who can still master the lost skill of rote learning in *Off By Heart*.

Audience-based talk shows have further problematized the coverage of contemporary affairs on television. Originating in the USA in the 1980s and popularized by Oprah Winfrey, first in the UK on Channel 4, they have become a familiar daytime format in Britain with the *Wright Stuff* and the *Jeremy Kyle Show* as particularly strong examples of the genre. Interviews and vox pops have long constituted part of journalism's repertoire but in these programmes the element of the popular voice, the non-expert, is foregrounded to the exclusion of nearly everything else except the celebrity status of the presenter and his/her skill in weaving together the range of views on a particular aspect of the audience's collective experience. Holland suggests (1998: 92): 'In these newer, more open forms of journalism, the audience is no longer merely "imagined" and the programme is never completely finished. Authenticity is no longer to be found simply within the text itself.' In the words of Livingstone and Lunt (1994: 36), such formats challenge 'traditional oppositions of programmes and audience, producer and subject, expert and laity'. They extend the techniques first pioneered by the radio phone-in and yet it is doubtful whether their democratic and participative ambitions outweigh the desire of networks to provide, as with docu-soaps – their current affairs counterparts – cheap and entertaining television. All of these types of programme offer a glimpse of what Dahlgren calls a 'postmodern condition' (1995: 66), in that they are self-referencing within the terms of the programme and detatched from the conventional methods of reporting a reality that is external to the framework of the programme and are, in contrast, rooted in the audience's experiences which the programme then selects and edits. This self-referencing can be extended back into the real (external to the studio) by the development of an audience – as in *Crimewatch UK*, from in 1984 – being asked to participate in real crime reconstructions with a view to solving them. This programme provides the vicarious pleasure of audience involvement in police investigations in an interactive update on the crime news periodical tradition of the Victorian era. Indeed the mysterious murder of one of its presenters, Jill Dando, developed into an extraordinary intertextual media event, hovering between the vicariousness of the programme's conventions and the external reality of the loss of a media celebrity.

Yet even if, as in Crissell's provocative slogan, 'Television news is naïve news' (1997: 154), it can still function usefully as a first port of call for audiences who can then go further in their search for information. However, because of its discursive and technological limitations, even experienced broadcasters such as Walter Cronkite have been clear in their assessment that those who get most of their news from television 'probably are not getting enough information to exercise intelligently their voting franchise in a democratic system' (1997: 2). Cronkite's experience as anchorman for CBS *Evening News* for nineteen years gives his perspective on contemporary television journalism a great deal of professional credibility. One reason for this is that the television version of journalism can only deliver a much smaller slice of information, certainly compared to newspaper journalism – given the delivery speeds for aural and visual comprehension – added to the fact that it is very expensive to provide equipment, personnel and editing facilities to cover even the basics of routine news production.

Another voice from within the industry, Jon Snow of Channel 4 News, has expressed his anxiety concerning the acceleration of television journalism's tendency to edit down reality:

> *The technology enables us to package, graphicise and meld five minutes of old TV information into 60 seconds of new TV time – the whiz and bang of such presentation may be enticing but the content reduction is so acute that normal debate is in danger of being degraded to the absurd. (Snow, 1997: 3)*

The academic commentator John Hartley (1996: 43), from a more positive cultural perspective, is keen to dispel such binary distinctions by arguing that journalism has always foregrounded its presentational aspects and its visuality. According to this viewpoint, considering it as a version of factual realism is naïve, unhistorical and also unhelpful for analysing its actual purpose, which has always been essentially bound up with the ways it constructs popular communication.

Newspapers: Technological Change Delayed

Despite the improved integration of printing and photographic technologies (with the best example being *Picture Post* from 1938 to 1957, which provided photo-illustrated, socially engaged reporting and maintained a steady audience of over a million readers) and using a layout and structure for stories in much of the press which made better use of the visual elements of journalism, World War Two restricted any further development (particularly in the daily press) because paper was in such short supply. Post-war restrictions on paper, in fact, continued until 1955 and kept printing and paper costs low and advertising space at a premium. What did not change though was the extremely high production costs in what remained a labour-intensive industry. From as early as the 1970s, technology had been available to reduce the dependency of newspapers on a volatile and disruptive workforce, but the well-drilled organization made up of print unions and journalist chapels ensured that management remained locked into a labyrinth of archaic production practices. Proprietors and managers were aware of the new printing systems that could have reduced staffing. However, print workers knew about these too and were determined to retain their jobs by preventing the introduction of cost-saving (or in their terms job-destroying) technology (Greenslade, 2003: 245).

Once paper was back in plentiful supply some things moved quickly while others continued to stagnate. The colour-printed *Sunday Times* dominated the 1960s with its serializations and its Insight team of investigative journalists. The *Guardian* rose to prominence within a left-leaning culture of specialist writing for the expanding public sector professions such as education and the social services. An advertising expansion also brought about extra pagination which allowed for more analysis and commentary, thereby changing the content and scope of much of journalism particularly in the elite press.

The Wapping Revolution

As 1896 had suddenly triggered the first mass newspapers, 1986 marked the beginning of a radically new era for newspapers and – albeit obliquely – for journalism in general. The events which began on 23 January 1986 were not termed the Wapping Revolution flippantly, as these were to trigger a literal overnight change in the organization of an entire industry despite the fact that, as with most revolutions, things had been smouldering on for a decade or so before they erupted. Murdoch moved his entire production and distribution operations from a site off Fleet Street over to a new purpose-built facility in the Docklands area of East London. The *Sun*, *News of the World*, *Times* and *Sunday Times* were all relocated without any consultation with either printers or journalists and certainly not with their unions. Murdoch used this as a way of introducing computerized printing technologies which in turn allowed journalists to input their copy directly onto a computer screen and subeditors and page editors to compose the pages on screen. Predicting the trouble this action would cause, the new site was surrounded by barbed wire, security fencing and other high-tech facilities to protect it throughout the period of protest, demonstrations and picketing which ensued in the following weeks and months. Rothermere caught the abruptness of this change when he claimed, 'There was before Wapping and there was after Wapping' (MacArthur, 1988: 106), and it has been correctly described as the 'decisive moment' in the history of the British press (Eldridge et al., 1997: 37), mainly on account of the impact that these changes had on the rest of the newspaper industry as other owners followed Murdoch's lead on both technology and printers. Computer-based typesetting replaced the linotype production which had necessitated skilled and experienced printers, and allowed for the immediate dismissal of 5,000 of them (Goodhart and Wintour, 1986: xi), which lowered costs, promised less interference in production, increased profits and quickly led to a more supine workforce of journalists on what were often referred to as individually negotiated contracts – but where the negotiation process flowed more often than not from institution to individual rather than in the other direction.

Despite their revolutionary impact, Wapping's 'new' technologies were simply not that new. In 1973 the *Nottingham Evening Post* had been first in experimenting with the technology that allowed journalists to input their copy directly. The Royal Commission on the Press as early as 1977 had also identified that the new technologies available, even at that point, would have enabled the improved management and profitability of national newspapers. Technologically, Fleet Street was at least behind the potential of the times. Reuters and the Stock Exchange were already using electronic transmission but any sudden shift to a modernized method of producing national newspapers would have to depend on political manoeuvring as much as technological innovation. By the mid-1980s, the available technology benefited from a political climate dominated by Thatcher's Conservative administration, which was extremely favourable to employers and also appeared to have customized anti-trades union legislation to smooth the way for a profitable transition to new production practices on behalf of favoured newspaper owners, most especially the Conservative-supporting Rupert Murdoch.

Direct journalist input without printers had been trialled by Eddie Shah's Messenger group of provincial newspapers in 1983 when he emerged victorious from in his conflict with the NGA print union. This new journalist input allowed for late corrections and updates to be included, thus giving much more flexibility than before, along with a significantly reduced wages bill which no longer required printers. The 1984 Trade Union Act further eased the introduction of this technology. For instance, it restricted picketing to one's own place of work and limited the numbers entitled to picket. Henceforth there could be no secondary action such as sympathy strikes in support of sacked or suspended workers and since Wapping was constituted as a separate company any picketing by Murdoch's staff would have been illegal. In addition, through his use of an Australian road haulage company – Thomas Nationwide Transport – Murdoch also eliminated any potential solidarity action from the rail unions.

This combination of new technologies and new industrial relationships, combined with the suppression of a disruptive print workforce, meant that it became much easier to produce additional sections and extra pagination as well as to update stories right up to their deadline. Colour printing was also easier to incorporate. As a direct consequence of the Wapping Revolution, the 1990s saw various trends accelerate towards the inclusion of more features as a proportion of newspaper content, which has been described as a 'big expansion in "non-news"'

(Tunstall, 1996: 155). Buoyant advertising markets assisted the extension of consumer journalism with less traditional news as a proportion of papers and more sections on lifestyles and consumer issues and greater cross-fertilization with other aspects of the entertainment industries (e.g. sport, fashion and motoring). Post-1986, newspapers were to double or even treble their number of supplements, and these sections contributed significantly to the identity of a paper and the image they wished to project to their readers and of course advertisers. As part of the heavyweight branding and identification of newspapers in an extremely competitive market, there was an increase in the number of columnists in a variety of styles – polemical, analytical and satirical (McNair, 2008a: 116). It is no surprise that Richard Littlejohn, as a columnist on the *Daily Mail*, is reputed to be the highest paid journalist in the country, reflecting the commercial importance of a successful columnist to a newspaper's market identity.

The *Independent*, founded in 1986 as an immediate beneficiary of the new technologies, foregrounded photography and boasted the most complete arts and leisure listings of any national daily, while the *Guardian* pioneered second and third daily sections and especially its tabloid *G2* from 1992. Yet it was to be a weekly newspaper – the *Independent on Sunday* – which in 1990 introduced innovations that were to accelerate many of these trends in the daily press. It perfected a technique for heat-set colour printing on cheaper larger format paper which allowed more space for adverts but also allowed for the inclusion of more review material from journalists than could previously have been accommodated. Together, the growth in supplements, length of reviews and the shift towards a greater amount of consumer-driven, lifestyle journalism meant a proportionate reduction in old-style news and even in the traditional reporting style as a proportion of the content. This did not mean the disappearance of the inverted pyramid but it has certainly contributed to its gradual marginalization within the totality of a newspaper. However, the great economic and cultural benefits promised for journalism by advocates of the new technologies have not come to pass. Most new launches have either folded or struggled to maintain their circulation and profitability. The more diverse ecology of smaller-circulation newspapers has not emerged. Bigger players have also made it increasingly difficult for newcomers to the market by using predatory pricing strategies or the tactic of bloated pagination to discourage them, and this has reinforced a newspaper journalism led by a commercialized consumer choice rather than one led by an altruistic vision of a contribution within a public sphere. The move to Wapping represented a decisive political and technological step in that direction.

One of the consequences of the accelerating market-orientation of journalism has been the decline in the reputation of investigative journalism because it is expensive, politically and economically risky, and not as immediately popular as other staples of news. Furthermore, in a corporatized media world there is pressure on journalism to conform to the beliefs and standards of corporate ideology itself. One aspect of mainstream journalism's repertoire has been curtailed, not as a direct consequence of any technology but as a result of the strategies which have been chosen to introduce new technology within a specific political economy:

The ability of the media and journalism to act as a 'watchdog' from the 1990s has been challenged by technological change, the new structure of broadcasting which works against serious and challenging journalism and programming, the concentration of ownership in Fleet Street and other parts of the British media, the increasing competition between media and the decline of resources, manpower and time available for campaigning journalism. (Williams, 1998: 249)

In fact, many of the changes of the late 1980s and early 1990s had much more to do with the ratcheting up of journalists' productivity and the lowering of their labour costs than with the consequences of the digital and electronic technologies themselves (Ursell, 2001: 184). An example of this was the Birt-inspired bi-media policy initiative of the late 1980s, whereby BBC correspondents were expected not only to produce material for regional television news but also to feed stories to BBC local radio and – where the story warranted it – also to BBC network radio, national television, online and News 24 (Ursell, 2001: 188). Cost-effectiveness rather than quality of journalism was the driving force. These were predominantly economic decisions to justify the BBC's continued existence in a hostile political environment with little to do with technology in itself.

Franklin has also stressed the implications of the imposition of technological innovation on journalists when this was driven by predominantly managerial considerations:

New technology also isolates journalists by removing them from the newsroom, encourages and facilitates freelance work, nurtures multi-skilling practices and empowers managers against journalists and other production workers. (1997: 102)

This is a point which has been reinforced by more recent quantitative research (conducted by a team including Franklin) which has concluded that more pages are being filled with material written by fewer full-time journalists. Lewis et al. (2008a, 2008b) and Davies (2008) claim that contemporary journalists have been increasingly driven by pressures of deadlines and profit-margins to provide more copy in less time which draws uncritically on agency and PR material, thereby leaving less scope for independent, investigative journalism than ever before. These findings are echoed by a similar survey at a local level (O'Neill and O'Connor, 2008).

Media Multiplication

On 10 July 1962 the communications satellite Telstar was launched, an event which inaugurated the era of satellite broadcasting and allowed sound and pictures to be relayed around the world. This was the beginning of a technological process which would begin to rapidly shrink the world journalism had access to. Hood and O' Leary (1990: 35–36) have argued that it was the images of military hardware readied for action on the decks of freighters during the Cuban missile crisis in 1962 which demonstrated once and for all the superior capability of television as an immediate channel for journalism.

The use of satellite technology on ITN to bring pictures of the 1973 Yom Kippur War to television viewers on the day of action was a further demonstration of the increasing obsolescence of newspapers as the best providers of overseas news. This process of increased speed of news delivery was accelerated towards the end of the 1970s by the introduction of electronic newsgathering, which bypassed the need to develop film as events could be recorded directly onto videotape. During the 1980s such technologies were combined under a suitably sympathetic deregulatory regime to break up the older patterns of control over television broadcasting. The first cable and satellite channels were launched in 1983. In 1989 SkyTV began, followed by British Satellite Broadcasting early in 1990. These subsequently merged to form BSkyB in November 1990 – a move which mounted the first sustained challenge to the BBC/ITV duopoly. Digital television kick-started a second wave of technologically-increased programme choice and has supplemented satellite and computer technologies to usher in an era of news media surfeit in contrast to the previous scarcity of wavelengths which was the technological determinant of the British government's approach first to radio and then television journalism in their public service modality.

From as early as the 1990s, restrictions on the space available to fill with news were no longer a consideration. In practice, there was no longer a need to limit the hours of output or the number of outlets for broadcast journalism. As with print, the limitations were eventually to be set simply according to the patterns of market demand as predicted by media owners. The BBC was drawn into this market reflex because its audience share has been plotted against its commercial competitors to test its own position in terms of value-for-money and competitiveness. As we move through the twentieth-first century, increasingly efficient and capitalized technology creates more competition among news providers, who are under pressure to deliver the news more efficiently and more profitably in a less regulated market. Technological change has led to a proliferation in the amount of broadcast journalism as well as changes in content designed to make it more commercially attractive. However, there is nothing necessarily new in this apart, perhaps, from the intensity of contemporary changes. The demands of the market have always been paramount in the structuring of the formats and technologies of journalism as it is shaped and reshaped as a site of informational activity. Bourdieu interprets the 'journalistic field' as inevitably linked to the economic field:

> ... like the political and economic fields, and much more than the scientific, artistic, literary, or juridical fields, the journalistic field is permanently subject to trial by market, whether directly, through advertisers, or indirectly, through audience ratings (even if government subsidies offer a certain independence from immediate market pressures). (1998: 71)

Other writers – rather than stressing the reality of journalism's location within the sphere of capitalism – have chosen to critique the increasing convergence between profitability and provision in broadcast journalism as detrimental to the fundamental public service ethos of British broadcasting in an attempt to prompt the consideration of alternatives (Curran, 2003; O'Malley, 2001). Dramatic changes in technology combined with the liberalization of the market for broadcast journalism came at a time of almost total credulity, at the end of the 1970s, about the benefits of free market approaches to the delivery of all sorts of public information, including journalism, on both sides of the Atlantic Ocean, meaning that there was little mainstream political or commercial opposition. Broadcast journalism's priorities have been dictated through a consolidated political push towards deregulation from the early 1990s onwards. This trend is currently being continued in the discussions led by Ofcom about further media regulation and ownership liberalization, where the public continues to be constructed in terms of consumerism before any concern for its requirements as citizens. This increasing ideological momentum towards the deregulation of news media ownership and control has become established as natural and inevitable within political and economic circles, with only peripheral resistance. Control has increasingly been handed to major media conglomerates which have been be trusted to act as allies for the neo-liberal political groupings in power in Western Europe and the United States. This consensus has also proved highly influential in Asian markets and constitutes something akin to a contemporary global hegemony. This lightly regulated market approach has become the new consensus between politics, commerce and journalism. It is a replaying by different rules of the nineteenth-century liberalization of the print journalism market and has had a similar effect in reducing real choice as the market narrows to concentrate on profitable and predictable formats and the content for its broadcast news and current affairs, illustrating what Williams has observed:

> *Serving democracy, encouraging diversity or expanding citizenship are very much in the back seat as entrepreneurs have to confront the increasingly competitive market-place for global information. (1998: 240)*

The Ironies of Instant Access

Satellite and video technology have combined to give us truly live reporting from overseas in areas where using traditional cameras has been unsuitable. The reporting from Afghanistan in 2001 and Iraq in 2003 by videophone brought instant news within reach and has been refined via the use of weblink reportage where journalists are unable to work openly, such as in Iraq in the early summer of 2009. Technologies have had important implications for the content of journalism and its associated proximity with front-line forces as part of the process of 'embedding' (Tumber and Palmer, 2004), yet once again we can remark that the impact of technologies of communication on war reporting continues to give rise to serious commercial and ethical concerns which have more to do with the implications of how the journalism produced has changed to fit the technology available that with the specifics of that technology.

Some commentators have expressed doubts that the semi-edited nature of some 'real time' coverage does anything to enhance our understanding and that this is compounded by the ways in which this technology reinforces the myth of immediacy while at the same time masking the constructed nature of the reports on screen (Dahlgren, 1995: 56). The proliferation of information which the technology allows, and the speed and density of the flow of that information, now mean there is more access to information which has had less editorial intervention. Web-based gossip, videophone content and rolling news channels all add to the availability of this raw material. Recent developments in hand-held digital cameras and mobile phones, lightweight portable computers and text messaging have each driven these changes further and faster. The media companies best equipped to exploit this material continue to produce ever quicker coverage with less time for the journalist or editor to reflect on its content. This has been demonstrated during the recent Iraqi conflict where the role of war correspondent was often reduced to that of an uninformed speculator, precisely because of the immediacy of events being transmitted. Twenty-four-hour news sometimes brought to the screen poorly sourced, insignificant reports that were often based on rumour. Reporters fronted this speculation on camera as unprocessed information – from smoke in the background and air-raid sirens in Baghdad to on-screen deliberations as to whether or not defections of Iraqi troops had taken place; all of this was paraded as evidence of the profoundly disturbing mismatch between technology and reliable television journalism.

Speed is in danger of becoming the ultimate aim of such journalism. The post-telegraph economic compulsion to beat competitors to a story, accelerated by the new technologies, can mean that it becomes more important to be first than to provide an adequate assessment of context. The pace of breaking news drives the possibility of in-depth analysis further down the list of priorities, adding to the fears of commentators like Bourdieu that 'Competition on the [journalistic] field creates a "sort of permanent amnesia"' (1998: 72). Technology can extend journalism's tendency, under pressure of time and a perception that audiences need sense to be made for them, to frame new occurrences in terms of familiar and already-constituted sense-making strategies (Schlesinger, 1978), leading inevitably to a reliance on points of view embedded within the narrowing range of a political status quo. Speed also necessitates an increasing efficiency in locating the probable sites for news in advance, and this means a growing concentration on predetermined locations and sources, with the consequence that television news in particular becomes confined to highly polished renditions of a fixed news agenda and enlivened by the familiar interplay between anchorperson and reporter on the spot. The proximity of the commentator brings nothing particular to the quality of the story but an expectation that news organizations will have their people placed at predetermined sites around the globe and can have them reporting live from these privileged locations for news production. Sources of news are, as a consequence, culturally and politically selected for their ease of accessibility to large newsgathering organizations and therefore their cost effectiveness, their predictability, and their closeness to the fulcrum of the political status quo. All of this compromises the incredible speed and technological sophistication of the journalism produced, as it is often lacking in any corresponding analytical depth or political variety.

Convergence and Journalism

Despite the technological changes centred on the internet – referred to as convergence – there is no automatic quality dividend in sight for journalism unless owners invest in resources. Media platforms may be converging but the professional attitudes of journalists and business managers within the media companies that employ them are diverging between the poles of quality and cost effectiveness:

> For convergence to work properly, it will take an increase in resources ... unless these news organizations are willing to put the resources and manpower into their news-gathering operations, convergence will not be the panacea many news executives suggest. It will just become a way to produce and present news more cheaply. (Kaplan, 2003: 518)

There is, in addition, a split in approaches to convergence which illustrates much about the nature of journalism in the early twenty-first century, suspended as always between technology and profit but this time with a new intensity:

> Viewed as a business model, convergence appears attractive to some editorial managers and publishers ... to produce more news for the same or little more money ... Seen from the journalists' perspective, convergence offers a chance to do better journalism by giving reporters the tools to tell stories in the most appropriate medium. (Quinn, 2005: 29)

Fitting the News to the Customer

Above all, technological changes have had an impact on the immediacy and the availability of journalism as it has proliferated as a mode of communication. There is literally much more of it about. Even before the satellites of the 1970s and the digital and computer technologies of the 1990s, the development of the transistor in the 1960s provided the technological impetus which was to profoundly alter the way that journalism could be delivered to its target audience. This initially meant a complete reconsideration of the reach and content of radio. Portability and the installation of radios in cars meant that the concept of background listening was extended. Journalism was in the process of developing a culture of news reception which would lead to the contemporary format of drive-time news, and once the restrictions on commercial radio were removed in 1973 this became the cheapest and most popular form of news for millions. Radio journalism also undertook an experiment in audience participation with the phone-in, introduced in 1968 on BBC Radio Nottingham. The fact that it was pioneered on local radio was significant in the way that, unlike letters from readers – a highly edited and slow form of communication with a newspaper – this interactive format was ideally suited to local issues and also added a sense of immediacy to reporting and commentary on current affairs. It was to be developed as an additional support to national radio and then television. These developments provided a form of journalism that was increasingly being designed to engage with the lives of people on the move who were in need of more concise bulletins and greater choice in patterns of information reception. Patterns of expectation towards the consumption of journalism were to continue to be extended through other technological innovations (such as teletext in 1974, updates on mobile phones and digital news menus), while breakfast television news and rolling television news were further acknowledgements of the continually fragmenting and diversifying viewing patterns of audiences.

Although 24-hour news channels can illustrate the increasing popularity of this style of presentation – as ambient news which fits around you (Hargreaves and Thomas, 2002: 51) – initially, this had only lukewarm success. In 1996, seven years after its launch, *Sky News* had a weekly reach in Britain of only around three million (Hargreaves and Thomas, 2002), but by May 2005, the BBC's *News 24* had achieved a weekly reach of eleven million, *Sky News* ten million, and *ITV 24 Hour News* six million. This could be directly contrasted with a decline in the viewing figures for mainstream news services in Britain. According to Hargreaves and Thomas (2002) this fell by 6 per cent between 1994 and 2002, with the largest decline taking place among younger people, while Ofcom's (2004) figures suggest that between 1998 and 2003 the audience shares for the early evening news programmes on BBC and ITV declined by 16 per cent and 37 per cent respectively. Lewis et al. (2005: 461) have concluded that despite the increasing popularity of rolling news services, audiences are better informed and receive more in terms of background information on conventional bulletins which draw from a wider pool of expertise. The format has been criticized more generally, for example by journalist Ann Leslie (2004: 12), who bemoaned the systemic 'sloppiness' that 'arises from the relentless demands of 24-hour news'. Technology which affords an apparent surfeit of journalism on demand has not improved the overall quality of provision. We might argue that 24-hour news, despite its popularity, is a prime example of technology being used to boost viewing figures rather than to raise the quality of the service. Regulatory frameworks seem to work on the assumption that whatever the uses new technologies are put to, this must be good as long as they keep the providers of news happy rather than measuring their output against any yardstick for quality journalism. Being able to watch the news when you want does not necessarily make it better news from any objective standpoint.

Online Challenge and Change

The *Daily Telegraph* launched its *Electronic Telegraph* as early as November 1994, but this did little more than transfer content from the paper to the website. *Guardian*

Unlimited was launched in 1999 and has since become the most popular UK news-paper website – in May 2009 it had 27.2 million unique users (ABC Electronic). The *Telegraph*'s full conversion was from 2005 under the editorship of Will Lewis, at which point it had started to appreciate the need for a radical overhaul of its approach to the new medium and its interrelationship with the rest of the *Telegraph*'s output. The BBC's online service, although in operation from as early as 1994, was only offi-cially launched in December 1997 once it had been approved by the government that it could fund the service out of its licence fee income. Murdoch's conversion, which Cole and Harcup (2009: 179) claim was a highly significant moment for online jour-nalism, was signalled with his speech to the American Society of Newspaper Editors in Washington, DC, on 13 April 2005. From this point on his newspapers would fully engage with the digital revolution.

The internet is as radical a technological shift as journalism has ever had to deal with and has brought with it fundamental challenges to our social understanding of journalism's very function, while arguably changing our concept of the news itself (Lewis, 2003: 96). The social context of the internet is inevitably having a related impact on the form and function of journalism, corroding and even inverting previ-ously stable hierarchies of communication flow. However, we still need to reaffirm the fact that communication history indicates that we should not be too quick to pen the obituary of any contemporary journalism platform given the widespread evidence that the introduction of new media has rarely caused the elimination of existing media, although audiences and consequently their revenue bases have often shifted (Burnett and Marshall, 2003: 1). Nevertheless, the flight of advertising revenue from traditional journalism media which has been triggered by the inter-net may mean that there is a sustained challenge to journalism to create a business model for a product which can accommodate the demands of the new online envi-ronment. Print journalism and broadcast journalism are adapting to this paradigm shift in mass communications, partly by the incorporation of their product to an online format and partly by an adaptation of their traditional product to the struc-tures and capacity of the internet. It is interesting to note both that the importance of branding in this environment is crucial and that the only two British operations able to forge ahead here have been those guaranteed by something other than a raw market approach – the public-subscription-funded BBC and the Scott Trust-backed *Guardian*. In fact, *Guardian Unlimited* is the most successful UK newspaper website and is topped only by the *BBC News* online service.

A *BJR*/YouGov survey from 17–20 January 2006 found that while newspaper read-ership is continuing with its long-term decline, regular readers of newspapers are more inclined to imagine that they will continue to read newspapers despite the increasing availability of online and broadcast complements:

> *In cultural and consumer terms, as long as the newspaper industry can continue to offer something of real journalistic substance, our data suggest that it will continue to find a willing and substantial readership. (Barnett, 2006: 14)*

Jenkins is robust in his defence of the role of journalism even in this new technological era and sees its future associated with confidence in the 'brand':

> *I do not see the internet as rendering journalism obsolete. It puts it on its mettle. It converts the editing process into a search engine and website designer, and places an additional premium on brand trust. (2006: 47)*

Reinforcing this in the context of the radical approach to the digital revolution of the *Daily Telegraph*, Peter Wilby contrasts its suddenness with the steadier and more integrated approach of the more successful *Guardian* online project:

> *... media products depend above all on their brands, and on public confidence in them. The Telegraph brand has thrived for more than 150 years on its printed product with all its quaint eccentricities ... but a successful newspaper is a living system and you disturb its ecology at your peril. Destroy it, and you have nothing to take into the digital age. That is the danger of the Telegraph revolution. (2006: 21)*

The Visual Impact of Online Journalism

This convergence of journalism towards the online screen appears to align it to the seemingly democratic accessibility of the web, with its boxes, annotations, blogs, links, user-generated content and responses to journalists' pieces in virtual debate, all apparently promising to contribute to changes in the social nature of journalism towards a more participatory practice. The way people are accessing journalism is changing fundamentally, fracturing the traditional audience-design model (Bell, 1984; 1997) towards something much more fluid. Journalism needs to be much more dynamic and populist and use the new technological platform to provide a language which can couple the older idea of the mass with newer, more idiosyncratic, appropriations as articulated in Negroponte (1995) and Lasica (2002):

> *The interactive nature of the medium also demands new approaches and, for journalism, it has become clear that the tried and tested top-down forms, developed over the past three centuries around print, have been made obsolete by the new media and are increasingly irrelevant to the lives of many readers. (Hall, 2001: 2–3)*

Television and print journalism have imported and adapted the layout and design features of their web-based versions – side-bars, top-bars, breaking ticker tapes, references to hypertext and website material. The scannability of shorter paragraphs, bulleted lists, news pegs and simple headlines of the online variety is part of the converging journalism format. Journalism on radio and television spends a lot of time crafting its product across reception modes and alerting audiences of their websites, digital extension services, e-mail responsiveness and UGC. The lack of closure inherent in online news is impacting upon the length and structure of stories in traditional print and broadcast forms as they invite readers to cross-reference inside and across formats to online links but, paradoxically it may seem, elsewhere the commentary sections of newspapers are providing increased space for extended opinion pieces which would certainly not fit onto a screen version suitable for one viewing. On the positive side, elite newspapers in particular have benefited from their ability to provide what is missing in instantaneous reporting – a reflective and analytical mode of commentary. This continues a trend first seen in the 1930s under the impact of another technological innovation (the radio) and was amplified with the increased speed of television delivery of the news in the 1980s and 1990s through satellite technology.

The sort of authoritative commentary which newspapers can now provide is unavailable in most other news media, although it is largely framed by the values of the political and economic status quo on account of the realities of the corporate ownership of these papers, which has been discussed in a previous chapter. Furthermore, they have been able to offer spin-offs in the form of exhaustive web portals from their own archives to enable readers to pursue their interests with increasing depth. Thus, elite newspapers become enablers, opening up from their own output a range of parallel sources. For their part, television and radio journalism allow a more in-depth view of contemporary journalism in their on-line archiving of stories and their links to related news sites. All this is a boon for the engaged participant in the twenty-first century public sphere. News archives have now been opened up to more than the specialist researcher, with huge potential for a broader and deeper perception of how events in the world are interlinked. This indicates how an incorporation of online influences into the journalism mainstream is taking place, at the same time as further functional differentiations of newspapers, radio and television journalism are also occurring. This constitutes a complex re-engagement which is characteristic in its dynamics of the whole of journalism's history – dealing with alternative formats and changing technological demands as well as maintaining a language to engage socially with reconfigured audiences. Yet it seems clear that one pre-requisite which online and hard copy journalism will continue to share is a reliance on traditional methods of careful and unbiased reporting that use compelling writing based on authenticated sources (Barnett, 2006; Ward, 2002; Wilby, 2006) to provide 'the holy grail of journalism – quality content' (Quinn, 2005: 32).

Contesting the Achievements of Online Journalism

In addition to presentation, journalism's content has responded, for instance, to the challenges posed by blogging by attempting to provide its own journalists' blog-responses, the online versions of its products. The extent to which this, by itself, will succeed is open to question. The tug-of-war between the ethical claims on public communication between bloggers and journalists (Singer, 2007) does not seem to have fundamentally shifted the ground of the debate since Bardoel re-asserted the role of the journalist as the 'broker of social consensus' (1996: 297). Indeed the continuing primacy of mainstream journalism and journalists, as sources for online bloggers' own reports, suggests 'a more complementary relationship between weblogs and traditional journalism' (Reese et al. 2007: 235). Haas is much more robust in contesting whether blogs have provided anything new in journalistic terms:

> *From the telegraph to television, the advent of new communication media has prompted speculation about their potential challenges to prevailing journalistic norms and practices ... weblogs do not represent a radical departure from more established media of communication. (2005: 387)*

Weblogs continue to be satisfied in reproducing (as opposed to challenging) the discourse of mainstream news media despite the fact that there are a wide range of alternative news media available (Atton, 2002a) which could, in theory, destabilize the conventional hierarchies of topic and source provided by the mainstream media.

To offset these concerns, there are also potentially democratic bonuses to these developments. For instance, in what has been dubbed the first internet war (Kosovo, 1999) Lewis claims that the online publication of news provided journalism with a greater range of involvement beyond the usual and increasingly 'accredited' war correspondents, and demonstrated a dynamism through which local witnesses, freelance journalists, news agencies, academics and other interested parties could all use the internet to publish news, background and comment on the conflict (Lewis, 2003: 96). This was an excellent illustration of the potential of what Pavlik has termed the 'contextualized journalism' which online developments may facilitate (2001: xi).

All forms of journalism depend for their survival on being able to continue to provide a cultural approximation of the specifics of time and place in their idiom and values (Conboy and Steel, 2008). This is their attraction and the secret of their continued success – not to be swallowed whole within a globalized, technological monolith but to find ways to retain what makes them relevant to specific audiences. The traditional taxonomy of news values which include cultural proximity, socio-cultural values and consonance (Galtung and Ruge, 1965; Harcup and O'Neill, 2001) will all continue to structure what it is that particular communities want from their news and how this carries meaning for them. In many ways, the technological potential of the internet to provide a global, almost utopian model for news beyond the traditional constraints may prove illusory. It is the socio-cultural specifics of the language of the news which determine the shape of the news itself, often specifically within a national framework (Billig, 1995).

Technology, Journalism and Postmodernity

Partly as a consequence of the technological and economic changes of the late twentieth century, we are witnessing, according to many commentators, a shift in our understanding of how to make sense of the world – referred to as postmodernity – that thrives upon the increased speed and intensification of these flows of information. Postmodernity is characterized by a blurring of generic boundaries and a radical scepticism concerning the definitions, identities and motivations that have become heightened within the practice and reception of journalism. Furthermore, new technologies within broadcast journalism engender what Jameson has described as a 'fragmentation of time into a series of perpetual presents' (1985: 125). The postmodern news seems to skim over the surface of things and is infected by a greater range of intertextual entertainment media at a faster rate than ever before. For all this, journalism may resist calls to feel included within postmodernity's scope because several of journalism's core functions, as they have emerged over four centuries, are deeply embedded within the more stable narratives of the preceding era of modernity. The political emancipation of journalism, for instance, can be considered as one of the grand narratives of modernity, and it possesses – in its myths of the Fourth Estate and objectivity – the twin pillars of this tradition. Claims which underpin these narratives inform journalistic standards which continue to be given frequent rhetorical emphasis by broadcasters: 'eye-witness news', 'live to air', 'on the spot report', 'the day's most comprehensive news round-up', 'that's the way it is' and so on (Langer, 1998: 7).

One of the most problematic elements of postmodernity for journalism is the relativization of truth. This was explored recently, appropriately enough in the pages of the *Guardian*, by the philosopher David Cooper:

> *'Comment is free, but facts are sacred'. When CP Scott, one of this newspaper's greatest editors, wrote his famous lines, he could count on general agreement – confident that intelligent readers were responsive to well-documented evidence and honoured a boundary between truth and interpretation, facts and their evaluation. Eighty years on, journalists no longer share that confidence. (2000: 14)*

This theme is taken up once again in a leading article on the complexities of a world in which Al Jazeera and the Western news media provide their contrasting and potentially incompatible versions of the world: 'Truth may, indeed, be the first casualty, but there is usually more than one version of the truth' (*Guardian*, 2003: 29).

Certainly the mulitdimensionality of the truth in an era of great cultural and technological changes provokes critical questions about the nature and function of journalism as a truth-telling 'grand narrative'. To a large extent we may consider journalism's responses to this current configuration less the fall from a 'golden age' and more an accommodation which enables it to maintain credibility in a media-saturated world of overlapping and contradictory styles. This is why the examination of format is such a crucial issue for journalism in its attempt to retain an identifiable coherence with its core continuities. It is the diversity and adaptability within these core functions which have enabled journalism to survive. Generic variation within the formats of journalism is not only a cultural response to shifting technological and economic conditions but also a struggle to maintain its definitional values in changed circumstances.

Conclusion

There has been much hypothesis about the future of all journalistic formats under the influence of technological developments such as the internet. Such discussions may be considered as part of a much longer debate on the impact of technology on journalism. As has been noted on many occasions, no mass medium has completely supplanted an existing one. The process of media development has always tended to be an additive one. The trends in new-media influences on contemporary journalism, particularly for newspapers, seem to continue to demonstrate this. The elite press had been quicker to develop cross-referenced archives with sophisticated web-site material, but popular tabloid newspapers have picked up interest of late (Conboy and Steel, 2010) and magazines have also developed rounder versions of their printed products.

As another survivor of previous technological challenges, it also appears that radio, in both its standard box-on-the-kitchen-table manifestation and its online adaptation, can boast a distinctive enough service to enable it to survive:

> It seems certain that radio will survive as a medium ... because the imagination is less vivid than sight, radio is good at handling ideas and abstractions – not as good as the stable medium of print, perhaps, but much better than television – and ideas and abstractions are, of course, an essential element in the presentation and analysis of news. (Starkey and Crisell, 2009: 126)

Television journalism has responded to technological and economic challenges by developing newer variations on established generic patterns. Format itself, in this context, is not simply a stylistic variation. Within such a contested and complex medium it has hugely important political implications (Cottle, 2001). Questions of format are often central to the weighting of journalism between citizen access or commercial appeal. If journalism is not infinitely malleable and therefore a meaningless term, it must be located within a set of conventions that may shift or return over time but which also carry certain core continuities in providing information and opinion about the world that are expected by its audience and without which it becomes simply a form of fictional entertainment. McNair (1998: 4) considers these core continuities to be embedded within social expectations of journalism and to be intrinsically involved with questions about how format can deliver those expectations.

Although unfashionable in a historical account, it may nevertheless be acceptable to reinforce the implications of these observations on the development of journalism's technological past for the near future. Journalism is, as ever, exposed to threats to its survival. Modes of communication must adapt and have no guarantee of continuing beyond the next political, cultural or technological reconfiguration. Journalism was developed in response to an amalgam of these needs and it can just as easily exit the world of human communication under a different set of pressures. The formats of twenty-first century journalism need to be able to establish new ways of defending their definitional practices as they have had to throughout history, but with the added complication that the changes are now more intense than perhaps at any previous moment.

FURTHER READING

Briggs, A. and Burke, P. (2002) *A Social History of the Media*. Cambridge: Polity. The authors here engage throughout their longitudinal assessment of technology and the media with central questions about influence and the social patterns for the incorporation of new media technologies. Some of the historical detail can surprise us by demonstrating how new technologies were not automatically adopted by societies or political institutions as quickly as we might have expected.

Winston, B. (1998) *Media Technology and Society.* London: Routledge. This provides a provocative and sceptical account of the mutual influences of technology and social forces in the context of media in general, but it also supplies an essential sounding board for current discussions on the impact of technology on journalism.

6

Styling the Century: Tabloid Journalism

Introduction

The most pervasive influence on the form and scope of the journalism of the twentieth century has undoubtedly been the tabloid, especially in its elaboration of, first, an appeal to a broadly working class readership and, subsequently, its incorporation of a wider range of general popular culture. The language and style of both the popular newspaper in Britain and then the tabloid have had an incremental impact on newspapers generally over the last hundred years. Not only have broadsheet newspapers been driven for commercial reasons to adopt a 'compact' format but also the emphasis and style of the language of these elite newspapers have also been orientated more towards the news values of the tabloids as they try to emphasize their congruence with popular culture in an era of unprecedented competition in the media. It may be, as Bromley and Tumber (1997) have speculated, that after the gradual convergence of tabloid and broadsheet styles, a process of re-specialization may see different newspapers (particularly in their on-line manifestations) starting to diverge once again in their tone, style and coverage. Yet from our perspective the tabloid remains very much the story of twentieth-century journalism.

The emergence of a distinctive tabloid idiom indicated a shift in the social parameters of journalism. This idiom blends sensation and a calculated disrespect and suspicion of authority, particularly political authority, within an overall concentration on the broadest appeal to contemporary popular culture. This chapter will explore the nature of this sub-genre of journalism and reflect upon the social implications of its attempts to articulate a populist, media-centric version of contemporary society for a mass audience. It will root the evolution of tabloids within the general history of popular newspapers and also assess the intensification of the rhetoric of social class from the relaunch of the *Daily Mirror* in the 1930s to the reconfiguration of popular Conservatism in the *Sun* as a self-styled spokespiece for blue collar Britain from the 1980s. In addition it will evaluate the implications of the tabloid style for other journalistic media.

The Tabloid is Named

Like many of the developments within twentieth-century journalism, the tabloid has its roots in the nineteenth century. The pharmaceutical company Burroughs Wellcome and Co. copyrighted the term 'tabloid' in 1884 to advertise their marketing of compressed medicines in the form of small tablets. The term itself is a contraction of 'tablet' and 'alkaloid'. It was on New Year's Day in 1901 that the first copy of a tabloid newspaper appeared. Harmsworth had been invited to New York by the most powerful American newspaper owner of his day, Joseph Pulitzer, to oversee the production of an experimental, one-off, tabloid-sized version of his *New York World*. Harmsworth showed his appreciation of the commercial appeal of the instant news digest when his slogan boasted 'All the news in sixty seconds'. Presciently, he announced that it would be the newspaper of the century. In retrospect, we can see that this was not hyperbole but in fact an accurate assessment of the future – not only of the newspaper but increasingly of journalism in all its formats. Although the *Daily Mirror* (1903) and the *Daily Sketch* (1908) preceded it in terms of size, the first newspaper which we would recognize as tabloid in format as well as content was the *New York Daily News* from 1919. It provided an early combination of the sensation, brash sexuality, bold headlines, human interest and sport that would come to characterize the tabloid genre.

In the 1930s, under pressure from increasing competition for the attention of the popular reader, it was the incorporation of bigger and more frequent pictures into popular journalism which constituted the most significant change of the period. On 7 August 1933 Christiansen on the *Daily Express* produced a cleaner, better spaced newspaper with more and bigger headlines and more cross-heads to break up the page. It was followed by all its rivals including the relaunched *Daily Mirror*, which from 1934, under the editorial direction of Harry Guy Bartholomew, triggered the so-called tabloid revolution with its signature heavy black bold type for its headlines, pin-ups, its appeal to younger readers, its simplified language and the prominent use of pictures to reach a new readership. Curran and Seaton have argued that this constituted a 'key moment in the incorporation of the popular press by the entertainment industry' (2003: 53), with its slashing of political, social and economic news to formulate a newspaper of popular appeal to the politically unaligned working classes.

The *Daily Mirror*: A Commercial for the Working Class

In contrast to the success of the popular press of the 1930s in attracting the broadest range of lower-middle-class readers, the *Daily Mirror* was the first to redefine and then dominate the market with a proletarian language of specifically commercial appeal (Bingham and Conboy, 2009). By 1934 the circulation of the *Daily Mirror* was falling towards an unacceptably low 700,000. Its readers were predominantly the metropolitan middle class who might have been better served by the *Daily Express* and the *Daily Mail*: 'retired colonels, dowagers, professional gentlemen and school-mistresses' – in fact, Cudlipp called it the '*Daily Sedative*' (1953: 64). It was decided that something had to be done to revive the financial fortunes of the newspaper within an increasingly competitive popular market. It had been identified that there was an imbalance, with more right-wing newspapers than the market could sustain (Pugh, 1998: 426). Furthermore, the existing left-of-centre newspapers, consisted of more serious-minded and party-affiliated publications such as the *Daily Herald*, *Daily Worker* and the Liberal *News Chronicle*. A newspaper which could encompass a broader appeal to a working-class audience and spice this up with entertainment, humour and an engagement with the lived experiences of its readers could occupy a hitherto vacant position in the market. The success of the re-launched *Daily Mirror* was built on a formula based on two American tabloids, New York's *Daily Mirror* and *Daily News*, and skilfully adapted to a British cultural context following the advice of an American advertising agency, J. Walter Thompson, while deploying the old Northcliffe formula of the telegraphic sentence within a modern layout (Edelman, 1966: 40). The guiding light behind all of this was its editorial director, Bartholomew, who introduced the heavy black type which was to distinguish the *Mirror* from all its competitors from his first year in charge. Its 'Tabloid Revolution' of 1934–1937 had begun but it still needed to find an authentic voice to match its bold appearance. Engel has described its new-found appeal under his stewardship in the following terms:

> *In the fuggy atmosphere of a bare-floored pre-war pub, the Mirror was the intel-ligent chap leaning on the counter of the bar: not lah-di-dah or anything – he liked a laugh, and he definitely had an eye for the girls – but talking a lot of com-mon sense. (1996: 161)*

It soon began to pick up in terms of circulation, fulfilling its ambition to articulate the broad interests of the working classes, in a format which meshed with the language and aspirations of its idealized readers, as Smith has commented: 'a paper that will conveniently stuff into the pocket of overalls, and that can be read in brief intervals between manual work' (1975: 233). Edelman has tried to capture something of the man trusted with expressing that identity:

> *Though the 'Establishment' was still an object of reverence, 'Bart', as everyone called him, was against it. Long before the aristocracy and its imitators in Britain recognized that their authority was crumbling, Bart spontaneously pointed out to the millions of working-class and lower-middle-class readers of the* Mirror *that they mattered, that many of the old accepted and snobbish values were bunk, that stuffed prigs should not be taken at their self-assessment, and that you didn't have to be a public school man to have worthwhile views. (1966: 38)*

The paper came to articulate the views and aspirations of the working classes in a vernacular style which transmitted that solidarity even if it was delivered in an intensely commercialized form. A key element in this construction of a working-class voice was the use of letters such as 'Viewpoint', 'Live Letters' and 'Star letter', and later the 'Old Codgers'' replies to these letters, as a barometer of readers' views. Also key to its development of a demotic printed language were the columns of Cassandra (William Connor) who provided an abrasive, populist commentary with a political edge which railed against unemployment, any appeasement of Hitler and the complacency of the ruling classes in a language well able to provoke debate and stir up passions.

Speaking for the People

It was during the Second World War that the *Daily Mirror* was able to take up the mantle as a spokesperson for the ordinary people with a hunger for radical change that was in favour of their interests and against the damaging social and political prejudices of the pre-war era. Without hyperbole Cudlipp could claim that it became 'the newspaper of the masses, the Bible of the Services' rank and file, the factory worker and the housewife' (1953: 136).

In the words of historian A.J.P. Taylor it constituted for this period a:

> serious organ of democratic opinion [which] gave an indication as never before what ordinary people in the most ordinary sense were thinking. The English people at last found their voice. (Taylor, 1976: 548–549)

Much of its credibility in the early war years derived from an astute identification of the inefficiencies of the bureaucrats and their hindrance of the war effort. Cassandra's crusade against 'Army foolery', for instance, managed to continually strike a popular chord which was patriotic at the same time as it was disturbing for the wartime leaders. He carried it off because readers genuinely recognized the problems which he identified in the many cosy preconceptions of hierarchy and protocol in British society. In stark contrast to much of the conservative individualism of populist appeal in the *Daily Mail* or *Daily Express* – its main mass market competitors of the 1930s – there was a decisive shift to a collective and working-class perspective in the *Daily Mirror*. By 11 May 1945 it had adopted the slogan:

FORWARD WITH THE PEOPLE

This emphasis culminated in its coverage of the lead-up to voting in the 1945 General Election. In a stroke of populist genius the paper began a campaign of considerable power and subtlety – not mentioning the name of the Labour Party while focusing instead on the experiences and memories of ordinary people as a repository of folk-memory. The catch-phrase adopted (5 June 1945) was both memorable and convincing:

I'LL VOTE FOR HIM

The people and the nation were merged in a vision of radical change for the benefit of both. An editorial on 4 July read:

THE ONE OR THE MANY

When people all over the country go to the polls tomorrow for whom will they be voting? Not for this party or that, not for one leader as against another, not to express appreciation or gratitude. They will be voting for themselves. They will be voting to express confidence in their own view of the kind of world they desire to live in. They will be voting for the policies which they believe are likely to bring such a world into existence. This election is a national issue, not a personal one.

Post-1945 the *Daily Mirror* continued to articulate the aspirations of a class of reader who had emerged from the war with a strong sense of social solidarity and a determination that things would change for the benefit of ordinary people. The *Daily Mirror* – with its astute identification of a representational style and above all the voice to match its constituency – was to continue to play a key part in that evolution throughout the fifties, as it overtook the *Daily Express* in 1949 and by 1967 had reached the still unmatched pinnacle of 5.25 million daily sales (Tunstall, 1996: 43–45).

Its continued success was rooted in the 'successful projection of personality', about which Fairlie wrote in 1957 when describing the 'Old Codgers' section of the letters page:

No other feature in British journalism so superbly creates the atmosphere of a public bar, in which everyone sits cosily round the scrubbed deal tables, arguing the toss about anything which happens to crop up, while the Old Codgers buy pints of mixed for the dads, and ports and lemon for the dear old mums. (1957: 11)

As editor of the *Mirror* from 1948 to 1953 Silvester Bolam could stake a claim for the linkage of sensation and public service which continues to inform much of the popular tabloids' self-image (Deuze, 2005b, Rhoufari, 2000):

We believe in the sensational presentation of news and views, as a necessary and valuable public service ... Sensationalism does not mean distorting the truth. It means the vivid and dramatic presentation of events so as to give them a forceful impact on the mind of the reader. It means big headlines, vigorous writing, simplification into familiar everyday language, and the wide use of illustration by cartoon and photograph. (Daily Mirror, 30 July 1949, p. 1)

From 1953, Cudlipp was editor-in-chief and editorial director of both the *Daily Mirror* and the *Sunday Pictorial* and according to Geoffrey Goodman he transformed 'the feelings, attitudes, beliefs, prejudices, romantic aspirations and illusions, nostalgic dreams and awkward-squad absurditites of the post-war masses into a kind of national common currency' (Greenslade, 2003: 59). Yet the language which it used to maintain that sense of readership into the 1950s and 1960s has been criticized by Smith as having 'stylized working class language into parody' (Smith, 1975: 238) and he was not alone in decrying the popular press as culpable of a cultural drift from an authentic representation of the voice and interest of the working classes. Richard Hoggart's *Uses of Literacy* denounced a sensational, sex and entertainment-obsessed popular press for its part in destroying a serious working-class culture sustained by the 'old broad-sheets' (Hoggart, 1958).

The *Sun*: A Blue-Collar Vernacular for a New Generation

The most significant, recent development in the history of British tabloid journalism came with the relaunch of the *Sun* in 1969. Thomas has located the epoch-defining pitch for a new, downmarket popular newspaper in Murdoch's conviction that the *Daily Mirror* had become too highbrow for its readers by the mid-1960s. Cudlipp had by this point begun to reposition the *Mirror* – if not upmarket, then certainly towards a more serious market – with features such as 'World Spotlight' and 'Mirrorscope'. With former *Daily Mirror* journalist Larry Lamb, Murdoch set out to produce an alternative that was explicitly based on an updated version of their rival's irreverent approach of previous decades (Thomas, 2005: 72). Lamb (1989: 22–23) scrapped all the specialist news reporters except political journalists, and specialized in human interest, sensation and sex, significantly narrowing its news agenda. The *Sun* targeted younger readers, dropped the increasingly serious ambitions of the *Daily Mirror*, embraced the permissiveness of the age, and provided a disrespectful, anti-establishment, entertainment-driven agenda. It reinforced its popular credentials by advertising itself on television (a first for a newspaper) and by providing an intensified coverage of the off- and on-screen activities of the characters in soap operas on British television. Greenslade, who worked for a period as deputy editor of the paper, summed up its impact in the following overview:

> The *Sun* *had shown that there was an audience for softer, features-based material and heavily angled news in which comment and reporting were intertwined. It also adopted a more idiosyncratic agenda, presenting offbeat stories that fell outside the remit of broadcast news producers. It cultivated brashness, deliberately appealing to the earthier interests – and possibly, baser instincts – of a mass working-class audience. (2003: 337)*

It was the *Sun*'s ability to transform the language of populist appeal away from the *Mirror*'s left-leaning progressive brand of politics to a new articulation of the sentiments and policies of the right, an 'authoritarian populism' (Hall and Jacques, 1983: 22), which provided it with a trump card – employing Walter Terry, former political editor of the right-wing *Daily Mail*, and Ronnie Spark to provide a demotic language to shape the editorial ambition for Murdoch/Lamb's shift to the right from 1978. In the late 1970s the Tories gained the support of the *Sun* (Negrine: 1994), which

114

had become synchronized with the aspirations and identities of the classes which were credited with the swing to Thatcher in the 1979 election. This represented an astute mapping of the newspaper's idiom onto the hegemonic shift towards the ideological project of the Conservative Party in government. Its effect was contagious to many areas of the press, with its rabid anti-union stance becoming a perspective that would be maintained by most of the national newspaper press (Marr, 2005: 169). It soon perfected a style of vernacular address which highlighted the perceived interests of a newly empowered blue-collar conservatism. This was, however, nothing new according to some more historically informed commentators such as Seymour-Ure, who observed that 'Ever since its birth, the popular press has "bolstered capitalism by encouraging acquisitive, materialistic and individualistic values"' (2000: 23).

Kelvin MacKenzie, as editor from 1981, encapsulated this new mood perfectly. His preferred slogan was 'Shock and Amaze on Every Page' (Chippendale and Horrie, 1992: 332) as he displayed bombastic and hyperbolic language on all aspects of life in Britain and beyond. Fiercely patriotic and a staunch supporter of the Conservative Prime Minister, he was always unequivocally supportive of British military involvement. This was demonstrated most infamously by its jingoistic coverage in the Falklands: 'GOTCHA: Our lads sink gunboat and hole cruiser' (4 May 1982). The paper adopted 'Maggie', feted British soldiers as 'our boys', and ran front-page headlines more redolent of popular speech than ever before: SCUM OF THE EARTH – KINNOCK'S PARTY OF PLONKERS – SUPERSTAR MAGGIE IS A WOW AT WEMBLEY – 70, 80, 90 PHEW WOT A SCORCHER! The paper was, furthermore, able to extend itself into more extreme examples of parody for its amused readership and in the process probably contributed to a more general process of political trivialization (*Sun*, 1 June 1987):

WHY I'M BACKING KINNOCK, BY STALIN

From 1985 onwards, driven by the enthusiasm of influential features editor Wendy Henry, it used the launch of the BBC's *EastEnders* as fuel for an endless supply of features and gossip which came to engineer a new and hugely effective tabloid approach to integrating popular television and media celebrity into tabloid journalism.

Sexualizing Popular Culture

Changing times had brought with them changing attitudes to public discussions of sexuality. The *Sun* managed to capture perfectly the resonance of Hunt's (1998) 'permissive populism' of the 1970s and 1980s. Once the veneer of didacticism had been stripped away (Bingham, 2009), public discussion of the direct and vicarious pleasures of sexuality became commonplace within a language of vulgar celebration, best epitomized by the descriptions of the Page 3 Girl: 'Cor!', 'Wot a Scorcher!', 'Stunner!'. It provided a language appealing to women as part of a broader celebration of heterosexual pleasure for ordinary people. 'We Enjoy Life and We Want You To Enjoy It With Us' announced the first 'Pacesetters' section for women (*Sun*, 17 November

1969, p. 14) and to that end its women's department's provided in 'Pacesetters' advice on how to improve one's sex life. Holland (1983) has supplied a subtle reading of how the news agenda of the paper and its raucous appeal formed part of a linguistic endorsement of the potential of pleasure in the lives of working-class readers, presenting itself as the champion of sexual liberation albeit of a particularly narrow, heterosexual, male-dominated variety.

This sexualization of the language of what soon became the most popular and most influential newspaper in Britain grew even more pronounced in a more intensely competitive market. It seemed as if, as Snoddy has discussed (1992), the race was on to find the bottom of the barrel in terms of public tolerance. The *Daily Star*, launched in 1978, beat the *Sun* by a short head in the plummet towards the lowest tolerance point in the late 80s in the sexualization of popular culture (Holland, 1998). It attempted but failed to provide the *Sun* with its nemesis. It has been described as having 'a circus layout that fairly burst from the pages ... the paper used more italics, more reverses, and more graphics in conjunction with sensational heads and stories to give a sense of excitement and power' (Taylor, 1992: 45). Engel commented (1996: 17) that each generation of successful, popular newspapers was undercut by a new wave which had been able to capture the readership of a lower social grouping and integrate that readership within the widest range of appropriate other media such as advertising, cinema and television. The *Daily Star* certainly attempted to outperform the *Sun* in this respect in the basement of tabloid taste. It was aimed at the lowest end of the market in terms of sensation and dubious journalism ethics, with a raunchy approach guiding what it believed was its appeal to an even younger market than the *Sun*'s. Its limited success meant that with sales falling and advertisers withdrawing contracts by the early 1990s, the paper strategically stepped away from its policy of 'bonk journalism', thus demonstrating how continually coarsening content does not guarantee success for the next generation of popular newspapers. It was almost entirely the fault of the tabloids in their pursuit of the bottom of this barrel that the Calcutt Committee into Privacy and Related Matters was set up in 1989 as a final attempt to encourage some sort of responsibility from the newspapers, short of imposing legislation which would encroach upon the freedoms that the press had come to take for granted.

The Tabloids and Royalty: Declining Deference

The diminishing deference within British society in the post-war era was perfectly articulated in the popular press, especially the tabloids, and this found early expression in attitudes towards the monarchy. A greater aggressiveness in royal journalism was first demonstrated in the matter of Princess Margaret's relationship with Peter Townsend. In June 1953 the *People* was the first British newspaper to print an item alleging that Princess Margaret and Group-Captain Peter Townsend were romantically involved. On 14 June 1953 a particularly controversial headline captured a newfound assertiveness towards the Royal family in a popular newspaper when the *Daily*

Mirror urged: 'Come On Margaret! Please make Up Your Mind' (19 August 1953). At least they said 'Please' at this point!

The *Daily Mirror* ran a poll on whether they should marry or not. The Press Council was hugely critical of the paper's behaviour, as were conservative newspapers such as the *Times* and the *Daily Telegraph*, but there was to be no going back. As a supplement to this in the 1970s, the romantic saga of Prince Charles' various courtships was to provide the first sustained taste of this new lack of deference towards monarchy. The stories peaked in the 1990s with the colourful and controversial adventures of Diana, Princess of Wales, but there were still notable stories beyond that decade as the tabloids became more desperate than ever to milk a royal scandal or even to fabricate one to boost its sales, such as with the 'Spy in the Palace' coup by the *Daily Mirror*'s Ryan Parry in 2003 and the Burrell affair (Coward, 2007). Stretching for sales through accounts of celebrity misdemeanours as well as a continuing obsession with Royal tittle-tattle have led to spectacular libel pay-outs, most notably Koo Stark's award of £300,000 against the *People* after the publication of false allegations that she had had an affair with Prince Andrew.

Tabloidization: Process or Panic?

The history of twentieth-century journalism has shown a struggle between the forces of commerce and the interests of the people. Tabloidization may be an extended working-out of the process of a commercial logic within journalism as it enters its next developmental phase. Although tabloidization is a problematic label which includes the organization and production of journalism, as well as just format in its terms of debate (Esser, 1999), the tabloid popular papers have been the pioneers of this trend. Although the sensationalism and personalization of the popular press have long been the subject of discussion and complaint on a national basis, particularly in advanced capitalist democracies, what has happened over the last twenty years is that a combination of political, cultural and technological changes has triggered a series of ripples which have spread across national as well as media boundaries and caused a range of debate about how processes which were once confined to the lower end of the newspaper market are now perceived to have infected the whole news media market. As concern has spread within the elite news media, political circles and parts of the academic community, the perception of the acceleration towards 'tabloidization' has become a moral panic in its own right (Gripsrud, 2000: 287).

Sparks (2000) has identified three ways in which the term is used – to identify shifts in the boundaries of journalism, shifts within the priorities of journalism, and shifts in taste within media forms – while Paletz (1998: 65–68) has proposed four trends within tabloidization which impact upon subject matter – shifting priorities concerning content, forms of presentation, journalistic techniques, and ethics. Tabloidization may therefore refer to an increase in news about celebrities, entertainment, lifestyle features, personal issues, an increase in sensationalism and the use of pictures and sloganized headlines as well as vulgar language, and a decrease in international news, public affairs news that includes politics, a reduction in the length of words in a story and the complexity of language, and also a convergence with agendas for popular and in particular television culture. Tabloids are characterized as being primarily to do with a combination of format and language: 'editorial matter is presented in emotive language in easy-to-consume formats' (Rooney, 2000: 91). It is clearly, if nothing else, a composite growl-list of elements, some of which have haunted the minds of commentators on journalism over the centuries.

Changing Formats

The first key developments in the tabloidizing of British newspapers can be defined initially and literally by the reformatting into tabloids of the *Sun* in 1969 and the *Daily Mail* in 1971. The *Daily Express* completed the middle market shift to the format in 1977, the *News of the World* in 1984, and the *Sunday Express* from 1992. The next stage was the tabloidization of most of the elite press, with the *Independent* leading the way in 2004, followed by *The Times* and the *Guardian*'s shift to the slighter larger 'Berliner' format in 2005, now leaving only the *Daily Telegraph* holding out as a genuine broadsheet in the daily market if one excludes the specialist *Financial Times*.

When Taylor writes, 'Tabloid journalism is the direct application of capitalism to events and ideas. Profit, not ethics, is the prevailing motivation' (1992: 409), she articulates why the tabloids are such accurate barometers of what has become the reality of commercialized journalism in Britain today. The journalistic media are all trying to keep their market share in the face of increased competition driven by technological innovation and market fragmentation. Tabloidization may be the contemporary reformulation of the discourse of journalism as it engages with the politics, commerce and social configuration of a new era (Sparks, 2000: 35–36), or it may be the crystallization of longer processes into this contemporary crisis – a different mix of entertainment and information to attract large enough audiences to maintain an essential commercial credibility. This does not mean that it does not have implications either for journalism itself, in the alleged 'decline in standards' (Bromley, 1998: 25), or for the political functions of journalism in a democratic system, and it also illustrates that:

> *The competing (and often conflicting) priority of profit and service is the tension within journalism that has underscored so much of the recent enquiry into its social functions. (Harrington, 2008: 267)*

Changing Style

The second key development within tabloidization is the spread of the characteristic tabloid style and news values to the elite press. McLachlan and Golding (2000) have charted the growth in visuals in relation to text as one indicator of tabloidization, squeezing text out of the frame. Other strategies which conform to the tabloidization model according to their study have included the inclusion of more lifestyle and consumer coverage and an increasing number of their journalists getting the media star treatment with a photograph accompanying their by-line and a freer rein to write from a more personalized perspective. Tunstall argues that objectivity, even on elite newspapers, has shifted considerably towards more of a house-style orientation than anything absolute, and interprets this as part of a need to differentiate themselves within the media market: 'Newspapers, in any case, need to "take it further" than TV and radio. They need to go beyond the neutral and objective rituals of balance' (1996: 197–198). Bromley observed this trend as it gathered momentum throughout the 1990s:

> At first, the 'quality' press ignored the substantive issues of tabloid news; then decried them. These papers ... subsequently began reporting and commenting on the behaviour of the tabloid press, which led to the vicarious reporting of the issues themselves. Finally, the broadsheet papers, too, carried the same news items. (1998: 31)

Thomas (2005) argued that there was a direct correlation between aspects of the development of tabloid newspaper language and their reporting of politics, and that this has drifted into the elite press as it too has come to depend on the populist techniques of the tabloids to maintain their place in an increasingly competitive market. This has meant a move away from balanced reporting, positive, politician-centred communication to a more negative, journalist-dominated approach and one-story front pages, screaming headlines and short, punchy campaigning prose at the expense of more detailed text or long quotations from politicians. In this sense, Thomas claims, the tabloid medium has certainly affected the message and has also arguably impacted not just on the popular press but also on the wider reporting culture as well (Thomas, 2005: 154–155). Through these processes, it has been argued that readers have more than ever become constructed by journalism in terms of consumerism rather than than active engagement in politics (McGuigan, 1993: 178), meaning that political news has simply become another part of the scandal/entertainment industry (Franklin, 1997). Fairclough (1995) and Fowler (1991) have both observed a movement in news media towards what they term a 'conversationalization' of public language, including political language, while Marr (2005: 71) concludes that the consequent tone of mocking scepticism adopted almost as a contemporary default has eroded the credibility of democracy. Critics of these trends, which are so characteristic of the reporting of political life in Britain, see the shift towards sensation, emotion and scandal as a major element in what amounts to a crisis in public life – 'the negation of the kind of journalism that is essential to democracy' (Sparks, 1998: 6).

The Virtues of Tabloid Style

Yet the influence of tabloid techniques on the journalism of the elite press has not been uniformly negative. McNair sees changes in the content and style of the elite press as a positive move towards a more inclusive, even democratic journalism culture: 'Less pompous, less pedagogic, less male, more human, more vivacious, more demotic' (2003a: 50). Greenslade also implies a cautiously positive note when praising the success of the editor of the *Guardian* from the 1970s in appealing to a younger, professional readership:

> *The key to Preston's success stemmed in part from his subtle adoption and adaptation of tabloid techniques. He realised the importance of 'selling' the stories, the virtues of brevity and the benefits of being proactive in both news-gathering and features selection. (2003: 428)*

A further endorsement of the encroachment of tabloid style on the elite press comes from Preston himself. This benefits from a historical perspective longer than many critics can provide:

> *The truth – my dawning truth from 1976 – is that tabloid actually suits the current broadsheet news and feature agenda best. It's the natural way of seeking to address segments of a readership which itself is increasingly composed of segments. It forces editors to put their judgement on the line. It establishes its own priorities, not an order of news nicked straight off the 6 O'Clock News on BBC. Tabloid is much more than easy reading on the Tube. It is a means to a disciplined end, a clarity of mind.*

> *What took us so long, then? Why was it the autumn of 2003 before* The Independent *broke the British mould? (2004: 51)*

As has been argued elsewhere (Conboy, 2006) there is nothing necessarily reactionary or ignorant in the techniques used by the tabloids in themselves. A recent article in the *British Journalism Review*, addressed to a readership located predominantly in journalism, emphasized the positive attributes of this kind of journalism while expressing caution over its irresponsible handling of immigration, asylum and Europe within that idiom:

> *... thanks to the exploits of Parry and co – and, more recently, Mazher Mahmood's encounter with Sven-Göran Eriksson as described in the* News of the World *– I gained a new appreciation (and occasionally, a grudging admiration) for what the tabs do.*

> *There is a certain gaudy brilliance to stunts like these. A weird hybrid of investigative journalism and the print equivalent of reality TV ... whiff of old-fashioned muckraking ... the tabs appoint themselves the official voice of the people ... Reality tabloidism is bold, enterprising, lively and fun. But is it good journalism?*

> *There's no reason why it can't be. (Geary, 2006: 43)*

Within the newspaper industry itself, there is a clear acknowledgement that the trends towards tabloid strategy as well as tabloid content and format are well advanced: 'Since the 1980s broadsheet newspapers have adopted many of the commercial, as well as editorial, practices of the tabloid press, including promotional stunts, cover price discounts and brand exploitation' (Greenslade, 1996: 17). More recently the editor of the *Guardian* highlighted that it was the way that quality newspapers in Britain continued to adapt to the pressures of this commercialized and tabloidized market which would define the next generation of serious newspapers in this country (Rusbridger, 2005).

From Newspapers to the Wider World

The third key characteristic of tabloidization is the crossover of tabloid style and news values from newspapers to other news media. As the tabloid newspapers decline in direct sales they are nevertheless – and perhaps this in part explains their slow demise – exporting their stylistic traits, first, as we have seen, to other parts of the newspaper press and then to other journalistic media in general.

The BBC has always attempted to construct as wide a national audience as possible, chiefly to justify its public funding, although the tone of its address has shifted considerably from paternalist to populist over the century. This shift was in part because of an increased competition for the loyalty of the popular constituency which was ushered in by the introduction of ITN in the 1950s. From this period onwards, the format of television journalism has expanded from set times to accommodate more differentiated viewing patterns and has created newer styles to address audiences at different times of the day. In this proliferation of varieties, the imperative has become to popularize the format so as to best justify expenditure and retain market credibility. The first experiment in adopting television news to changing patterns of consumption and lifestyle was the regular breakfast television news in 1983. This saw a shift in the hitherto rather austere image of the newscaster. These new journalists – easy on the eye and with tones suited to a gentler, chattier style of 'sofa journalism' – were very different creatures to their counterparts in other broadcast news programmes. Breakfast television news introduced an accompanying softer range of human-interest angles on stories in the news, and because of its man–woman double-act it was soon dubbed 'Ken and Barbie' journalism (van Zoonen, 1998: 40). After the introduction of breakfast television news, the presentational styles and formats of mainstream television news started a process of rapid transformation. Regional journalism began to become more oriented to a lighter style with more human interest and good news stories. On the prime-time mainstream news there was an increased use of text on the screen, a sound-bite syntax which reduced the length of individual news items, the use of graphics to illustrate news, newscasters and reporters on first name terms with each other if not quite yet with the politicians they interviewed – all an indication of the popularization of the television news format.

Form 1987 the BBC went for more populist approaches to 'difficult' stories as part of the Birt revolution. In November 1992 ITN's *News at Ten* was relaunched in a new, visually more dynamic format, with one newscaster rather than two and a greater emphasis on 'human interest' in its stories. As a summation of these trends in mainstream news programming, *Channel 5 News* was launched in April 1997, fronted by the photogenic Kirsty Young and targeted specifically at an audience of 'younger adults'. It has been observed that it aggressively advertised its innovativeness by paying more attention to positive news stories and incorporating more human interest and lifestyle coverage into its programming (McNair, 1998: 117).

Barnett and Gaber (2001: 8) concluded that ITN and Sky operated to a more identifiable tabloid agenda, with shorter items, more sport, more celebrity-based stories and less foreign reporting, while BBC TV and radio continued to adhere to a more serious set of priorities. This has been reinforced by comparative research (Kadritzke, 2000) which has contrasted the greater contextualizing and informative character of BBC news against that to be found on commercial channels, which are more notable for their busy and personable style, broad range and, in many items, shallowness (Ursell, 2001: 192). Yet the BBC has not remained immune from moves to introduce more visually appealing television newscasters and reporters as part of this concentration on visual appeal over content. This has embroiled the corporation, in line with its commercial rivals, in arguments over the suitability of older women as newsreaders, in particular when Moira Stuart resigned in 2007 when it was alleged she was fearful of being moved out for a more photogenic and younger replacement. The logic of more aesthetically-pleasing TV presenters seems to fit within a general movement of broadcast news towards entertainment values, and it may even represent part of the bid to retain some of the younger audience which is turning away from mainstream news and politics.

Both Winston (2002) and Barnett and Seymour (1999b) have conducted research which makes the point that the tabloidization thesis is not borne out in any generalizable or incremental way by longitudinal studies of mainstream television news, which are in fact more complex in their editorial shifts and emphases. There have been changes in emphasis and presentational style but the content has not moved consistently in any particular direction. However, Barnett and Seymour did conclude that the drift to lighter content and more human-interest-driven presentation and theme was borne out by the state of current affairs. The most notorious example of this was when *Tonight with Trevor McDonald* replaced *World in Action* in 1998 as ITV's only current affairs programme. Current affairs programmes such as this, drawing on the celebrity status of an anchorman despite its poor ratings, are symptomatic of an increased perception that television journalism must appeal as widely as possible to maintain a popular appeal regardless of the quality of its content.

The perceived 'tabloidization' of television news and current affairs has generated optimistic assessments as well as negative critiques of these changes. Television journalism's contemporary developments fit easily into a catalogue of criticism attached to the perceived trend towards a tabloid format, content and philosophy: 'image crowding out rational analysis' (Bird, 2000: 221). This is especially so in the relative decline of older style Public Service Broadcasting and the rise of celebrity/docudrama styles of factual popular television and entertainment-led news. From the other end of this argument, Macdonald attempts to recuperate some of this generic material for positive ends. She explores the particular implications of 'personalization' in current affairs journalism in order to argue that when it is properly integrated and used to clarify otherwise abstract concepts, it can help to demystify complex and potentially arcane subjects for a broader and more democratic public appeal (2000: 264–5). She quotes Norman Fairclough as a pivotal voice in this debate, indicating how these processes, showing an increasing conversationalization in public affairs' discourse within the media, can either be read as a concession to market forces or as an opportunity for extending democratic access (Fairclough, 1995: 10–12).

Celebrity and Tabloid Culture

Celebrity news acts as a perfect conduit for the tabloids as it allows the fluid interchange between fact and fiction as well as the easy generic transfer from information to entertainment (Hill, 2005: 15) upon which its values are centred. Tabloid tendencies to cross-reference celebrity and entertainment issues can be witnessed increasingly as part of the repertoire of the elite press and broadcast journalism in all its forms, and they are part of a strategy to reach new audiences in a crowded market and a changing cultural and technological environment. Celebrities are increasingly providing an alternative public sphere where Jamie Oliver's tirade against the low nutritional value of school meals can generate hundreds of column inches across the elite press, and the political opinions of a member of the band Coldplay can be flagged on the front page of the *Times* in the run-up to a general election (11 April 2005). Both examples demonstrate that elite newspapers are not only in the business of reporting political issues from parliament. Peter Andre and Katie Price, the ultimate tabloid celebrity pair, had their trumpeted divorce covered in all the newspapers, not just the popular tabloids, and on all mainstream television news programmes, while the late Jade Goody's problematic life and tragic death were as much debated in the elite press and television news as they were in the popular tabloids who had first catapulted her to fame on the crest of her notoriety in reality television.

Tabloid celebrities are usually drawn from specifically national media culture, its music, sport and soaps. The form of intimacy thus generated between reader and tabloid journalism is an important element in establishing and developing a resonant sense of mediated community in Britain. Giles (2000) and Rojek (2001) stress the importance of 'para-social' activities such as media identification in the contemporary patterns of domestic existence, where increasing numbers of people are dependent on what they term 'second-order intimacy' to provide social recognition and belonging to replace older forms of direct social contact in real neighbourhoods. We need to consider whether celebrity coverage in this tabloidized journalism is merely parasitic and replacing other news values or part of a cultural amplification enabling audiences to better grasp the intertextual, media-heavy nature of the contemporary world. Turner summarized this critical stand-off succinctly when he wrote:

The more pessimistic accounts argue that the public sphere is progressively impoverished by such a shift; the more optimistic ones argue that the media are now simply serving different purposes than they used to. (2003: 102)

Conclusion

To many – coming at it from an elitist cultural perspective – tabloidization represents the lowest form of media life, a profane besmirching of the traditions and heritage of a liberal and politically committed journalism. To others – coming from an economic perspective – it is simply evidence of what happens at the end point of the marketization of popular news. From a more integrated, almost anthropological perspective, Bird sees the contemporary tabloids as unimaginable outside other historical and cultural phenomena:

They complement the star system, the other popular media, the class system, and the gender system. They exist because of television, newspapers, movies, and a vast range of folk narratives and values. (1992: 1–2)

Yet as the panic has unfolded, the perceived process of 'tabloidization' has begun to move beyond the description of a particular kind of journalism to become a portmanteau description for what is regarded as the trivialization of media content in general (Turner, 2003: 76; also McKee, 2005). This tendency is exaggerated because the process is not restricted to the tabloid newspaper but is connected to a more complex set of changes – a 'dynamic structural transformation' within the whole media sector from new technology to general social changes (Sparks and Tulloch, 2000: 160). Maybe it represents part of a broader 'communication chaos' (McNair, 2003b: 552) that is enveloping the whole of journalism in the twenty-first century.

To its critics, tabloidization signifies an inexorable decline in journalistic standards: to its admirers or even its pragmatic observers, it represents an amalgam of professional and economic compromises with the realities of contemporary mediated popular culture which has successfully colonized much of the spectrum of journalism in the twenty-first century. Dahlgren suggested in 1992 that journalism should be considered as part of and not separate from popular culture, and indeed the tabloidization of journalism is such an important feature of contemporary trends in the culture at large that we could say that tabloid culture can no longer be conveniently quarantined in an annexe some distance from the concerns of mainstream or even elite cultural activity. It touches the lives of all of us in some way even if our engagement is limited to bemoaning its very influence. It has long been acknowledged that the vicarious coverage of tabloid media in our elite press and by our public service broadcasters is a discreetly acceptable way for these institutions to keep their own idealized audiences abreast of what is commonly known to be going on 'out there'. To this extent, we are all populists now.

FURTHER READING

Biressi, A. and Nunn, H. (eds) (2007) *The Tabloid Culture Reader*. Milton Keynes: Open University Press. This provides a culturally rich assessment of the influence of tabloid culture throughout the media's output.

Conboy, M. (2006) *Tabloid Britain*. London: Routledge. An account of the specifics of the language of the tabloids as an explanation for their attractiveness to both audiences and owners.

Sparks, C. and Tulloch, J. (eds) (2000) *Tabloid Tales*. Oxford: Rowman and Littlefield. This locates the growth of tabloid culture as a global phenomenon as well as giving an impressive theoretical account of this process, providing the reader with a wide range of different tabloid experiences from around the world.

7

Journalism and Political Coverage

Introduction

Although the issue of political coverage runs throughout much of this book, this chapter will focus exclusively on this particular function of journalism, a function which distinguishes journalism from other related forms of communication in its ambition to inform an audience of contemporary political developments in order to enable people to make democratic choices about the world in which they live and work. It will concentrate on the coverage of politics beyond the attempts of media owners to control the content of newspapers, from Northcliffe to Murdoch. It will consider the implications of the shift from hard political coverage over the century and the increase in soft-news and lifestyle coverage. It will indicate something of the relationship between newspapers and political parties throughout the century and the attempts in other journalistic forms such as radio and television to provide a different model from the direct partisanship of the press so as to provide a counter-balance of 'objectivity'. It will explore key moments of tension between these ideals of public service from the BBC's coverage of the General Strike of 1926 to the Kelly Affair of 2004. As a more sceptical inflection of journalism towards politics and politicians has now become all pervasive, it is widely considered as threatening the compact between journalism and political life (Blumler and Gurevitch, 1995) which had hitherto guaranteed their mutual credibility and even sustainability. It will end by reconsidering the political role of journalism in a democracy and how the web might be offering fresh opportunities for a wider involvement in political debate beyond the confines of an increasingly corporatized journalism.

The Democratic Ideal

Some see the prime function of journalism as its relationship to reporting political events and discussion:

> The core purpose of journalism is and should be about producing and distributing serious information and debate on central social, political, and cultural matters.

Journalists regulate much of what the public gets to know about the world they inhabit, and this activity is vital to a functioning democracy. (Gripsrud, 2000: 294)

This is, in fact, a partial view of a form of communication which has always been a much more dynamic and varied set of practices. However, one can understand why political journalism and its most obvious expression – the reporting of the affairs of parliament – have become such a focal point for concerns about the health of politics and indeed the health of journalism itself. It was, after all, the reporting of parliament which had brought journalism into a consistent social engagement with regular readerships for the first time in the 1640s, and it was the struggle to provide accounts of the proceedings of parliament, as it was sitting, which were to dominate periodical publications' efforts to wrest prohibitions on this practice from political leaders for over one hundred years after the civil war had finished. But we can see that the decline of political coverage begins quite soon after it has become established. William Woodrow, or 'Mr Memory' as he was nicknamed, had been memorizing whole passages from the day's proceedings in parliament and regurgitating them onto paper – with, one imagines, a fair degree of imagination and stylistic licence – for the *Morning Chronicle* between 1769 and 1789. *The Times*, by the early Victorian period, had become accustomed to reproducing verbatim accounts of parliamentary debate for a readership who had the time and interest to consume these lengthy reports. However, no sooner had the taxes on newspapers been lifted in 1855 than the *Daily Telegraph* took the decision to launch itself with a much-reduced emphasis on this practice of verbatim reporting. In terms of the completeness of coverage of Westminster in newspapers, one could say it's been downhill ever since. Yet that is not really the point of journalism's relationship with politics. Once the market hit the practice of verbatim reporting of political speeches, it was the quality of the digest which was more important than the provision of uninterrupted accounts. The length of these reports became squeezed still further as the appetite of popular newspapers expanded into other areas of topical interest, meaning a dramatic reduction of the space available to political reporting from the introduction of the *Daily Mail* in 1896. From this point, as with much else in subsequent journalism history, politics was in competition for space with other matters of topical interest and – when it was covered – it was as much at the mercy of editorial processes which had audience share as their main focus.

A different model of political allegiance came to complement the newspapers' political role. As a public broadcaster the BBC brought a carefully constructed political balance, objectivity and attempts to adhere to a style of impartiality which newspapers had rarely even aspired to, let alone achieved. Broadcast journalism's set of political principles emerged as it had to cope with shifts in political pressure from the General Strike of 1926, the Munich Crisis of 1938, the Second World War, Suez in 1956, Northern Ireland, the 1982 Falklands War, and most recently Iraq. To a large extent the BBC's journalism, certainly from the 1940s, has provided a counterpoint to the diminishing centrality of political news to the bulk of the newspaper press, while ITN brought a refreshing decline in deference to politicians from 1955 to complement the BBC's high-minded ambitions.

The full televising of parliament combined with the advent of the internet has meant that once again full access is no longer the problem. In fact, this had rarely been journalism's goal at all. Even when editors and writers had risked prison and worse in order to report parliament, it was ultimately for the right to exercise control over editorial selection from the whole rather than to report the proceedings in their entirety.

The Lobby

After decades of informal access to politicians in parliament, the formation of the lobby system in 1885 formalized communication channels between senior reporters and politicians. The Lobby has been informed by off-the-record briefings from MPs in the Houses of Parliament and in the lobbies and corridors of Westminster to provide information and early sightings of documentation which it was hoped would provide a richer context for parliamentary debate. Originally, there was one reporter per paper and an informal set of rules of engagement – normally emanating from a loose tradition of custom and practice. Over years the grouping became less formalized, including broadcasters by the 1970s and allowing alternate members to enable more flexibility in personnel. One of its main shortcomings was the sort of clubbish symbiosis which developed out of this proximity, given the similar educational and class backgrounds of political editors and parliamentarians in what has been described as a 'collusive' relationship (Franklin, 1997: 30), and this is what led political journalist Henry Porter (1987, quoted in Barnett and Gaber, 2001: 1) to conclude that the Lobby system itself was at the heart of the corruption of the liberal ideal of press scrutiny of the political process.

Press Secretaries and Political Influence

Prime Ministers certainly did not need press secretaries to manipulate the press to their own ends in the early twentieth century, as Chamberlain demonstrated when coercing much of the press, through his own personal contacts, to collude in his preference for the suppression of anti-appeasement news in the 1930s (Cockett, 1989). Yet as this process of communicating politics through journalism has become more professionalized (Negrine et al., 2007), the role of the Prime Minister's Press Secretary has taken on a central importance. Francis Williams, once editor of the *Daily Herald*, was chosen to act as Atlee's communicator of the Labour Party's post-war vision, and since his tenure nearly all of these press secretaries have been former journalists. In the late 1950s, Tony Benn supervised the introduction of commercial marketing techniques into Labour political communications. As if to demonstrate that there was no political difference in the realization of the need for modern politics to manage journalism in this way, Joe Haines became a particularly influential pioneer of the role of Press Secretary for Harold Wilson in the 1960s, and Heath continued this for the Conservative Party from 1970. Under Thatcher, with her deployment of the ultra-modern marketing strategies of the Saatchi brothers, political communication had become more about selling the brand/product than the communication of policies themselves.

By this point, the role of Press Secretary had come to acquire much of its contemporary associations of power, manipulation and strategic political importance. With Thatcher's appointee, Bernard Ingham, accusations from political journalists of a cynical 'media management' became more pronounced and were amplified by his Draconian adherence to the lobby rules, withdrawing privileges on his own initiative. From 1989, Ingham combined the roles of Head of Government Information Services and the hitherto anodyne Central Office of Information – thereby monopolizing control over the government information flow and using this to mount a sustained pressure on journalists to see things his way, through the briefings which emerged from his partisan representation not only of the Conservatives in government but also of Thatcher's faction within the Conservative Party. In 1986 the *Guardian*, *Observer* and *Scotsman* withdrew from the lobby, refusing to obey Ingham's increasingly idiosyncratic and partisan interpretation of the rules. They were later brought back into the fold by the more consensual John Major once he replaced Margaret Thatcher as prime minister in 1990.

The Labour Party, in opposition, appreciated the urgent need to get its own message across via a press which it felt, with some justification, was skewed towards the right; it set Peter Mandelson, as Communications Director from 1985 to 1992, the task of winning back lost ground in the strategic management of the media in their reporting of the politics of what became branded as New Labour. The role of Press Secretary for the incoming government was taken on by another former journalist, Alastair Campbell, from 1997 to 2004. Despite hostility to Campbell in his role, from both politicians and journalists, on account of his aggressive briefings against opponents both inside and outside the party and his generally authoritarian attitude towards the control of information flow, it has been claimed that he did, nevertheless, a great deal to open up the political processes of the Lobby (McNair, 2004: 335).

Newspapers and Political Reporting

The political slant of newspaper reporting over the past century has become mostly more indirect and more associated with the innate bias of wealthy owners and their corporate priorities than with any specific party affiliation. In 1923 Angell had identified such proprietors and the State as the twin threats to the liberty of the press, but one half of this perceived dual threat became rapidly eroded as a direct political affiliation became sidelined on account of increased competition in the 1930s – particularly in the popular market – which led to a 'shift away from the traditional concept of a *news*paper' (Curran and Seaton, 2003: 45) dominated by news of public affairs. The ambitions of powerful owners to exert political influence were no longer enough as the need for newspapers to sell outweighed such personal vanity. A benchmark moment for this realization came when the Duke of Northumberland discovered that, having bought the Tory *Morning Post* backed by Conservative party supporters, he could do nothing to prevent its closure in 1937 because he could not find a way to make it pay as a predominantly Conservative political organ. After the Second World War only the *Daily Telegraph* and the *Daily Worker* maintained their direct political affiliations and only the former had a role as a genuinely mass medium.

Throughout the century there have been few daily newspapers whose political preferences have been allied to points of political conviction for the centre and the left, if not strictly speaking to political parties. These include the *Manchester Guardian* (later the *Guardian*), the *Daily Worker* (*Morning Star*), the *News Chronicle*, the *Daily Mirror*, the *Daily Herald* and the *Independent*. Of these the *News Chronicle* and the *Daily Herald* went out of business in the early 1960s as their blend of politics and ageing reader profiles were not attractive enough to advertisers to consistently deliver big enough profits. Other papers have been consistently Tory. As television was increasingly bringing instant news to large audiences, newspapers from the 1960s onwards began to concentrate more on opinion and commentary and even – for a short period, with the *Daily Mirror* and *The Times* – on investigative journalism. It was however this ambition of the *Daily Mirror* to become more than simply a populist organ of entertainment which was to be exploited by Murdoch when he re-launched the *Sun* in 1969, suspecting that the *Mirror*'s political ambitions were now shooting over readers' heads. Consequently, one of the fist tasks of the *Sun*'s new editor Larry Lamb was to make deep cuts in the number of specialist political reporters. After Wapping, newspapers across the board produced more supplements and had more pagination than ever to fill and this was to provide a counter narrative to the decline in the coverage of policy debates in parliament. One of the ways the elite press filled the space was by increasing the amount of political commentary, meaning that if they were no longer first with the news and if they were less concerned with the stuff of policy debates in parliament, they were to become significant brokers of political opinion on behalf of their readers. There was consequently much more in the press coming from political journalists and much less from the politicians (Thomas, 2005).

There have indeed been occasions when political coverage in the press has been overtly political, most notably in the campaign led by the London press in the 1970s and 1980s (Curran, 1986; Curran et al., 2005) and in the boast of the *Sun*'s editor in 1992 that it had been his newspaper which had swayed the country to vote Conservative with the notorious headline 'It's the Sun Wot Won It'. Beyond these examples, however, it has generally been a more subtle set of influences which has shaped the political perspective of most of the press:

> *By regularly reporting political and economic news as disconnected events, it encouraged acceptance of the power structure as natural, part of the way things are. Embedded also in its entertainment features were values and assumptions that were not quite as apolitical as they appeared to be at first sight ... consumption is a way of expressing self in a world far removed from, and transcending, structures of power ... to offer individual-moral rather than collective solutions to problems. (Curran and Seaton, 2003: 103)*

The Style of Political Reporting

Political journalism was also influenced by a style of reporting which had become increasingly personalized and had shifted towards the tabloid end of the spectrum over the course of the late twentieth century. By the time of the 1992 general election, for instance, it has been calculated that 80 per cent of voters were reading a tabloid newspaper compared to fewer than half in 1970 (Seymour-Ure, 1991: 222) and that the language of these newspapers was inclined to be reductive in style. In terms of news content, Dick Rooney has estimated that the current affairs element of popular newspapers between 1968 and 1992 declined in the *Daily Mirror* from 23 per cent to 8 per cent, while showbiz news increased from 13 per cent to 28 per cent and a similar trend in the *Sun* saw current affairs reduced from 1968 to 1992 from 33 per cent to 8 per cent, with showbiz news increasing from 10 per cent to 25 per cent (Rooney, 2000: 101–103).

Tendencies within popular journalism which downplay the importance of the traditional general newspaper in the provision of contextual political and social material and in-depth debate on issues of public concern, and which also allow such matters to be consigned to a specialist or elite readership, have profound implications for the breadth of democratic involvement. The specific attributes of print journalism are not considered expendable by many critics who will insist upon its special place even within a multi-media news environment. There are implications for the overall contribution of news media to political debate if newspaper coverage declines, which are not compensated for if other media take up this coverage in their place. Some years ago, Bairstow pointed out that it was the written form of journalism that allowed for the greatest degree of reflective engagement with the contemporary world:

> ... with its unlimited capacity for comprehensive investigation of a situation and the detailed unravelling of complex issues beyond the scope of the oral bulletin, its unrivalled quality as a forum in which ideas can be exchanged and pros and cons set out and argued ... [the newspaper] must be the most important safeguard of the democratic process. (Baistow, 1985: i)

In response to any claim that all the information you could actually ever need is out there – somewhere – the decline of coverage in generalist publications can be criticized for the reasons Dahlgren has articulated. He argues that one consequence of the restriction of political debate to a narrow range of elite broadsheets and specialized journals is that, by default, analytical, contextualized journalism becomes a source that will be accessed only by the political and economic elites who will continue to value print media for their robustly analytical information content (1995: 58–59).

Of course since 1992 – the end point for Rooney's research – we have seen a further intensification of the influence of tabloids and an almost total embrace of the 'compact' form among the elite press, with a corresponding reliance on the prominent headline and on increasing image size (McLachlan and Golding, 2000; Sparks, 2000). Far from this being confined to the popular tabloids, it was in the elite press in particular that changing trends and styles of reporting were combined to oust the centrality of parliamentary coverage. Labour MP Jack Straw has monitored a decline in *The Times*, the self-appointed 'newspaper of record' itself, from between 400 and 800 lines of daily coverage to fewer than 100 lines between 1988 and 1992 – a steep fall indeed! In 1991 the editor of *The Times*, Simon Jenkins, dropped the parliamentary page and told the Nolan Committee that this was due to the fact that he wanted to provide news and not a specialist service for parliamentarians: 'We are not there to provide a public service for a particular profession or, for that matter, a particular chamber ... Newspapers, are about providing people with news' (Negrine, 1998: 2). Where *The Times* led others followed, meaning that by the mid-1990s no British daily newspaper had a dedicated parliamentary page or section which included verbatim extracts from speeches made by MPs in the House of Commons (Negrine, 1998: 2).

Another significant democratic deficit in the British press has been identified through research carried out by Anderson and Weymouth, who consider – with some considerable justification – that the coverage of the European Union militates against an appropriate level of understanding for British voters to be fully informed in political debate on these matters. They argue, drawing upon Marquand (1995: 189), that the style of coverage or the absence of appropriate coverage reflects a post-imperial vacuum with regard to how Britain engages with the realities of the modern world (Anderson and Weymouth, 1999: 8) and its diminished status within this new world order.

Newspapers have moved from being providers of news to miscellanies of analysis, commentary, lifestyle and entertainment. This has meant that their politics have become more abstract, more removed from the direct words of politicians, and indeed have moved away from the policy agenda of political life to offer more of a politics refracted through the dominant concerns and angles of the time (i.e. lifestyle and personality).

Broadcast Journalism and the State

It was the General Strike of 1926 which first enabled the British Broadcasting Company to develop its own news service and to navigate accusations of bias from both sides in the dispute by self-censoring and trying to settle on an appropriate balance between conflicting accounts. The following year – on its foundation as the British Broadcasting Corporation – it pledged itself not to editorialize and to seek a political balance as part of its commitment to the public interest. One of the ways which it evolved in order to ensure this sort of political balance was the 14-day rule which was introduced formally in 1944, as the wartime coalition between the political parties began to show signs of strain, in order to avoid the corporation's independence being compromised by ministers who wanted to broadcast something of advantage to their own political position concerning current legislation. By 1947 this rule had become a polite agreement not to broadcast discussions or statements on any issues during the fortnight before they were to be debated in either House, showing the broadcasters as subservient in the strict sense of the word by 'deferring to a crudely literal notion of the sovereignty of parliament' (Seymour-Ure, 1996: 185). The gradual erosion of adherence to this 14-day rule was part of a cultural shift from the deference of the 1950s and 1960s which ITN's approach to its political journalism helped to accelerate.

Broadcast technology has forced a reconsideration of the relationship between journalism and the State over the last century. As the narrative of this book has shown, different eras can be defined by this relationship (Siebert, 1965). The confluence of technological and commercial pressures on journalism in the late twentieth century has produced a very contemporary set of challenges with regard to the relationship between journalism and politics. Within this relationship, broadcast journalism is even more sensitive because of its longstanding commitment to a model of public service ethos which is based on the concepts, some might say ideals, of independence and impartiality. Whenever broadcast journalism seems to be challenging the boundaries of these conventions politicians have always been swift to accuse them of bias and of deserting the principles which the public expects from them. Indeed the status of the independence of television journalism has been strained at many points in recent years, notably throughout the prolonged military intervention in Northern Ireland (especially with the 1988–1994 Sinn Fein broadcasting ban) and the war in the Falklands. Since this point, Keeble (1997) has chronicled a general trend within the news media to self-censor genuine political criticism once hostilities have started, as part of a process which – in negotiation with the state – allows for a condition of crisis to be declared on behalf of politicians through the news media (Raboy and Dagenais, 1992). The recent dispute between the BBC and government over coverage of the Iraq war (Lewis et al., 2004), and the debate on the contents of the intelligence dossier which the government claimed justified its decision to go to war, is a striking contemporary illustration of such tensions.

The Broadcasting Paradox: Increase and Decline

Parliamentary reporting has become the dominant form of broadcast political journalism, moving initially from *The Week in Westminster* which had first been aired in 1929 to daily reports of parliamentary proceedings that had begun in 1945. *In the News,* which began on 26 May 1950, was based on an entertainment model and was broadcast first as a weekly programme. At that point it was the only regular political programme on TV; it featured politicians among its panel of guests, discussing various issues in the news. The party conferences of the three main political parties have been covered in some shape or form since 1954, which was five years prior to the first coverage of an election campaign. A by-election in Rochdale in February 1958 was the first time that a political campaign had been covered by television when ITN produced both reports of the candidates campaigning but also arranged for a question-and-answer session between them and a panel of journalists. The effect of this was to test the Representation of the People Act provision that had been designed to prevent the undue influence of news media on the outcome of an election. It was deemed not to have prejudiced a fair electoral process and so the practice picked up momentum. In 1959 there was the first televising of a general election campaign – again by ITV – and this process of opening up political campaigning to public scrutiny provided by broadcast journalism was reciprocated by politicians when, during the same campaign, Labour introduced daily press conferences (quickly followed by the Conservatives) as an attempt to set the agenda for broadcasters. Increasingly, politicians were being groomed to be televisually literate.

The interpenetration of politics and broadcast journalism continued with the first election phone-ins on commercial radio in 1974. Such a symbiotic relationship, though, is not without consequences for journalism. Politicians have become more aware of how they need to perform in the mediated public eye and are suitably coached and styled for TV appearances and radio performances. More and more political reporting has become a commentary upon the rhetoric of politicians as the main party political agendas have converged towards the middle ground. Policy substance is consequently subordinated to policy rhetoric, and journalism colludes with this by its own concentration on how politics is represented rather than on issues of substance. The new journalism medium and its popularity with viewers had also had an impact on politicians, particularly backbenchers, who saw the advantages of a brief TV or radio appearance over a Commons speech that received no coverage (Seymour-Ure, 1996: 170). This could however be a tendency which can be double-edged. Such televisualization of politics tends towards a media spectacle in which power becomes more a display than the rationalization of argument. You appear on TV because of who you are, not because of what you have to say. It is part of a longer-term shift which Habermas refers to as the 'refeudalization of society' (1992: 231).

The Televising of Parliament

Gradual progress towards full coverage of events in the Houses of Parliament began from the first regular radio broadcasting of parliamentary debates in 1976, to the televising of the House of Lords in 1985 and finally the televising of the House of Commons in 1989. This constituted a staged journey of increasing intrusion on behalf of the public into the processes of political debate and thus assisted the credibility of broadcast journalism, but it also generated in response an increasing sophistication by the political media machinery in responding to and preparing for this opening-out of the processes of politics.

The first live images from the House of Commons came with the state opening of Parliament on 21 November 1989, but despite the democratic promise there remains an issue of the place of both live televised politics and the use made of such coverage on subsequent news programmes – where severely cropped highlights are regularly used in evening news bulletins to add a bit of entertainment or an illustration of debates which are far removed from the slow, long and measured deliberations that categorize these in politics:

The ultimate telos of television is judged to be entertainment, which is most readily achieved by stressing the trivial and the sensationalist. By contrast, the Commons is concerned with informed and rational debate, based on the forceful presentation of a particular case. (Franklin, 1992: 7)

Serving the Public or Fostering Cynicism

Some of the most vociferous complaints about radio journalism's political coverage have concerned the tenacity and intensity of interviews with politicians on Radio 4's flagship news programme *Today*, which still averages six million listeners per week and has been acknowledged as a vital part of the setting of the daily political news agenda. Television's high profile bearpit for politicians is *Newsnight* on late-night BBC television. *Channel 4 News*, as an exemplar of good practice in the commercial sector, provided some particularly sustained questioning of political and military personnel early on in the Iraq war. There is obviously a commercial as well as a public service motivation if such coverage can attract viewers/listeners within a provision which is often judged on its popularity. As well as interviewers – probing in the time-honoured role as watchdogs acting on behalf of the public – television producers are aware of the gladiatorial spectacle of such interviews and the thrill of the event for the audience as well as the commercial appeal of such adversarial political journalism, together with the carefully constructed role the interviewer plays in this (Blumler and Gurevitch, 1995). As politicians, in their turn, become more adept at playing the media's games, analytical attention and a corresponding increase in self-awareness and reflexivity among journalists themselves have seen a tendency for both politicians and journalists to protect their own sectional interests first and foremost, often it would seem to the exclusion of the electorate. One solution suggested for this current stand-off has been to follow the lead of newspapers and modify or even drop the rigorous requirements for impartiality and objectivity in broadcast journalism. Indeed, Hargreaves and Thomas (2002) suggest this may be one solution to alleged political apathy among the public. Channel 5's *News on Five* is already experimenting with a mixture of news and debate, with speakers from well-flagged political orientations giving their views of the topic under discussion.

The economic imperatives of broadcast journalism, in particular, have led news media organizations to concentrate increasingly on tried and tested routines and sources. In mainstream news programmes on television we can now see increasingly formulaic representations of political events. The sight of reporters standing in front of the important locations of public life – relating the events of the day – has become a familiar yet dull part of television reporting routines. Such approaches converge on Westminster as if it were the sole site of politics, and have had detrimental implications for the quality and range of discussion in a democracy. These presentational conventions generate an increased reliance on sound-bites from political communicators which reduce the content of policy debate to the particular formats that broadcast news specializes in. In doing so they tend to 'frame' the political process from the perspective of what journalists need rather than from what democratic participation requires. Exploring the contemporary structure of political interviews, leading researchers from Cardiff University concluded that interviews were more likely to be used for the purpose of *creating* rather than *informing* the news:

> *generally by asking senior figures – typically politicians – to comment on or react to a story ... too often, we would suggest, interviews are there to prompt a newsworthy statement rather than to increase understanding ... journalistic pressure (for a 'good story') works against audience understanding. (Lewis et al., 2005: 470)*

It has also been demonstrated that journalists themselves play a part in the political alienation of audiences, as they prefer journalistic 'common sense' about public opinion over widely available data on public opinion, and rely largely on their own hunches, remaining confident about their ability to speak independently on behalf of people rather than engaging with them as active participants in the democratic process (Brookes et al., 2004: 72). According to Brookes and colleagues this leads to:

> *the discursive construction of the apathetic electorate [which] works ideologically to legitimize a situation in which media and political elites are the key players, while citizens are incapable of making meaningful contributions to the debate. In this way, the political and media establishments produce the alienation they claim to deplore. (2004: 78)*

The public have increasingly been locked into a 'penumbra of cynicism' (Blumler and Gurevitch, 1995: 220) about media manipulation which may in part be responsible for a decline in interest in hard political reporting and involvement in politics itself, contributing to the decline in numbers voting in general and local elections. From the politicians there have been attempts to put the blame squarely on the broadcasters while attempting to increase the efficiency of their own media management. Much of the journalistic response has consisted of an attempt to counter the strategy of political media presentation known as spin. From the broadcasters within political discussion programmes there have been increasingly forceful attempts to brow-beat politicians into submission on air – which squares conveniently with an increasingly entertainment-led news media agenda that is masquerading as public-spirited enquiry.

Yet from the perspective of the journalists, one might claim that this intense shaping of politics – now even between elections – leads them to be constantly bombarded by pressures to present the information they receive in a way which highlights the preferences of the political parties in what Jones (1995: 1997) has referred to as a framing process. In turn, journalists have attempted to create strategies to resist this incorporation into what they perceive as a strategy of manipulation. This has also led to claims by the journalists themselves that they are in the business of clarifying what has become an extremely complex communicative form. In their own defence, prominent political editors (such as the *Sunday Times*' Michael Prescott) have been reported as claiming:

> *We are not spin doctors – we are professional decoders ... Politicians speak a strange language and it is up to us to decode it. (Cockerell, 2000: 11)*

This dynamic of action and reaction between politicians and journalists has meant that the professionalization of political party communication strategies (Negrine et al., 2007) has found its mediated counterpart in the professionalized routines of political journalism which has become, at the same time, as interested in entertainment and the potential of personalized intra-party conflict to fit that bill which all broadcasters find as newsworthy as in the questions of political policy themselves (Stanyer, 2001: 6). Together these developments constitute a profound problem at the heart of modern political journalism (Barnett and Gaber, 2001: ix).

Quality Decline or Dumbing Down?

Despite the fact that there has been an increase in the volume of political programming and newspaper coverage since the 1990s, it is the narrowing of the range within a competitive media environment which is of greatest concern to democratic discussion. In an intensely commercial environment, cost-cutting and the rise of the unattached freelancer at the expense of the staff reporter have meant there is a shortage of funds to direct towards longer-term investigative projects which might get behind the politicians' need for a sound-bite and the hard-pressed journalists' need for a headline.

There has been a reduction in political journalism in peak-time programming and in particular a reduction in serious investigative political current affairs at the same time as there has been an increase in the Sunday morning and lunchtime political interview. These slots tend to highlight conflicts and personality clashes between politicians rather than the substance of political differences. Such a concentration on the adversarial nature of politics has in turn crowded out issues of policy difference and magnified our suspicion that politicians must be withholding the truth because they cannot deliver simple answers which conform to the sound-bite expectations constructed by the news media. Increased competitive pressures have led to a tendency to cover politics within the framework of existing orthodoxies (consider, for instance, the paucity of real debate on the current economic crisis), where complex perspectives are routinely ignored because they are either ideologically challenging or too expensive to investigate (Barnett and Gaber, 2001: 73).

Jeremy Paxman endorsed these observations when he wrote in the *Guardian* on the restrictions stifling good political reporting in the contemporary climate:

> *good journalism is bad business and too often bad journalism is good business ... for journalists to function properly, they have to be given freedom and resources. And those will come only from organisations which believe that their first duty is disclosure, not entertainment. (2000: 10–11)*

Yet at the same time as complaints proliferate among both journalists and the public (Temple, 2008: 172–187) about 'dumbing down' in peak-time broadcast across all news media, and especially on the publicly-funded BBC, there has been a great deal of analysis of the processes involved and a probing of the rhetoric of politics rather than the straightforward reporting of political events and policies as facts. Such coverage is as available for elite audiences as it is for the readers of elite print publications and is widely available online as well, yet it provides quality political journalism for a niche rather than a mass market, and the question which needs to be resolved is how to integrate more of this quality provision within mainstream, primetime programming in order to maintain the broadest reach for high-quality political coverage.

PR – Complement or Enemy?

Edward Bernays was the self-declared founding father of PR in the early 1920s as it emerged as part of a general appreciation of the political and commercial potential of using the propaganda techniques in peacetime which had been developed as part of the pursuit of war aims (Cutlip, 1994). PR became an established part of the landscape of public communication, first in the United States where the Public Relations Society of America became in 1947 its largest and longest established forum for debate and self-promotion. Techniques pioneered in the USA spread to Britain post-Second World War where they were then developed by politicians in order to establish better representation within a more organized and more technologically pervasive news media environment. Despite its presence within British journalism and politics for over half a century, there is currently an intensifying debate about its relationship with journalism and even the extent to which the two can be meaningfully distinguished given that the pressures on journalists to process more copy within even shorter timeframes lead to an almost inevitable increase in a reliance on PR material. PR is thus one of the drivers of a process which has seen journalists shift, once again, from being reporters to being 're-processors' (Harrison, 2006: 150).

Habermas (1984; 1987) distinguishes journalism from public relations by reference to their ultimate goals. Journalism has a communicative goal – aiming to bring about an understanding of the world. Public relations, on the other hand, has a strategic goal – affecting the actions of others. According to Habermas journalism aims to produce communication for a public while PR does so for a client.

The self-conscious role of journalists as a counter-balance to the public relations and 'spin' of politicians and public spokespeople is located very much at the core of the self-legitimation of the journalist. In addition, the oft-proclaimed tension between journalism and PR or the 'spin' of politicians can be used to enhance the entertainment value of journalism, as it helps boost the credibility of a journalist's organization as opposed to the machinations of adversaries in the pursuit of truth. Many journalists see this as a fundamental difference even in these changing times:

> *Revelation and conflict are thus instinctive to journalism. Public relations can never be real news. (Jenkins, 2006: 46)*

However, it is often pointed out that the boundaries are no longer as fixed as they might once have been:

> The border between journalism and public relations is being eroded in the context of a more general decline of normative inquiry and its replacement with inquiries into mere instrumental effectiveness … I argue that there is quite an explicit danger of merging public relations and journalism that can only diminish the effectiveness of journalism in fulfilling its normative role. (Salter, 2005: 90)

Salter might see the issue in terms of a contrast of missions and styles while others have developed possibly more nuanced views of the interrelationship between PR and journalism, considering that PR puts journalism on its mettle and is, in fact, 'a necessary dimension of the modern political process' (McNair, 1996: 53).

Regardless of the arguments which would seek to demarcate journalism from public relations, research carried out by Lewis et al. (2008a) and O'Neill and O'Connor (2008), together with the polemic indictment of Davies (2008), all demonstrate that under intense commercial pressure to produce more news within less time using fewer resources, journalism is increasingly turning to PR to shore up this information deficit in much of its content. They might operate according to 'different logics' (Salter, 2005: 103), but their interdependence is increasingly part of the process of contemporary journalism and it has been evolving as such for some time. PR advocate Julia Hobsbawm goes further to suggest that:

> Interdependence is not unhealthy. It is simply a fact. Unless practitioners and journalists recognize this, and stop treating it like a dirty secret, the reputation of journalism will continue to be compromised and PR will gain more of the powers that journalists would least like it to have. (Hobsbawm, 2006: 129)

Rather than threatening the role of journalism as a Fourth Estate, McNair posits public relations as the Fifth Estate and concludes that it has merely generated a tension which maintains a healthy relationship of enquiry and professionalism between the culture of politics and the changing culture of journalism (McNair, 2004: 337).

Political Reporting and the Web

The online environment would appear to promise accessibility of access to the stuff of political debate more efficiently than ever before. Parliamentary websites, streamed content from parliament, party political blogs and many more outlets provide a surfeit of content. Yet such technology lacks the sociability necessary for the sort of genuine political debate that journalism can foster when it edits politics within the framework of balancing counterposing arguments and giving historical contexts, and targets this to a particular demographic. Gaber has asked of the internet's delivery of political content, 'Where is that national political conversation taking place?', and expresses anxiety about the resultant 'individualised politics' (Gaber, 2005: 28). Before the internet, television had personalized politics (Scannell, 1996: 165), but it had also collectivized it as part of the same process. This collectivization is the missing social aspect of this technological cornucopia. There is also the question of social access to the technology addressed by Murdock when he points out that 'Wi-fi nodes are more likely to be concentrated in airport lounges and leisure hubs in business and entertainment districts than in bus shelters and hostels' (2004: 22), while even those who may have access are less likely to be using it to access political information despite its prevalence. Lusoli, for instance, has discovered that less than 10 per cent of the population who use the web regularly access the internet for political information (2005: 247–265).

Conclusion

The political role of journalism as a generator of political discussion and in enabling the education of an active citizenship has certainly changed over the twentieth century. Newspapers became more interested in the provision of a much more varied menu which included but did not prioritize political information as it once had. Broadcast journalism came to provide an initial attempt at balance and even objectivity within political reporting, but this too has been influenced by the growing entertainment agenda of much television coverage. In providing closer and closer scrutiny of the motivations, characters and lifestyles of politicians, journalism has provided fuel for a cynically disengaged public. Certainly the professionalization of political communication has demanded that journalism adapts counter-strategies to maintain an independent channel of scrutiny, but John Lloyd (2004) has argued that this has pushed the news media too far. In accusing the media of destroying public trust in politics he sees journalists as the central problem, who in order to shore up their own sense of purpose and professional credibility create the impression that politicians are seeking to avoid telling the truth. He considers this such a structural disposition that it has come to corrode our trust in both politicians and the political process itself. Other commentators, such as Brian McNair (2002), see current trends as leading to more transparency with regard to the mechanics of politics, yet this process can by its very transparency often engender a cynicism and distrust in both politicians and journalism for an audience without a sufficiently well-developed understanding of the context of either politics or the news media. Both processes are interconnected and both tell of cultural shifts in politics and the public reception of politics via journalism rather than the latter's decline from a high point of public service. This surely calls for an increased concentration on both political and media literacy among the wider public.

Martin Kettle has pointed out the self-interest of the profit-hungry press in reporting the scandals and the personalities in politics rather than the processes and the political arguments:

> In the end, one has to confront the following serious question. What aspect of the restoration of trust in politics would be in the media's interest? The answer is no part at all. A media that have become progressively less engaged with serious

political argument and progressively more focused on personal frailty, foible and failure is one of the shapers of the nation's political problem, not the deliverer from it. [sic] *(2009: 33)*

Journalism throughout the twentieth century has become more socially pervasive, providing the potential for more people to access a wider range of information and entertainment in the construction of citizens/consumers of a global public sphere. There continues to be a fair range of probing political investigation but this tends to be broadcast outside the prime time band of mid-evening viewing – reserved for guaranteed peak audiences. The century has also witnessed increasingly sophisticated attempts to harness journalists' disruptive potential through media management and manipulation and by bringing journalism ever closer to the sources from which it seeks to retain a critical distance. This has the additional consequence of bringing pressure on journalism to present source material favourably as the threat of withdrawal of such privileged access may threaten cooperation from essential suppliers of political or other institutional news. The current complex relationship between politics and journalism certainly does not represent a permanent stalemate when viewed from a historical perspective. More likely, it is a momentary pause before one side or the other develops a new set of strategies in order to take the initiative in a struggle over information and control which is even older than either journalism or the print media. In this present predicament the missing ingredient is the voice of active citizens as both politicians and journalism wrestle for their attention.

FURTHER READING

Blumler, J. and Gurevitch, M. (1995) *The Crisis in Public Communication*. London: Routledge. Although a little dated, this still provides an essential grounding in how scepticism about the journalistic portrayal of politics grew in the late twentieth century.

Corner, J. and Pels, D. (eds) (2003) *Media and the Re-styling of Politics*. London: SAGE. This outlines a range of approaches to the communication of contemporary politics as an antidote to simplistic narratives of decline.

Davis, A. (2007) *The Mediation of Power*. Abingdon, Oxon: Routledge. This gives a fine analysis of the role that journalism plays in the broader mediation of political power.

McNair, B. (2003) *An Introduction to Political Communication*. London: Routledge. This is an excellent starting point for students considering this area of journalism.

Muhlmann, G. (2007) *Political History of Journalism*. Cambridge: Polity. This is an internationally-focused account of the specifics of political journalism over time, with some useful case studies from France, Britain and the USA.

Sparrow, A. (2003) *Obscure Scribblers*. London: Methuen. This is a British-based account of the development of political journalism which gives a good context for contemporary understandings as well as for concerns about its future.

8

Alternative Journalism

Introduction

The triumph of liberal capitalism as a model for the newspaper market in the mid-nineteenth century after the ending of the taxes on newspapers from 1855 led inexorably to a narrowing of the field of potential for alternatives to what was rapidly becoming shaped as mainstream journalism. This was increasingly profit-driven and dependent on advertising revenue to supplement the income from its cover price. Put simply, advertising keeps down costs. Nevertheless, this market has been populated by different experiments within this capitalist environment at different times, but commercial success has always remained the single overriding imperative for longevity. This didn't mean that the alternatives that did appear did not weave their influence over the longer term but that any such influence tended to be at the margins of journalism or was incorporated within the mainstream, if ever it proved to be a successful addition to the commercial blend.

This chapter will provide a brief account of some of the twentieth-century's varieties of alternative journalism. It will do this not in any attempt to provide a definitive chronology or analysis of this range of journalism but – more in keeping with the aims of this book – to allow us to reflect on the ways in which mainstream commercial journalism has been practised as well as challenged through the century. It will move from the advocacy journalism of the suffragettes, through to the Trades Union tradition of the *Daily Herald*, the campaigning of organs as different as the *Daily Worker*, *Morning Star* and *Socialist Worker,* and the periodical radicalism of the 1960s and 1970s and *Red Pepper* in the 1990s. It will explore how technological variants of alternative journalism have begun to militate within this radical tradition.

Defining an Alternative Tradition

The definition of 'alternative journalism' which we will use will be a pluralistic one, highlighting both the organizational features as well as the editorial content or political perspective of journalism which we can term 'alternative' to the mainstream. Along with Atton and Hamilton (2008: 1–2), we will define 'alternative' as existing outside the restrictions of the capitalist system and being produced to challenge that system of information provision. Unlike them, this chapter will also consider those alternatives that have attempted to challenge the commercial paradigm of journalism from within, especially when they try out what Downing et al. term 'prefigurative politics' – attempting to practise socialist principles in the present and not merely to imagine them for the future (2001: 71).

Exploring the history of alternative journalism demands a complementary critique of the social construction of mass-mediated journalism that is based on a complex of newsroom routines and rituals, conditions of production and notions of professionalism and objectivity, as well as rehearsed standards of writing and editing (Allan, 1999). Curran and Seaton (2003: 15) highlight the antecedents of the sort of journalism which challenged the mainstream during the period of the English radical press (c. 1790–1835) that resulted in papers characterized by pauper management and in which journalists saw themselves as activists rather than as professionals, and where there was an overriding determination to expose the dynamics of power and inequality rather than simply reporting the facts of 'hard news'. This stance was eloquently expressed in the sub-title of the *Poor Man's Guardian*, a radical weekly from 1831, 'For the People. Published In Defiance of "Law" To Try The Power Of "Might" Against "Right"'.

Despite the demise of the radical press of the early nineteenth century there was a historical continuity in that these features also ran throughout all twentieth-century alternative journalism as well as through contemporary alternative media, as we shall see. The Royal Commission, in fact, observed in 1977 that there had been 'a persistent tradition of small radical publications' (40) from the early nineteenth century on.

Radical Women's Press

One of the most sustained attempts to prefigure alternative practices as well as alternative content came in the newspapers and periodicals of the women's movement. It was out of the movement for women's suffrage and wider social and political rights that much of the organizational effectiveness and editorial commitment of the alternative press of the twentieth century were to emerge. The Suffragettes were the first to provide a modern exemplar of journalism that was organized outside the mainstream and with a commitment not only to critique the workings of commercial journalism but also to act as a challenge to it and its refusal to cover issues of interest to women as political and social actors. They drew together the strands of radical women's publications of the previous fifty years to militate for wider social and political reform. It was no surprise that such a journalism which attempted in its prose and in its production to prefigure a way of working outside the confines of traditional capitalist models should be of interest to other systematic analyses of questions of power and representation in the early twentieth century. The women's movement shared much of a common cause with socialist politics and this led to the production of periodicals which combined into a double-fronted attack on capitalism and patriarchy in magazines such as the *Women's Dreadnought* from 1914 (Tusan, 2005). However, there were those who did criticize one of the main Suffragette publications, *Votes For Women* (1907–1918), because in order to consolidate its low price and its high circulation, of up to 40,000 a week at its peak, it included much advertising of a conventional nature which was identical to that targeted at women across the range of bourgeois publications (DiCenzo, 2000: 121).

The Trades Union Model

While struggling to fund a formula which would enable the interests of working people to be disseminated cheaply and broadly enough to have a real political impact on a mass scale, the early twentieth century provides one of the richest examples of an engagement with an alternative form of journalism for the politically aware working classes. This was produced out of a profound disillusionment with commercialized models that were perceived as ignoring or even deliberately misrepresenting the interests of such people. Within the Labour movement there had been a growing clamour for the foundation of a newspaper which could regularly articulate the viewpoints and interests of the workers. Out of a cluster of alternative publications and proposals one publication emerged which was to provide a longer-term solution than most. A newspaper called the *Herald* was first published as a strike sheet in 1911 during a lockout of print workers in London. After the strike sheet folded, its name was taken on and the *Daily Herald* was founded as a regular publication in 1912 by a coalition of trades unionists, with the independent radical George Lansbury as its editor and propagandist-in-chief. From the start it was identifiably targeted at a different set of interests to the mass market popular dailies, with industrial rather than parliamentary matters dominating its news and editorials:

> It is clear who the paper was calculated to appeal to – a serious-minded, well-informed and possibly highbrow trade unionist and political activist with more interest in the latest news from the Genoa conference or a strike than in the most lurid murder or court case. (Richards, 1997: 36)

The *Daily Herald* reduced itself to weekly publication during the First World War and mainly on account of that slightly lower profile survived and continued to thrive despite rumours of subsidies of 'Moscow gold' and an advertisers' boycott in its early years after 1918. The same was not true of *The Worker* and *Forward* in Glasgow which were both suppressed in 1915 because of anxieties about their socialist politics at a time of national danger and the rise of the Russian Bolsheviks. Another publication to survive was the *New Statesman* which had been brought out in 1913 as a weekly and was to become over time a leading voice of the Labour movement.

Despite its unique place in the hearts of trade unionists and radicals, the *Daily Herald* was not able to survive without some longer-term investment to obviate its lack of commercial appeal to advertisers, and so to remedy this precarious financial situation in 1922 it was taken over by a combination of the Labour Party and the TUC who together guaranteed its future funding. Landsbury was replaced as editor by Hamilton Fyfe and from this point its editorial position was more in keeping with official Labour Party policy. However, despite its political backers it continued to suffer from a lack of finance and advertising until 1929 when the TUC took it into partnership with the commercial publishers Odhams.

Socialist and Communist Publications

Other voices to the left of the Labour Party were keen to be heard in the aftermath of the First World War. The General Strike of 1926 saw something of a blossoming of alternative publications and Harrison has recorded a wealth of socialist journalism in over 100 factory papers which were especially remarkable in their geographical range across the UK (1974: 198–198). The *Sunday Worker* was launched in 1925 and run by the Communist Party of Great Britain which also found funds enough among its membership, supporters and those broadly sympathetic to its politics to found a daily newspaper, the *Daily Worker*, in 1930 in order to compensate for the realignment of the *Daily Herald* to being more of a successful commercial operation and therefore clearly less inclined to subscribe to radical anti-capitalist positions. Emerging from the war with a reputation for engaging with popular struggles on behalf of the Labour movement, and with much public sympathy on its side following its suppression during the war, the *Daily Worker* relaunched itself under the co-operative ownership of the People's Press Printing Society in 1945 and achieved sales of over 100,000 in its first year. The *Morning Star* replaced the *Daily Worker* from 1966 and the CPGB made circulation its top strategic priority. Close to the political line of the Communist Party until the fall of the Berlin Wall and the break-up of the Soviet Union, it has subsequently broadened its approach to socialism to include green politics, environmentalism and community politics while remaining the longest-standing, most successful reader-owned newspaper in the country.

The Commercial Consolidation of the *Daily Herald*

Despite its unique appeal to the Labour-supporting masses, the *Daily Herald* continued to struggle both in attracting advertising and in its circulation compared with other popular mainstream newspapers. This of course was no surprise in the commercial environment which had dominated British newspaper production, particularly since the arrival of Harmsworth and his *Daily Mail* in 1896. The question remained whether it was worth finding some sort of compromise between a popular newspaper of the left and the demands of the market. In its attempt to locate a sustainable solution, the *Daily Herald* was sold to a commercial publisher, Odhams, on the understanding that no matter what its commercial path its politics would remain

Labour/trade union in its emphasis. In 1930 its relaunch with Odhams as a mass-circulation daily, with a trade union affiliation and an official Labour line, led to the most intensive period of newspaper competition yet seen. Within its first fortnight it had reached a circulation in excess of one million, yet despite this it did not guarantee electoral success for the Labour Party which went down to its worst ever defeat in 1931. In 1933 it beat the *Daily Express* to the two million mark still with a blend of politics that was more industrially oriented than parliamentary (Curran and Seaton, 2003: 126–127). Its success in terms of circulation was certainly due to this mix of traditional popular newspaper fare and an approach to politics that – despite its earnestness – could hold on to an audience which wanted just as much entertainment as information from their journalism. Other experiments in the purer sort of political journalism which were successful at the time included the *Tribune,* which launched in 1937 as a left Labour weekly initially to support the Socialist League.

The Long Decline of the *Daily Herald*

The decline of the *Daily Herald* in the post-war period was down ultimately to its inability to match the resounding success of the *Daily Mirror* which had by then perfected a blend of populism and political sympathy with the underdog that made it attractive to younger readers. By contrast, the *Daily Herald* has been characterized as having fallen down in its 'utter failure to appeal to the young' (Richards, 1997: 169). It closed in 1964 with a circulation of still well over the million mark, but with declining advertising revenue and an ageing readership of little interest to the youth-oriented newspaper advertisers. It was relaunched as the *Sun* and sold to Rupert Murdoch in 1969. Richards claims that ultimately, and despite its commercial failure, its political ambition has been vindicated in its wider contribution to attempts to make a better world as:

> *... the one mistake it never made was to assume that the world is unchangeable. The* Herald's *struggle was to ensure that change should make it fairer, more equal and more humane. It lost battles more than it won, but the struggle was, and is, well worth it. (Richards, 1997: 187)*

Other left-inclined newspapers suffered the same fate as they struggled to find the combination of circulation and readership profile which the advertisers demanded, including the *Sunday Citizen* (formerly *Reynold's News*) which was closed in 1967 by its Co-operative movement managers as its losses piled up.

The 1960s: Contexts and Titles

The 1960s saw the beginning of the largest scale of innovation in alternative publications since the early nineteenth century – the 'heroic age of popular Radicalism' (Thompson, 1979: 660). Spiers (1974) has produced a bibliography which reflects the diversity and sheer volume of these developments. The cultural and political context of the post-war era was fertile ground for the growth of a wide range of alternative forms of public expression including journalism. In the USA from 1955 onwards the *Village Voice* provided a meeting point where beats, jazz enthusiasts and political radicals explored the articulation of alternative lifestyles. This radical energy spread through the Anglophone world, and the British establishment was rocked by Penguin's publication in 1960 of D.H. Lawrence's *Lady Chatterley's Lover.* This publisher had proved to be the victor in a subsequent trial under the Obscene Publications Act. The vindication of a novel that had been banned in the UK since 1928 – which dealt with the taboos of cross-class relationships, extra-marital sex and the use of a sexually explicit vocabulary – indicated how rapidly previous moral and social restrictions were being swept away. Politically, a new generation found its voice outside traditional party and even class politics with the orientation of *Peace News* (first published in 1936) towards the growing influence of the radical, left-wing, anti-nuclear CND formed in 1957–1958.

In 1961 an anti-establishment Oxbridge theatre satirical performance called 'Beyond the Fringe' opened in London and began to have an impact on the boundaries of accept-able humour, which was to shape a generation. 1961 also saw the launch of *Private Eye* whose satire, while mostly ex-public school and containing nothing politically sub-versive or radical, still contributed to a growing mood of disaffection with convention. In combination these cultural strands led to the growing prominence of what became termed the 'counter-culture' or the 'underground' – and their vision of seizing power through seizing the means of communication made it important for alternative publi-cations to vie for the minds of the people or at least the youthful student demographic. While America turned in upon itself in emblematic struggles such as the Detroit Race Riots or rallies in opposition to the Vietnam War, Richard Neville drew these indica-tors of the new times into his publication *Oz* in London from 1967. From 1968, as stu-dent rebelliousness spread to the streets, factories and universities of France, radical publications began teeming onto the streets of towns and cities in the UK. *Oz* became ever more linked to alternative movements, radical politics and especially 'liberated' attitudes towards sexuality. *New Musical Express* was beginning to show how musi-cal journalism could feed into the radical debates of the time on lifestyle and alterna-tive cultures, and *Black Dwarf* appeared as a radical monthly – researched out of the original nineteenth century journal by Sheila Rowbotham, among others – while the International Socialists revamped their fortnightly *Labour Worker* to create the weekly *Socialist Worker* which still survives today. *Time Out* also began publishing its alterna-tive guide to London for a more radical readership than previously targeted by tourist magazines, developing in time gay, black and gender strands to its agenda.

Local Alternative Journalism

Most of our attention is focused on metropolitan experiments with journalism in this period but many of those listed by Spiers (1974) bear witness to a sense of dissatisfaction with the mainstream in areas as geographically and demographically distant as Rochdale and Brighton, Glasgow and Bristol, Stoke-on-Trent and Devon. By the late sixties and early seventies Manchester had its *Grass Eye* and there were publications cropping up across the land, from the *Cardiff People's Press* to *Inside Out* (out of Dundee – 'Scotland's Alternative Magazine') and the *Aberdeen Free Press* (Fountain, 1988: 177–179).

The *Manchester Free Press* was originally produced by professional journalists in the city during a newspaper strike in the early 1970s and was then continued by them, surviving for four years with an alternative news-based agenda summarized by its masthead 'The News You're Not Supposed To Know'. It was dedicated to the exposure of the innate corruption of the political system by revealing those facts which would otherwise never be revealed in regular newspapers (Franklin and Murphy, 1991: 109).

Harcup (1994) uses a case study of his own experience on the Leeds radical newspaper, *Leeds Other Paper*, to explore how different news values and uses of sources meant that the journalism produced by this paper was in truth very different from that of mainstream journalism products. This co-operatively run radical weekly publication survived for more than a decade, from the 1970s to the 1990s, combining the radical press staples of satire and the political contestation of anti-working-class politics.

Murphy (1988: 5) has estimated that by the late eighties there were 120 alternative newspapers with sales of up to 4,000 weekly. Born out of the counter-culture of the 1960s they were structured around a magazine format, incorporating a listings guide and featuring artistic contributions from radical cartoons to psychedelic artwork and often built around anarcho-democratic principles of production. It is said that 'They espoused an alternative political agenda which was usually left wing, supported sexual and racial minorities and increasingly focused on green and ecological concerns' (Franklin, 1997: 110). The demise of this rich network of publications in the 1990s came not because of a lack of impact or popularity but more because the way that they were run did not allow them to accumulate the capital necessary to invest in the technological resources which would have made them financially viable in a changing news media environment.

McChesney (2000) has often make the argument that the exigencies of traditional news production mean that longer-term public issues such as racism, social inequality or urban sprawl are not adequately dealt with or even taken as given, since the historical and ideological context required is inimical to the news values of mainstream profit-making journalism. Along with other commentators on alternative media (Atton, 2002a; Downing et al., 2001) he concludes that practice always impacts upon the traditional routines of news gathering and that this becomes expressed in the content.

Red Pepper

If content and sources are two main differences between alternative journalism and the mainstream, some would argue that the third is organization. Is it possible for an alternative publication to flourish and survive without having to resort to traditional commercial frameworks? In the early century, as we have seen, the decision to play commercial interests at their own game on behalf of the working classes – in the experience of the *Daily Herald* – did not in the long-term guarantee success.

The Comedia group had been established in 1978 under the name of the Minority Press Group to explore the perceived failure of alternative publications to become established on a longer-term basis. In their report they identified how two magazines, the *New Socialist* and the *New Internationalist*, had managed to thrive by embracing 'such "capitalist" skills as marketing and promotion … to further this political ambition' (Comedia, 1984: 101).

Khibany (1994) however explore the launch and readjustment of *Red Pepper* as a radical political and environmental project of the left and discovered that the market-oriented model Comedia espousea was not the way in which the magazine became a relative success and that, on the contrary, it made editorial or institutional decisions based purely on 'market-appeal'. In fact, *Red Pepper* provides a case study of the efficacy of a 'Lenininst' model of alternative journalism as opposed to a model emanating from studies of alternative media by Comedia (Khiabany, 2000). It was dramatically more successful when it operated on 'politicized', agitprop lines (Khiabany, 2000).

Alternative Journalism as Social Empowerment

The *Big Issue* was launched in 1991, first as a fortnightly and from 1993 as a weekly. It provided a blend of propaganda, self-help, agit-prop, awareness-raising and journalism. Its distinctive organizational feature is that it is sold by the homeless themselves on the streets in part to offer them a way of making a viable contribution to ameliorating their lives and in part to bring attention to the national scale of homelessness and, in conversations with vendors, the complexity of its root causes. It was perceived as a way of allowing the homeless themselves to tackle the issues raised by the social exclusion they experienced. By 1997–1998 it had become the weekly current affairs magazine with the largest circulation of 280,000. There are now Scottish, Welsh, Northern and South West editions as well as the original London edition. In addition to campaigning against homelessness it is also a publisher and film maker, taking a 'business-like approach to social problems' and seeing itself as part of a 'social business' approach to homelesseness (Swithinbank, 2001: xiv). It is a good example of what Atton has termed a more hierarchical and centralized form of alternative 'advocacy' (Atton, in Cottle, 2003a: 43).

An important element of the less hierarchical structures of alternative journalism is the role of the native reporter who takes the voice of the first-person narrative to act as an authority within a community, talking in a partisan fashion on behalf of that community (Traber, 1985: 3). According to Atton (in Cottle, 2003a: 46) the use of native reporters inverts the usual order of authority within the mainstream journalism community where traditionally only the most experienced of reporters is allowed to voice his/her experience. Within this inversion a radical populism which validates the experience of the community being reported is asserted against the conventions of media professionalism which act to distance it from the interests of a community as a point of principle. The potential of the role of the native reporter has been galvanized within the contemporary technological environment where video clips, recordings of interviews and still images can be posted on the web with the minimum of fuss and a potentially huge impact.

Alternatives Within the Mainstream

There is a long tradition in journalism of alternative voices being incorporated within the mainstream. Orwell (Keeble, 2001) was a regular newspaper correspondent, John Pilger has made a name as both a television documentarist and popular propagandist, most notably in his recent work on the Iraq war for the *Daily Mirror*, while Paul Foot played a similar role for the *Daily Mirror* and Naomi Klein and George Monbiot are frequent contributors to left-leaning newspapers with views that are certainly to the left of those papers' usual spectrum. John Fisk has also provided a wealth of radical critique of the rationale and conduct of the war in Iraq for the *Independent*.

Mainstream media also find time to include parodies on both the content and the formats they employ. Charlie Brooker is one good contemporary example of this but the most striking illustration of an assault on the sacred cows of contemporary journalism has come from Chris Morris. The Chris Morris satires have radically reviewed the whole area of investigative journalism itself as the claims of television journalism are held up to sustained mockery from within the very conventions they employ. Morris had started with *On The Hour*, a spoof of the *Today* programme, and with Armando Iannucci he produced and fronted *The Day Today* which in 1994 ran parallel to the BBC's *Nine O'Clock News* and boasted it would, 'knock[s] current affairs broadcasting off its axis, then blow a hole in its spluttering head'. One reviewer clearly appreciated the tendencies within television journalism which could provoke such a satirical onslaught:

> The editors of the Nine O'Clock News, News At Ten *and* Live At Five *may find it uncomfortable viewing. And viewers who fear we are sliding towards a TV news agenda dominated by soundbites and trivia could find* The Day Today *too close for comfort. (Cuff, 1994: 9)*

His television work on *Brass Eye* (from 1997 on Channel 4) deliberately preyed on the genres and conventions of television to satirize its truth-telling claims and especially its documentary and investigative journalism. Commenting on the success of Morris's satire one television reviewer, Will Self, knowingly located it within the tradition of contemporary referential scepticism with regard to the media in general:

> So why did these people fall for such fakery? ... Because they aren't real people any more – they're hyperreal. They've made the Faustian pact of being that oxymoronic incarnation, 'television personalities' ...

The other important point to be made about Morris's elision of 'real' and 'unreal' is that it's at the very core of his attack on television itself. What Morris realises is that television isn't a 'medium' in any meaningful sense at all. Rather it's a skein of different media imprisoned in a bogus proscenium. (1997: 8)

Web-Alternatives

Internet-based forms of alternative journalism have provided the impetus for a wide range of production which is facilitated by the free-flow of information and images between geographically distant communities of activists. These are enhanced by the role of witnesses (Couldry, 2000) to events who might otherwise be ignored or marginalized by the mainstream media and by the 'native reporting' which challenges conventional hierarchies of believability within journalism (Atton, 2002b). Nevertheless – and despite the radical potential of such an interchange – a global journalism institution, the BBC, has been moved by the energy of these new channels of communication to incorporate some of this energy, if none of its political motivation, in its *Your News* site. The most influential of such internet-based communicative communities is *Indymedia*, a world-wide, web-based, radical media project which provides more than 140 interconnected weblogs (emanating from 50 countries) which emerged from the anti-corporate protests against the World Trade Organization in Seattle in 1999. According to Kidd (2003b) it has become one of the main alternative news sites with between half and two million readers per day.

One of the facilities of these new media technologies with the most potential to provide alternative forms and fora for journalism is blogging. This communication form creates an undeniable tension between the amateur citizen-contributor and the professional journalist as a mainstream producer of public information, since it appears to threaten the specialist role and expertise of the traditional journalist. Under attack from such practices, institutional journalism may attempt to repair the perceived gaps in its provision or its credibility by the incorporation of blogging (Lowry, 2006) or by demonstrating its professional and even ethical superiority (Singer, 2007) – its 'value added' one might say.

Such free-flowing sites for political and civic expression have enormous potential to change the engagement of citizens with more open forms of journalism, if they can manage to move beyond a tendency to group around single-issue politics and also find ways for more effective groupings of material which do not submerge the passing browser. At its best, journalism has always been able to edit down, meaningfully, for a specific target audience; at its worst the internet opens out into a dizzying multiplicity of fragmentation. Either journalism will find ways to harness that vertiginous potential or the diversity of demand from online users will fragment the very consistency of audiences that journalism has always depended upon, meaning either the renewal of a radical new paradigm for journalism or its eclipse as a medium of generalist public communication as we become more attuned to the demands of Hartley's (2000) 'readactional society'.

Conclusion

Throughout the twentieth century, mass market newspapers have effectively constrained the field for any realistic and sustained challenge to the political or economic status quo. They have narrowed the market both in a restriction of content and in ensuring the prohibitive costs of entry to the market. The expense of provision of high quality journalism in a broadcast form has consolidated this trend. There have however been striking examples of alternatives throughout the century and often mainstream journalism has had to deal with the impact of these. They have provided a complex range of experimentation and a contestation of the status quo – from the Suffragette press to the women's liberation publication *Spare Rib*, the *Daily Herald* in its various incarnations, Communist Party daily newspapers, and the upsurge of a local alternative press in the 1970s and 1980s. All of these have left their mark on the broader culture of journalism and it is that tradition which gives impetus to experiments on the internet as it seeks to involve citizens in the communicative process of democracy while trying to find ways to enhance a credible alternative discourse for public communication in a new century. Harcup (2003) has concluded that the technology and language may change but the existence of a counter-hegemonic journalism in alternative media demonstrates, in practice, that there are other ways of seeing the world and therefore other stories to be told. He takes issue with those who might decline to acknowledge the importance and impact of this range of journalism let alone its future potential, claiming:

> … the attitude of radical websites in the 21st century would be familiar to those who wielded golfball typewriters in the 1970s … both echo the attitudes of those who laboured to produce the likes of the Northern Star *and the* Poor Man's Guardian *in the 19th century. To label such a tradition a 'failure' is to take a very short-sighted view indeed. (Harcup, 2003: 372)*

Any approach which brands the generic variety and political contribution of alternative journalism as a 'failure' also betrays what can happen if a proper historical perspective is not applied to considerations of the nature of mainstream journalism itself.

FURTHER READING

Atton, C. (2002) *Alternative Media.* London: SAGE. This provides a lively and engaging account of the range of alternatives to mainstream media, how these have developed over time, and some of their achievements in constructing alternative political spaces.
Atton, C. and Hamilton, J.F. (2008) *Alternative Journalism.* London: SAGE. A development of previous work by these authors within the specific frame of journalism.

Fountain, N. (1988) *Underground: The London Alternative Press, 1966–74.* London: Comedia/Routledge. An exploration of the social and cultural causes of radical journalism of the sixties and seventies as well as an assessment of what remains of the energy of this interlude in journalistic practice.

Harrison, S. (1974) *Poor Men's Guardians.* London: Lawrence and Wishart. This is an excellent and politically-engaged assessment of the rise and impact of journalism addressed to the working classes over two centuries. It provides an excellent contextualization for alternative practices in the present.

Richards, H. (1997) *The Bloody Circus: The* Daily Herald *and the Left.* London: Pluto. This gives an insider's overview to the contribution by this newspaper 'of the left' to socialist debate and mainstream journalism for over half a century.

Swithinbank, T. (2001) *Coming Up From the Streets: The Story of the Big Issue.* London: Earthscan. This gives an excellent account of one particular form of journalistic enterprise in pursuit of a wider social awareness of the issues surrounding homelessness.

9

Magazine Journalism: The Most Influential Genre

Introduction

Magazine journalism – despite being obviously located at the most aggressively commercial end of the journalism spectrum – is most definitely a form of alterative journalism, at least when compared to some traditional views of journalism as primarily a political form of communication. As the emphasis within contemporary news media representations of politics has shifted to more personalized, lifestyle orientations and away from big politics and an interest in the machinations of Westminster and the local council, so too has magazine journalism come to be appreciated more for its broader approach to a more consumerist attitude to the politics of everyday life.

This chapter will consider some of the crossover influences between magazines and newspapers and other forms of journalism over a long twentieth century. Newspapers have had to react to the increased attractiveness of magazines to advertisers and also to the increased appeal to readers of consumerist perspectives on daily life. Although there had been many successful variants of general magazine journalism in the nineteenth and early twentieth centuries, it was not until the increasing affluence of the post-Second World War era that consumerism and journalism really began to combine to full effect. This culminated in the explosion of lifestyle magazines which matched the rise in identity politics in the 1980s. It will be argued that this boom in the demand for lifestyle magazines provided an important indicator of changes in British society as more people came to identify themselves through their individual lifestyle rather than through broader, social identifications such as class, region or employment. Under pressure from the expansion of this style of magazine, newspapers have incorporated more lifestyle features as part of their own content, thus changing the character as well as the layout of even the elite press. In a similar fashion, television, radio and web provision has been influenced by magazine formats which prioritize a general appeal and an emphasis on personalized, soft-focus news with a celebrity emphasis where possible – from breakfast television news programmes on all television channels to programmes as varied as *The One Show* or *The Wright Stuff*.

Women's Magazines: Setting Patterns of Expectation

Although the first named magazine, the *Gentleman's Magazine* from 1731, was a miscellany aimed predominantly at a cultured male audience, the magazine became an arena for the development of a type of periodical journalism aimed exclusively at a female audience. Women had been identified early on in the history of printing as the subjects for specific publications. Some of the first printed publications designed for women were beauty treatises, such as the Jacobean translation of Buoni's (1606) *Problems of Beauty*. Early examples of miscellanies specifically addressed to women include the *Ladies Cabinet Opened* from 1639 which explored 'Physicke, Surgery, Cookery and Huswifery' and the *Queen's Closet Opened* from 1655. The market for women's magazines was to remain strong and yet they were often owned and sometimes even written by men. Dunton's first miscellany for women in 1693, *The Ladies' Mercury*, required writers who could produce interesting material for women readers more than it needed actual women writers, and although it did employ women it did not do so exclusively. This trend was consolidated in the early nineteenth century (according to Hunter's research) into the influential *Lady's Magazine*, which indicates that as little as a fifth of its content was contributed by women in its early years despite claims that it was written for and by ladies (Hunter, 1977: 109).

Much of what has developed as women's journalism has come to us out of the complex evolution of the women's magazine, as it has adapted both its formats and definitions of the female within – and occasionally against – the grain of consumer expectations. Beetham has summarized this complex relationship between female identity and its representation in journalism:

> *Just as the meaning of femininity was always being re-made, so was the meaning and the form of the magazine and its conventions. (1996: 5)*

The journalism of women's magazines has shaped the debate around a public and private visualization of the female, constructing a network of imagined communities for readers. To this extent they constitute an important aspect of the public sphere, although according to critics one that is determined by 'biological determinism' (Ferguson, 1983: 186). They continue to have an important cumulative effect on mainstream newspapers and broadcast journalism as part of a gendered cross-over between concepts of the popular and the quality, and between the personal and the political. This has been, in part, due to an economic pragmatism, responding to a realization that women as audience and consumers have steadily become more important to the success of news media in general. Dancyger (1978: 163) makes the point that, in addition to entertaining and informing, women's magazines have played a third role – 'to reassure' – which indicates how they are often located within the discourses of journalism, complementing its traditional informational and entertainment roles.

In this more restrictive way, they have functioned to educate women into their social roles and even determined the borders of acceptable protest and dissent.

Late Victorian Era

As with much else in print journalism, it was the Victorian era which gave us the pioneers of many of the magazine formats we take for granted today. *The Field* (1853) is often cited as the first special interest magazine, while new inventions quickly generated sufficient specific advertising and consumer interest to spawn their own dedicated publications such as *Autocar* (1895) and *Motor* (1903). The *Illustrated London News* was an early Victorian pioneer of illustration and general interest combined with topical news, founded in 1842 and running uninterrupted until its closure in 1989. *The Grocer*, appearing in 1861, was the first trade magazine – an often neglected but substantial part of journalism's range.

Following the Compulsory Education Act of 1870 the biggest expansion of periodical publication came in the category of women's magazines, with 48 new titles entering the market between 1880 and 1900 (White, 1970: 58). These were aimed at the lower ends of the economic spectrum, at the increasing numbers of women employed outside the home in service, factories, offices and shops as well as at working-class housewives intrigued by a diet of escapist entertainment, thereby providing 'a glamour later supplied by the cinema' (Dancyger, 1978: 94). There were also technological innovations which ensured this new readership could be better provided for in terms of quality and an increasingly accentuated visual appeal. In the 1880s wood-pulp paper was introduced, replacing rags and dramatically cutting the cost at the same time as improving the texture of paper even at the cheaper end of the market, while making it more suitable for illustration. By 1882 the half-tone process had been introduced, which helped raise the presentational standards of advertisements in women's magazines that in turn required a matching sophistication in writing about fashion and domestic consumption. Display advertisements and in particular brand names became an increasing part of the landscape of periodical publications from this point on, bringing with them a leap in profitability that would not go unremarked for long by even the most staid of newspapers. Across this miscellany of magazines a rejuvenated female public sphere was being consolidated within a specifically domestic economy.

The New Journalism and Women's Magazines

Newnes' *Tit-Bits* (1881) and Harmsworth's *Answers to Correspondents* (1888) were to demonstrate – drawing upon experience of this expanding market – how the astute exploitation of advertising within a magazine miscellany could show the way forward for popular newspapers. In terms of true mass markets for woman's magazines there was a further development in the introduction of the penny weekly.

Home Chat, published by Harmsworth from 1895, claimed that the 200,000 copies making up its first print needed to be supplemented by 35,000 additional copies in order to meet demand. It was lively and entertaining, as was the Harmsworth aim for all his publications – previewing his ambitions for the new magazine in the *Daily Mail* he is reported as claiming that it would provide 'a weekly woman's journal for a penny which should be the equal in the quality of its contributions both editorial and pictorial to any of the sixpenny journals' (White, 1970: 76).

Inevitably, all the major publishing players wanted to participate in this lucrative market. This kind of journalism built upon the patterns of the previous sixpenny monthlies and also extended its reach to a larger readership. It was characterized by the familiar strategies of breaking up information into short and memorable fragments together with the well-rehearsed intimacy of its tone, enabling it to appear closer to the lived oral experience of many of its readers in that it replicated how they exchanged information themselves in their social lives. This reinvigoration of the oral tradition of news exchange was one of the key shifts in journalism at a popular level at this time and was to become ever more pervasive across the twentieth century. It formed an integral part of the style of the New Journalism, as it had become established by the time of *My Weekly* which was launched in 1910 for working-class women with the following editorial:

> *My editorial experience has left me impressed with one thing in particular and that is the need for what is called the 'personal note' in journalism ... I will try to appeal to readers through their human nature and their understanding of everyday joys and sorrows. For I know well that, in order to get into active and intimate relationship with the great public, one must prove oneself fully acquainted with its affections, sentiments and work ... I understand, too, that human nature is strangely and pathetically eager for friendship. I mean willingly to become the confidant of readers, young and old, rich and poor, who can safely trust me with their ideas and difficulties. (White, 1970: 87–88)*

In the context of the traditional address of these magazines to a commercially orientated sense of commonality with the reader, Mary Grieve has observed: 'This close contact with the reader has been our gold-mine since the first journals made their genteel début to the present day' (1964: 96).

Mid-Century Developments

Woman was relaunched on 1 June 1937 as a 2d weekly and changed the woman's press in Britain completely (Reed, 1997: 189) by extending its brief to include a more broadly defined social conscience for a middle-class women's magazine. In market terms it saw an initial drop in circulation of 30 per cent which thereafter soon picked up to become a market leader, forcing other magazines to develop this part of their appeal (White, 1970: 11). In extending the range of journalism in these popular women's magazines to include topical questions such as divorce, social issues, birth control, parenting and women at work through the war years and beyond, the women's press was seen as entering something approaching its own golden age, as indicated in this extract from *World's Press News*, 7 October 1943:

> *Only some forty years ago the woman's magazine was an inconsiderable factor in journalism. Today it has won a dominant and very adult place in the periodical field, and is rivalled in sales and social influence only by the newspapers. This phenomenal growth of the woman's magazine is directly due to – and has been largely commensurate with – the advance of woman herself as a political, economic and moral force in the life of the nation. (Ferguson, 1983: 19–21)*

Good Housekeeping, which had been a dominant feature of the landscape of women's magazines since 1922, took on responsibility for a middle-class debate on the sort of women's issues launched by *Woman*. In May 1946 it made the following stalwart call to women to play their part in the post-war reconstruction, which could have appeared in the popular daily newspaper the *Daily Mirror* of the same era, illustrating the extent of the interpenetration of writing about women within popular news media at this point:

> *'... if we are to survive as a nation, Britain will have to allow our women as well as our men to use their energy and ability ...*

> *'Yet now the war is over, some people seem to think that women should go back to just the kind of jobs they did before the war and accept once more the same old artificial reasons and limitations. To my mind that would be disastrous ... We women must assume the responsibility of making our full contribution in the field for which our personal capacity fits us. Many women will rightly choose marriage and motherhood and feel that under present conditions the making of a home and bringing up young children is a job to which they wish to give the whole of their time. Others, many of whom are professional women, wish to combine marriage and motherhood with at least a part-time career ... we do need an adequate supply of women with first-class qualifications to serve on policy-forming bodies ... If we can carry forward into the future the spirit of individual efficiency shown by British women in the war years, then we need not fear the problems of tomorrow.'(White, 1970: 136–137)*

From the Swinging Sixties to Teen Mags

From the 1960s we can see a trend towards a much more intensely commercialized version of lifestyle publication which used advertising and editorial to position women readers as consumers and as lucid participants in the selection and maintenance of specifically gendered lifestyles. *Flair* (1960) and *Honey* (1961) were two early examples of this development. In addition, the growth in disposable income and the virtual invention of the new consumer category of youth culture saw the creation of more niche markets for women's journalism. These exhibited a similar intensified linkage of writing, editorial and consumption. Such specialization meant a reduction in general interest articles and a newly configured retreat by women's magazine journalism from more broadly social themes. *Cosmopolitan*, launched in March 1972, was the high point of this modern trend and the paradigm for subsequent women's magazines aimed at and constructing at the same time the newly 'liberated' sexual and economic woman. Helen Gurley Brown was quoted in the *Guardian* on 20 June 1977 as saying:

> '*Cosmopolitan is every girl's sophisticated older sister ...* Cosmopolitan *says you can get anything if you really try, if you don't just sit on your backside and gaze in on life with your nose pressed to the glass ... we carry our profile, one piece on health, one on sex, two on emotions – we had a good one the other day on the Good Luck Factor – one on man/woman relationships, one on careers, one short story and one part of a major work of fiction, as well as our regular columns.'* (Ferguson, 1983: 37)

Women's magazines have retreated, in the main, from engaging with broader social issues to concentrate on the increasingly lucrative combination of 'advertorial' journalism supporting the commodity lifestyles at their core. Within this commodification of lifestyles in women's magazines, a lucrative sub-genre of journalism was launched with magazines such as *Jackie* from 1963 to *Just Seventeen* from 1983, signalling the development of a hugely significant and controversial wave (McRobbie, 1991) of publications aimed at a distinctive teenage female market containing advice, features and music. Against the rising tide of increasingly commodified women's magazines, there were also influential minority publications which offered radical alternative critiques to mainstream commercialized views of women. The most significant of these was *Spare Rib* from 1972. Critics have argued that magazines like *Company*, *Cosmopolitan* and *Elle* have fostered in women an individualist pursuit of aggressive sexual pleasures and material indulgences to the exclusion of responsibilities and caring for others. Yet even within the consumerist focus of the mainstream, Smith (2007: 531) can make the case that these magazines have hit back by focusing on their informational base and the ways in which a changing sexual climate and sexually transmitted diseases demanded the sort of frank public discussion which these magazines claim to have provided.

The ambivalent potential of women's magazines within journalism has been well expressed by Shevelow:

> But in looking at the periodical, which was then and remains now one of women's principal – and for many women, the only – means of engagement with print culture, we are reminded that the tools of liberation are not in themselves liberating. Print culture can provide the bricks and mortar for constructing a prison – or the dynamite for shattering its walls. (1989: 198)

The Tradition of the General Magazine

It is useful to recap what the attractions of magazine journalism are:

> The process of finding and fostering a group of readers which can coalesce into a community generally follows five phases. A magazine will always target a precisely defined group of readers and will base its content on the needs, desires, hopes and fears of that defined group, thus creating a bond of trust with their readerships. Using that bond, a magazine will encourage community-like interactions between itself and its readers, and among readers. Finally, because they are close to their readers, magazines can respond quickly and flexibly to changes in the readership and changes in the wider society. (Holmes, 2007: 514)

These features of a publication are particularly attractive in an era which has seen the intensification of 'para-social' activity (Giles, 2000; Rojek, 2001) substituting media consumption and imaginary relationships with media celebrities for real contact with the social world and a corresponding shift of many relationships to that para-social level. These are trends which are reinforced by other patterns of technological development such as social networking sites, mobile phones and e-mails which generally enable virtual communication to predominate over actual contact. In addition magazines can provide topical and in-depth coverage for their own specialized communities which would be prohibitive to a more generalist provider of journalism. They must provide an acceptable balance between editorial and advertising in order to retain a credibility of appeal to both readers and advertisers; and in doing so they are an excellent illustration of the combination of information and entertainment into a hugely pleasurable product whose attractiveness is amplified by the glossy, tactile characteristics of the magazine and the provision of high quality illustrations which further enhance the feelings of pleasure in indulging in the enjoyment of one's niche of choice.

There was a surge in magazine launches from the late 1940s, as newsprint restrictions were lifted for magazines more quickly than for newspapers. This saw the heyday of the picture magazines *Picture Post*, *John Bull* and *Everybody's Illustrated* whose format stood out against the newspapers, bereft of their pre-war quantity of pictures under their paper-rationed restrictions. These all folded in the 1950s once the lifting of paper rationing and increased advertising enabled newspapers to adjust to a more pictorial mode of presentation, and television had also been introduced thus providing competition for the general picture audience, meaning that as Hartley (2007: 556) has argued, as photographs became ubiquitous the picture papers became defunct.

Tunstall (1983: 89) suggests we should consider Sunday newspapers as magazines even before the advent of the first glossy Sunday supplements in the early 1960s and particularly at the popular end of the market. Indeed the circulation figures of both forms of journalism match this assertion, with both peaking in the mid to late fifties with *Woman* at 3.49 million in 1957 and the *News of the World* maintaining its circulation above eight million until 1954.

> *Magazines sales boomed again between 1952 and 1958 – as advertisers with goods to sell, magazine publishers with plentiful paper, and housewives tasting unfamiliar affluence, all participated in a great consumer boom ...* Woman's Mirror *(1956),* Woman's Realm *(1958) and* Woman's Day *(1958) each quickly reached sales of over one million. (Tunstall, 1983: 93)*

At first generalist magazines were clearly threatened by the launch of commercial television in 1955 but television's advertising caused more of a ripple effect than a ravenous devouring of other media's advertising share. For example, as a consequence of astute interaction with the new medium, daily newspapers such as the *Daily Mail* and *The Times* at least trebled their TV schedule space between 1959 and 1966 (Tunstall, 1983:100), at the same time as the most popular magazine genre in Britain – the woman's weekly – declined from 12.21 million in 1958 to 6.26 million in 1982 (Tunstall, 1983: 89), hit by the encroachment of newspapers into a territory they had considered their own. Sunday newspapers began launching their own magazine supplements motivated by the obvious financial attractiveness of a magazine approach blended with their own brand identity to enhance their appeal in the increasingly affluent post-war consumer wave. The *Sunday Times* launched its colour supplement from 1962 soon to be followed by the *Observer*. These were copied in the popular market by the *Sunday Express*, the *News of the World* and the *Mail on Sunday* between 1981 and 1982.

From Generalist to Specialist

Trade and technical magazines survived and even thrived. Those with sales of over 100,000 were unusual but in 1980 there were some 72 consumer magazines in Britain with sales over this figure (Tunstall, 1983: 102), including *New Musical Express*, *Motor Cycle News* and *Garden News*. *Farmer's Weekly* acted as a leading representative voice for a whole rural community with a loyal and wide readership based on its editorial strengths which combined to make it a powerful trade magazine. The 1980s witnessed the rise and rise of targeted, specialist magazines for a more niche and less mass market – women, teenagers, music, hobbies, computers, lifestyle, motoring, supermarket, cooking, fashion and life events (e.g. weddings). At the same time we have seen the growth of politically and professionally specific titles (*Economist*, *New Statesman*, *Times Educational Supplement*, *Times Higher Educational Supplement*) which continue to thrive even as they distinguish themselves from the appeal of the expanding magazine sections of the daily and weekend elite press.

Men's Magazines

Gill writes of broad-based men's magazines:

> *For years, people working in the fashion, magazine, advertising and retailing industries had fantasized about the creation of a magazine which could be targeted at affluent male consumers – but it was seen as an impossible dream. (2003: 43)*

It was largely assumed that men did not constitute a separate general magazine market for three main reasons. First, newspapers provided general reading matter for the male market. Second, men's magazines were targeted towards specific hobbies. Third, generalist magazines had perfected an intimacy of approach to both reader identity and advertiser which was broadly viewed as 'feminine'. This did not mean that there had not been efforts made to attract such a generalist male readership but these had inclined mostly to some variation of approach to titillation. *Vogue* had been launched as early as 1916 and remained an idiosyncratic success until it was joined by *Esquire* in 1933 with the high production values characteristic of the women's fashion magazine, thus staking a claim to being the arbiters of taste and leaders in fashion for the wealthy or the aspiring. The inevitable opposite end of this particular spectrum was *Lilliput*, launched in 1937 with a combination of nudes, amusing anecdotes and light-hearted features by celebrity authors. Along with *Men Only* it sold particularly well during the war, encouraging further experimentations at the border between masculine lifestyle and soft pornography. Most notable were *Pall Mall* from 1950, which changed its title to *Clubman* and blended nude photographs of an artistic nature with film star pin-ups, humour and general features. This was marketed as 'Britain's favourite entertainment magazine for discriminating men' (Osgerby, 2003: 80), while *Man About Town* (1951) possessed a blend of restaurant guides, fashion advice and travel features for the sophisticated urban male. The genre probably could be considered to have settled for the editorial blend provided by *Penthouse* from 1965 which was modelled on the globally successful American *Playboy*.

There was little change in the formula until the 1980s which saw the rise of a new range of consumer-oriented journalism, following the introduction of new technologies in printing and colour and an unprecedented expansion in diverse and affluent youth markets emerging from alternative journalism, fanzines, listings magazines, fashion, music and lifestyle. This was a cultural mimicry of the fragmenting personality politics of the seventies sold back as commodified, lifestyle journalism. After Thatcher's claim that there was no such thing as society, her policies seemed directed towards the creation of a more individualistic culture and the rapid fragmentation of older traditions of mass forms of identification produced a social order where identity was far more dependent on consumption (Giddens, 1991; Hall and Jacques, 1989; Jameson, 1985). One significant area where the breakdown of a traditional identification around work and social identity was most acute in a period of mass male unemployment was that of young men. Masculine identities became increasingly articulated through lifestyle, music and fashion during these years (Mort, 1996; Nixon, 1996; Stevenson et al., 2001). The most striking example of these sorts of identification can be seen in the phenomenon of the men's magazine.

Nixon (1996) claims that *The Face*, launched in 1980, was of primary importance to the development of these publications. It promoted itself as a style magazine rather than a men's magazine, although the vast majority of its readers were male. It was organized around fashion, music and any kind of social commentary chic enough to fit into its pages while adopting a suitably 'laddish tone' to address readers as 'mates' (Gill, 2003: 43–44). It built its journalism around the concept of the 'New Man' – a caring and sensitive variation on men's social and consumer identity. This 'New Man' was the ubiquitous media-driven label that embodied these 'caring and sharing' middle-class, white, male consumers for whom, it was argued, a narcissistic concern with the body and fashion played a more central role in their sense of self (Craik, 1994: 249).

As a reaction to the New Man, in 1994 James Brown and Tim Southwell provided with *Loaded* a younger, more street-wise, and most of all more vulgar extension of this tradition. Wheaton (2003: 193) claims that it provided the reaction of the 'New Lad' to the 'New Man' phenomenon, centred around football and indie pop music (Wheaton, 2003: 193). Its tone appeared markedly less earnest and more celebratory in its portrayal of masculine culture than its predecesors (Crewe, 2003: 95). By the mid-nineties *FHM*, *Men's Health* and *Maxim* were all vying in competition for readers and advertisers in this new generation of men's lifestyle magazines on a monthly basis. These had proved so successful that *Nuts* and *Zoo* took the genre further downmarket, back to the glossy version of soft porn whence the man's general interest magazine had emanated, with weekly publications which now regularly sell a combined total of over 400,000 copies. Free sheets have also spread to the free men's magazine market with the 2007 launch of *Shortlist*.

Conclusion

It is clear from walking into any branch of WH Smith's that magazine journalism is in vigorous good health. There are over 8,300 magazine titles (PPA Marketing, 2008) in the three defined sectors of consumer, business-to-business and customer magazines, yielding an annual sales total of over 81,000,000 (ABC July-December, 2008). Magazines continue to modify their appeal and are taking full advantage of the attractiveness of their niche advertising by providing online versions of their products as well as seeing the continuing success of subscription and off-the-shelf purchases.

Magazine journalism thrives because of its ability to match a particular submarket with very particular and well-identified interests or even passions. It is targeted at those particular readerships and brings a buoyant amount of advertising which can be considered money well spent by the advertisers concerned. It also continues to provide a range of writing on a whole range of contemporary lifestyle issues which have become more important to consumers. Over the course of the last hundred years magazines have played a key part in the development of journalism as a whole. First, they provided a template for the broader appeal of the mass newspapers at the turn of the century. They then provided a parallel commentary to the lifestyles, professional interests and consumer patterns of the British population as they moved between affluence, austerity and consumer boom and bust. Ultimately, it was the magazine format which began to impact upon the early versions of commercial television and thence to newspapers in their post-Wapping exploitation of the growth in pagination that was available to satisfy a branded approach to a broader concept of their readerships. It is because magazine journalism is so closely affiliated to the precise requirements of consumer identities that it continues to provide a rich source of information on the culture in which we live. This had been the case on the appearance of the first named magazine in the eighteenth century, through the blossoming of popular miscellanies into the Victorian era, and also continues to be the case as contemporary journalism across the board maximizes the magazine potential of its content.

FURTHER READING

Benwell, B. (ed.) (2003) *Masculinity and Men's Lifestyle Magazines*. Oxford: Blackwell. This supplements the work of Stevenson et al. with a more historically informed chronicle on the emergence of a variety of magazines aimed specifically at the men's market.

Gough-Yates, A. (2003) *Understanding Women's Magazines: Publishing, Markets and Readerships*. London: Routledge. This gives a good insight into the ways in which content, institution and culture come together in these particular magazines.

Holmes, T. (2007) Special Issue, *Journalism Studies* 8 (4). This emanates from the two 'Mapping the Magazine' conferences organized by Cardiff University. This special issue provides a selection of papers drawn from across the world, and across times and genres, to demonstrate what a rich and provocative range of journalism that magazines can provide.

Reed, D. (1997) *The Popular Magazine in Britain and the United States, 1880–1960*. London: The British Library. This is simply the best overview of the development of this particular form of journalism.

Stevenson, N., Jackson, P. and Brooks, K. (2001) *Understanding Men's Magazines*. Cambridge: Polity. This provides a ground-breaking assessment of a new form of magazine.

10

Hacks or Heroes?

Introduction

The role of the journalist is a complex and sometimes contradictory one. This situation is becoming even more challenging in the contemporary world as journalism's tectonic plates shift to reveal a radically altered landscape. Yet the role of the journalist has never been straightforward, simply because it is too broad a range of activities and motivations to be encompassed by one word. Neither on the side of the angels of democratic engagement on behalf of the people, nor unequivocally in league with the devils of corporate finance in pursuit of the bottom line of profit, the journalist is constructed in history and in the present as scuttling somewhere between hack and hero.

It would appear that as more and more is expected of journalism as a mode of communication, less and less is expected of the practitioners themselves as they continue to struggle in terms of credibility with the public. At a time where journalists are increasingly expected to be educated to degree or even postgraduate level, much of the work they do appears to be more often connected with the trivial and the scandalous or with routinized duplications of items that must fit a pre-determined news agenda which leaves little room for investigation or imagination. Fictional mass-media portrayals of journalists as well as high profile accounts of the trespasses of senior journalists such as the Royal Correspondent and Editor of the *News of the World* – together with coverage of the recent shaming of the BBC in the wake of its reporting of the events which led to the death of Dr David Kelly in the Hutton Report (2004) – have put journalism in the dock under the public's gaze as never before. This chapter will take a look at the evolution in the role of the journalist over the century and it will also chart the related implications of recent moves to professionalize the function and education of journalists.

The Rise of the Hack

'No man but a blockhead wrote, except for money', complained the famous Samuel Johnson in 1776 (Fleeman, 1970: 731) at a time when those whose work could earn them the description of 'journalist' were perceived generally as 'hacks' – a metaphor derived from the 'Hackney cabs' that could be hired for short journeys across London and therefore applied to those writers whose skills and opinions could be purchased for any short-term writing job if there was money in it for them (or even better, money and a drink). The routine work of the scribe from the Middle Ages, copying out pre-ordained texts on behalf of wealthier clients, developed during journalism's nineteenth-century heyday into the lowly labour of the 'penny-a-liners', often women, who were as denigrated as any of their eighteenth-century relatives, the 'hacks'.

Yet despite these lowly beginnings, the increasing industrialization of the periodical press meant larger profits could be made, and this necessitated – as in most other areas of commerce – a greater degree of differentiation and specialization of roles within journalism. Some parts of the work became suitable for highly educated editors drawn from the upper echelons of society while there still remained a need for lowly paid but industrious writers. The complexity of the role has since deepened as the range of journalism and its technological platforms have multiplied. Across the stretching spectrum of journalism, the function of the journalist has also been increasingly polarised – from the elite, celebrity opinion brokers and nationally recognized editorial leaders, to the freelance contributors, editorial assistants and unpaid interns dealing with routine jobs, often with little job security and even less status.

The standing of journalists in the twentieth century bears the hallmarks of a complex sedimentation of public communicators in general. There have been at least five different sorts of journalist, each with a different level of social standing. There was the radical pamphleteer, a Cobbett or a Paine; there was the enlightened editor such as Delane or Perry; there were men-of-letters who dabbled in journalism as they plied their literary careers in parallel such as Dickens or Hazlitt; there were the populist scribes who went on to develop an eye and an ear for both audience and advertiser such as Harmsworth or Newnes; and finally there were the hacks, the scribblers descended from the scribes of the sixteenth century, the penny-a-liners with little financial security and little social standing given their role as purveyors of low-grade information, writing for money in the short-term, and lacking the private incomes, patrons or privileged backgrounds which allowed gentlemen writers their amateur and therefore more refined status (Pinkcus, 1968: 14–15).

This complex history means that there has never been a need to define what exactly a profession of journalism might consist of. It would continue to require those at the top of the pile as well as those at the bottom and it would likewise continue to require skilled political and commercial operators who were able to maximize profits and economic opportunities as well as others who were more inclined to rattle the cages of politicians and celebrities. Despite this duality, journalists themselves have taken a number of steps to become more professionalized in a similar fashion to other trades and occupations in the twentieth century. Whether these steps have moved them any closer to the status of a professional class and what the public thinks of them are questions which we can begin to address here.

Reputation and Reflection

This mixed history is reflected in assessments of both the abilities necessary to do the work and the status of the job. These problems lie at the heart of what Elliott (1978: 172) has termed a 'conceptual dilemma' for journalism. Success in journalism depends, according to one oft-cited quotation, on the possession of three assets: 'rat-like cunning, a plausible manner, and a little literary ability' (Tomalin, 1975: 77). However, the subtly self-congratulatory message masked within such a summary is in fact the very aspect of journalism which makes it difficult for the public to trust such practitioners. This has implications which some journalists are themselves aware of. Kevin Marsh, editor of BBC Radio 4's *Today* programme, provided a view of his industry and his anxieties for its future if it could not address public concerns about its self-image in a speech to the Society of Newspaper Editors in October 2004:

> *Journalists are members of Britain's least trusted profession: the press. More than 90 per cent of the population trust their doctor to tell the truth; less than a fifth trust the press to do the same. It's not an essential condition of journalism. Trust in broadcasters is very much higher and trust in the BBC higher still ... Government ministers and MPs share the lowly standing of the press – we don't trust those we've chosen to exercise power for us; and we don't trust those who tell us how the chosen are doing it .... The crisis of trust cannot be any great surprise to anyone. Why should anyone trust a practitioner of any craft or profession who doesn't seem to know and is unable or unwilling to articulate what that craft or profession is for? Or who wears indifference to the effects of that craft as a badge of honour? Or who seems to relish the denial of responsibility, playing the romantic maverick, happy to be identified only as someone who kicks against authority, just out to make trouble and get up people's noses? (Marsh, 2004: 17)*

This decline of trust in journalists (Worcester, 1998: 46–48) has been a steady process over the last thirty years, given its impetus by various scandals – from cheque-book journalism to the intrusions into the private lives of the rich and famous which led to the brink of legislation in the wake of the Calcutt Report of 1990. This appears to have accelerated recently according to a *BJR*/YouGov survey. This suggested that journalism's reputation, never particularly high in the eyes of the public, had suffered massive damage over the previous five years (Barnett, 2008: 5). In the wake of, for example, the imprisonment of Clive Goodman, royal correspondent for the *News of the World*, in January 2007 and the scandal of 'Crowngate' at the BBC, figures showed declining public confidence across the board compared to a similar survey five years before, with the largest decline showing for broadcast journalists. The reason we should be alarmed about this decline in public esteem is that it is widely believed that the good reputation of journalism makes a difference to the kind of society we live in, and a distrust of journalism can lead to the slow poisoning of the social values journalism purports to serve. It is no use cackling cynically while professing the centrality of one's role to the democratic process and the state of the nation as Marsh has highlighted.

Despite its current rather dubious self-image and the complexity of journalism's historical functions there are those who would make claim for its centrality to the democratic process itself and conversely would argue that damage to its reputation does damage to this process:

> *For journalism is not just a craft or a profession. It is the lynchpin of the found-ation of democracy: an informed citizenry making informed judgements about how they will live together. (Dates, 2006: 145)*

Further to this, it has been noted that high standards in news are not a given in a democratic society – especially not a global, capitalist one – and that journalism needs explicit protection if it is not to deteriorate and decline (Moore, 2006: 51). Public discussion of the role of the journalist in these processes is absolutely pivotal to the future good health as well as the prosperity of journalism.

The National Union of Journalists

Professionalization in the Victorian era meant, among other things, the ability to demonstrate that a practice was restricted to gentlemen, excluding both the work-ing classes and women (Beetham, 1996: 43). Journalism posed problems for this process of selectivity as it entered the twentieth century. It was precisely during this period that the role of the journalist was crystallizing around the modern practices of professional communication techniques which had jettisoned older conventions of advocacy and instead collected information from authoritative sources and aimed to present this in as entertaining a form as possible to the reader (Smith, 1973: 41). This role – a blend of showman and social commentator according to Smith – already presented the sort of duality which would constitute problems for any consideration of the journalist as a member of a profession.

Elliott (1972) has argued that occupations have traditionally sought to reconcile varying individual and collective situations by identifying themselves as profes-sions rather than through any trade union activity and association, and yet journal-ists appear to have taken what could only be described as an oblique route at best towards this long-term goal. This second route could be said to have originated in 1886 when the National Association of Journalists was founded by the newspaper owners, subsequently changing its name in 1890 to the Institute of Journalists, and was awarded a Royal Charter.

In its early years the Institute sought to gain professional status by pushing for better conditions, better education for its members, and better standards in part by insisting on a certain level of qualification for entry, but it struggled to find a suitable test of profi-ciency which could encompass the wide set of practices which could all claim to form a part of journalism (Taylor, 1940). There was then, as now, a struggle to define what the entry knowledge (such an important part of the definition of a profession) should be. In 1895, a Society of Women Journalists was formed and in 1907 the National Union of Journalists was created to differentiate itself from the corporate aims of owners which dominated the Institute of Journalists. While the newly formed union concentrated on the living standards of its members, it was in effect inverting the usual route to professionalization. Its main objective was at first to establish legally binding minimum wages for different categories of journalist (Elliott, 1978: 175) which appeared to demarcate lower sections of the workforce from a more professionalized vision of universal expectations from the start. Yet this was to a large extent made inevitable because of merit pay, freelance earnings, the gentleman contributor and especially the well-connected theatrical and literary reviewers and the political lobbyists. All this, plus the potential to become a 'star' within an increasingly massified market, meant that collective approaches were limited in their efficacy. Ambitions concerning the objectives of these new representative bodies were expressed by contemporaries who were clear about where the emphasis of a journalist's professional allegiance should lie:

> *The professional organizations of journalism should fight for a completely new conception of the obligations of the journalist. That obligation is not primarily to the man who pays him, any more than the judge's obligation is primarily to the Government that pays his salary. The obligation is to the public – and to professional conscience. (Angell, 1923: 269–270)*

One part of the process of the professionalization of journalism can be seen in the ways in which journalists have attempted to draw together the common purpose of their activities, but tensions have remained between the NUJ's role as a 'traditional' trade union on the one hand and its role as an almost quasi-professional body on the other (Harcup, 2002: 103).

Another approach to a collective professionalization came in 1934 with the Code of Professional Conduct first debated at the annual meeting of NUJ delegates. It was referred back with amendments to the next annual meeting and finally adopted as the official code of the union at the 1936 Annual Delegate Conference (Frost, 2000: 175). Yet the original goal of a liberal profession of journalism has proved a chimera in every sense and this in spite of the efforts of the Institute of Journalists, which twice sponsored a Journalists' Registration Bill in the 1930s. In 1949 the Royal Commission on the Press espoused the goal but not the Institute's method (Elliott, 1978: 189), looking forward instead to a General Council of the Press (the Press Council) 'which, by censuring undesirable types of journalistic conduct and by all other possible means, should build up a code of conduct in accordance with the highest professional standards' (Royal Commission, 1947–1949: 170).

Boyd-Barrett applied the conventional definitions of a profession to the work and careers of journalists and found that:

> *Applying this framework to journalism we find that these five attributes are either non-existent or exist only to a very limited degree. (1970: 181)*

169

In another study, Tunstall found that many of the ambitious strategies aimed at professionalizing journalism which had been initiated from the 1960s had been reversed by the 1990s because of a range of factors, including the erosion of job security, increasing workloads, a de-recognition of the NUJ and its associated consensus, and the preponderance of macho management styles (1996: 136–141). Particularly after the watershed of Wapping, we find that more and more journalists had been asked to sign new, individualized contracts with their employers which negated the collective power and related status of belonging to a trades union.

Technology and the Erosion of Professional Territory

In broadcasting, the BBC is more unionized than the commercial sector with pay scales and a career structure negotiated with the National Union of Journalists (NUJ), while at the same time it is generally more professionalized with professional and regulatory codes of practice such as the National Union of Journalists' *Code of Conduct* (2004) and the BBC's *Editorial Guidelines* (2005) setting standards and norms of professional practice which the corporation expects journalists to observe (Starkey and Crisell, 2009: 64). However, radical innovations in digital technologies, satellite and cable delivery systems have provided opportunities for a convergence in journalism that has encouraged large corporate news providers to employ 'multiskilled' (or is it 'deskilled'?) journalists who are now often obliged to produce journalism to 'conventionalized formats' (Cottle, 2003a: 16). These 'permanent part-timers' (Keeble, 1994: 3) tend to package the news in a way that tends to do nothing to enhance the reputation of either journalism or journalists. In addition, new technologies make it seem as if amateurs can step unproblematically into the erstwhile territory of the professional and displace them in the process. This is most marked in the area of blogging where the traditional professional autonomy of journalists is being challenged by amateurs keen to take on the role of watchdog themselves, external to the routines and traditions of journalism (Singer, 2007: 79). Technology appears superficially at least to be able to liberate journalism from the routines and restrictions of its industrial past. It promises a future in which in principle we can all become journalists, and free journalists themselves can work more independently from large corporate structures and expectations.

It's not as simple as this of course. To a large extent journalism is the sum of its restrictive boundaries. There are good blogs but there are also unreliable and unaccountable blogs which do not need to answer to anyone for their reliability or even veracity. And then there is the question of how one sources independent information while sitting in one's attic. It's fine to argue that journalists themselves do little of this work themselves these days, but at its best, journalism does provide this sort of consistent scrutiny of information and its sources, while, at their worst, bloggers can never hope to acquire the skills and networks to enable them to come close. Journalists may not have succeeded in creating a profession from their practice but there are still professional imperatives at the heart of much of what they do even within the challenges of a new technological era.

Education as a Professionalizing Trend

One of the principal ways in which journalism and indeed journalists can reflect upon the importance of journalism for society as a whole is both through education and through an engagement which the issues that journalism education generates. There was an increasing professionalization of journalism caused by a growing speciali- zation within many of its activities during the nineteenth century, yet this was still marked by the division between the upper echelons which had dominated as they do today, with their ease of access to senior politicians and financiers contrasting sharply with the status of the more lowly journalists who did not require any formal training. The most common route into journalism for much of the twentieth century remained an informal apprenticeship on a local, most often weekly, newspaper. This has been described as 'Sitting by Nellie' (Allen, 2005: 318) – an odd expression in a workplace so dominated by men – and consisted of a traditional craft approach based on learning by watching. In the 1930s there had been an experimental postgraduate course at the London School of Economics but this was discontinued after a couple of years.

The turning point appears to have come, belatedly, in the wake of the first Royal Commission on the Press which reported in 1949, as the end product of wide- ranging post-war debate about the relationship between the level of education of journalists and the standards of the journalism they produced. Despite the fact that the Commission's report had led to the first systematized education for journalists through the National Council for the Training of Journalists – which was founded in 1951 and provided the first formal post-entry training for new entrants and also some linked courses with FE colleges to provide pre-entry training – a noted history of journalism has remarked sardonically: 'the first Commission [on the press] had hoped that the reform of journalism education would instil a spirit of public service among journalists [it didn't!]' (Curran and Seaton, 2003: 357). This was almost cer- tainly because of the conservatism of the skills approach the NCTJ adopted, which had the effect of disassociating journalism as a practice from its broader social and cultural contexts. The 1960s saw the growth of more formal courses. National and local newspaper groups started to provide a limited number of training schemes. The Thompson Foundation Training College in Cardiff started as a six month course followed by an internship at one of the Thompson group's regional newspapers, and soon became linked with Cardiff University as a postgraduate course. This ini- tial postgraduate alternative to traditional journalism education was supplemented in 1976 by the founding of the Graduate Centre for Journalism at City University. By the 1990s, with the rapid growth of students at universities and an increased emphasis on vocational courses, the provision expanded at both postgraduate and undergraduate level with degree courses at over 60 institutions by the end of the decade according to UCAS statistics. It had already become a substantially graduate occupation since the university expansions of the sixties and seventies with over 70 per cent of journalists now holding a degree (Delano and Henningham, 1995), while even more recent figures from the Journalism Training Forum assessed that in 2002, 98 per cent of entrants possessed a degree (2002: 4). Education has moved more formally onto the agenda of the BBC as it opened its College of Journalism in 2005 in response to the Hutton Report in order to demonstrate its continuing commitment to the evolution of excellence in its public service journalism and to secure the elaboration of its own liberal version of a global public service journalism.

Scepticism from Within

Journalism itself however remains more than capable of dismissing attempts to professionalize its practices through education, as was evidenced in a comment in one of the more media-friendly elite newspapers: 'This paper regards a degree in media studies as a disqualification for the career of journalism' (*Independent,* 31 October 1996). What this article did not care to mention was not only the high international standing of British media studies degrees, media studies research or the high levels of employability of media studies graduates but, perhaps most importantly, that students wanting to study journalism at university have a large choice of specifically named journalism courses. This general theme was combated by research commissioned on behalf of the Association of Journalism Education by Tony Delano (2008) and published in the *British Journalism Review*, where he eloquently made the case that journalists should be more informed by the facts of the contemporary journalism education environment and less willing to parrot ignorant prejudices which do nothing to help young people discover how they might aspire to gain a foothold in journalism.

Journalism education is a key component of the ongoing professionalization and even socialization of journalism (Deuze, 2006b: 24). However, if journalism is to attain the respect and professionalism it aspires to it must also seek to embrace – in addition to essential skills and knowledge – an awareness of debates among critics outside its practice about its relationship with social, political and cultural realities if it is to fully engage with the expectations of citizen and consumer in a complex and changing environment for public communication. Journalist educators might well agree that we need to start at the ground floor with higher expectations of what journalism education should aim to deliver if its practitioners are ever to improve their currently plummeting reputation:

> ... *a journalism course – even a practical, introductory journalism course – should include a critique of journalism. (Stephens, 2006: 152)*

This education needs to encourage an excavation process to move beyond the clichés and platitudes that newsrooms use to ward off critics (Glasser, 2006: 149), literally a 'leading out of', an e-ducation, which leads students to an understanding of where such practices emanate and whose interests they serve. A rounded education should be based around training in the skills and knowledge needed to perform within current paradigms but should also provide the context for future practitioners to operate critically within society's wider expectations. Yet at the same time as these courses should include an engagement with practitioners and an intimate familiarity with the state of news media practices today, journalism students should need to be able to respond to critiques of their practice because their customers are increasingly critical of it. As Glasser writes: ' ... journalism studies will only make a difference if they make journalism better and help us understand what journalism means' (2006: 146). Such courses already exist in the UK and Delano is correct in the view that the news media should be more aware and supportive of them if journalism's professionalization is to continue.

Social Composition – Who Are They?

In 1971, Tunstall provided a rare but detailed examination of the professional lives of journalists at the point where their working lives were on the threshold of radical change. Over half of young recruits wanted to write a novel. Prominent among reasons to choose journalism as a job was a perception that it did not tie one into a routine. In the late 1960s only 12.1 per cent of recruits to provincial newspapers were graduates, only 11.5 per cent had three or more A levels, and only 30 per cent of specialist reporters held university degrees (Tunstall, 1971: 59). There was also an elite and extremely opaque path, parallel to the traditional three year local indenture, for prestige positions such as foreign, financial and political journalism and thence to national editorship which by-passed the local apprenticeship and often any previous experience of journalism at all.

It is also still today – in the case of senior levels of editorial responsibility – an almost exclusively male occupation and at all levels resistantly white. Journalism in Britain is dominated by white, Anglo-Saxon Protestants, with only 1 per cent of the research project's sample of Indian and Pakistani origin in 1995 and only 1 per cent black African or Caribbean (Henningham and Delano, 1998: 148–149). From the perspective of ethnic inclusivity, it is clear that elite racism, institutional racism and textual examples of everyday racism continue to provide, particularly in contemporary newspaper journalism, a significant obstacle to a more accurate social portrait of Britain in the twenty-first century:

> *Hugh Muir, a senior reporter at the Guardian ... says that being a member of an ethnic minority is no longer a novelty, though most newsrooms are still run by white, middle-class men who are highly educated and share a set of assumptions that shape the news agenda. (Francis, 2003: 70–71)*

This is, however, hardly surprising when one considers the evidence of the Society of Editors' (2004) report *Diversity in the Newsroom* which demonstrated how a tiny proportion of journalists from ethnic minorities were employed on a range of local newspapers in areas with significant ethnic minority populations. This reinforces the point made by Van Dijk (1991, 1993) that within the news industry there exists a patterning of selection of both news content and personnel which is oriented towards a particular set of assumptions about the ethnic composition of the country. It is therefore no surprise that his research has been endorsed by more recent findings about the patterning of news about ethnic minorities in Britain in recent times (Conboy, 2006; Greater London Authority, 2007; Richardson, 2004; Runnymede Trust, 2008). There may be bold attempts by broadcasters to include a more representative range of news presenters on our screens, but despite this literal façade it remains a predominantly white version of the news which they read from the autocue.

As well as in its public discourse on ethnicity, journalism continues to exclude as much as it includes in its representation of gender. Up until the postwar era there was, according to Greenslade (2003: 628–629) very little that was directly targeted towards a female audience. This has not changed to a large extent since Tuchman identified in her withering assessment (1978) the 'symbolic annihilation' of women in the elite press – to which we could add the almost complete 'sexualization' (Holland, 1998) found in the popular mass dailies. Van Zoonen (1998) has observed that journalism is changing, but within newspapers and their online variants this change has merely provided more opportunities for the development of 'feminine' styles of writing in consumer-oriented and market-driven news, such as human-interest and emotional investment and the rise of the female confessional column (Heller, 1999). There is significant evidence that 'real' news continues to remain stubbornly 'androcentric' (Simpson, 1993) and this can still be observed in the fabric of journalism's language today and is underpinned by the role of photogenic news readers on television who are deployed to obscure any lack of a shift in emphasis towards a male-oriented news agenda.

In Delano and Henningham's report (1995: 50) two-thirds of all newly recruited journalists described themselves as 'middle-class'. The Journalism Training Forum confirmed this recently, concluding that only 3 per cent of journalists come from families headed by parents in semi-skilled or unskilled jobs (Francis, 2003: 72). National readership surveys continue to indicate the extent to which newspaper readership is demarcated along social class lines, while patterns of ownership and control have meant that diversity of public representation has been severely stunted (Curran and Seaton, 2003: 102). The Sutton Trust's (2006) *The Educational Background of Leading Journalists* found a similar tale of under-representation of a wider social base, with independent schools and an Oxford or Cambridge university background seemingly distinct advantages in seeking advancement in the news media.

Heroes

Despite its lowly public esteem and the resistance to professionalization within parts of journalism, there are a variety of expressions of journalism as a heroic enterprise. In the 1930s foreign correspondents had become 'the veritable, ideological James

Bonds of their time' (Gannon, 1971: 3). Yet this was a point at which, from a different perspective, the role of journalist was more than ever becoming incorporated into institutional expectations, and nowhere was this more evident for Seaton than at the BBC as it developed its highly influential pattern of journalism in the 1930s:

> *Journalists stopped being passionate advocates, saw themselves rather as independent professionals, and their writing as a negotiated product of conflict between partisan views. This self-image and its practical consequences were most fully developed in the BBC. (Curran and Seaton, 2003: 123)*

The derring-do emphasis on the work of the foreign correspondent shifted to representations of investigative journalists as the wise-cracking, hard-boiled seekers after truth found in *Hold the Front Page* (1931; 1974). By the 1970s they had become the politically-driven upholders of democratic values, notably in *The China Syndrome* (1979) and most famously in *All The President's Men* (1976). Since then, the trope of journalists as flawed but sincere seekers of the truth that the authorities want to hide has remained a commonplace – from *The Killing Fields* (1984) to the recent. Hollywoodization of Paul Abbott's television drama *State of Play* (2009) or *Frost/Nixon* (2008). Much of the narrative of these films emphasizes the dangerous, glamorous investigation of hunches which then lead the heroic journalist protagonists to uncover dark secrets within the political world (Ehrlich, 2006; Good, 2008). Reporters have been turned – partially through the agency of such films – into a collective myth in which they represent the individual in mass society and are able to mobilize the power of the press to right injustices on behalf of those wronged individuals (Elliott, 1978: 187). In fact, the fictional representations of journalists have become ever more idealized at the same time as their real-life reception among the public has declined. Such a dichotomy between idealization and reality has never been too far away from both the practice and perception of journalists.

This tendency to create heroes out of individual journalists, both fictional and real, creates ideal types against which it is extremely difficult to measure up in the daily routines of work. It is a tendency amplified by powerful narrators and representatives of journalism themselves. Often the history of journalism has been reduced to the glorified highlights and reminiscences of successful careers, narrated from the perspective and often from the pens of the owners and editors.

This tendency has been amplified now that more and more journalists are being encouraged to parade their market appeal as celebrities. The irony is that individual journalists have less opportunity to have a real impact in this idealized way as they become more prominently displayed as personalities across corporate media. Celebrity journalists because of their fame have far less chance of mounting serious investigative work. The development of the news journalist on television into a major national figure was probably the catalyst of this trend. Overall, however, the role of television journalists is characteristic of changes in journalism in general. They have moved swiftly from being able to provide probing questions and a sustained investigation, particularly in current affairs journalism, to supplying more personality/

populist entertainment approaches to the mainstream news. This trend has accelerated since Wapping with an increasingly entertainment agenda within a largely deregulated market that is eager for personalities to hang stories on. The celebrity journalist has become a stand-in for a more thorough and consistent investigative journalism.

A contemporary solution to this combination of the need to retain some radical investigative content to journalism with the inflation of the importance of the individual journalist in current affairs broadcasting can be seen in the campaign for a 'journalism of attachment' which seeks to question the traditional neutrality of the journalist. Martin Bell coined the expression, 'the journalism of attachment' in 1997 to describe a journalism:

> *that is aware of its responsibilities; and will not stand neutrally between good and evil, right and wrong, the victim and the oppressor. This is not to back one side or the other; it is to make the point that we in the press, and especially in television which is its most powerful division, do not stand apart from the world. We are part of it. We exercise a certain influence and we have to know that. The influence may be for the better or for worse, and we have to know that too. (Bell, 1997: 8)*

Contemporary journalism has a marked tendency to show more interest in the private lives of politicians and their husbands and wives than in the wider implications of public policy. Investigative journalism must occasionally be seen, for the sake of its own reputation, to be instrumental in exposing wrong-doing in high places, but stretched resources in a competitive, commercial environment and rolling news agendas militate against such sustained investigation. Successful investigative journalism – by which we mean sustained investigative journalism within the mainstream – becomes less likely the more that mainstream becomes commodified. Once investigative and critical journalism become edged out, the role and reputation of the journalist drift further away from their idealized public service. This structural shift in the work of journalists is well captured in the following:

> *... we believe that the pendulum has moved (and is still moving) away from the model of journalists as free professional agents towards a model of journalists increasingly beset and hemmed in by an array of different structural demands. (Barnett and Gaber, 2001: 2)*

Some would go still further, such as one of the most prominent spokespersons for the public relations industry, Julia Hobsbawm, who considers journalism's failure to engage with the realities of contemporary public communication flow as revealing that:

> *journalism has become, like the Emperor with no clothes, that most gullible of all entities: the organisation that believes it is immune from criticism or fault. (2006: 129)*

This is all in stark contrast with the high aspirations and tradition of high-flown rhetoric emanating from the industry itself – the 'freedom of the press' and the role of journalism in maintaining a healthy democracy, 'holding authority to account', 'watchdog function', 'telling truth to power' – and with the rather grubbier reality of providing information for profit as pragmatically as possible. But journalism needs more substantive evidence for its own contribution to the public good to counter-act the all-pervasive substance which informs the public's mistrust of many of its practitioners.

Conclusion

The hero or celebrity status of certain individual journalists and the fictional representation of journalists' work as campaigning against the powerful, as crusaders on behalf of the public and truth itself, need to be considered against the grubbier representations and diminishing status of the journalist. There is a degree of recognition that a perspective needs to be developed which is able to harness both idealism and pragmatism if journalism is going to be able to attain a level of public appreciation which, at its best, it would appear to deserve. Journalists' own resistance to thinking more laterally is captured as part of the problem by Monck when he admits: 'As journalists, we tend to sneer at intellectualism and value pragmatism', while concluding that as a profession it certainly needs, 'a little more philosophy and a little less marketing' (2008: 18). One of the best ways to do this is by concentrating on the core strength of journalism which Kovach and Rosenstiel identify as 'sense-making based on synthesis, verification and fierce independence' (2001: 197) while recognizing its responsibilities to the public it purports to serve to a far greater extent.

Despite the recognition that journalism needs to engage more consistently with the public as demonstrated by the successful experiments in public journalism in the USA (Haas, 2005) and also to professionalize – including raising its game with regard to engaging with education on a sustained basis – it is often the very institutions which journalism chooses to be judged by which act to draw more suspicion down upon its ability or even desire to police its own product in a socially and politically responsible way, as was highlighted with regard to the activities of the PCC by Moore:

> The PCC regulates newspapers on behalf of the industry, but it is, at best, a smokescreen to prevent government regulation and has no power either to promote standards or even to review them. (2006: 50)

As the demand for many of the products of traditional journalism and the business model for much commercial journalism continue to fragment, credibility among the public – as both citizens and consumers – is now a matter of economic survival as much as of professional respectability. Both extremes of the binary division of the hack and the hero are ultimately unhelpful for an area of public communication of such importance for the health of democratic culture.

FURTHER READING

Allen, R. (2005) 'Preparing reflective practitioners', in R. Keeble (ed.) *Print Journalism: A Critical History*. Abingdon, Oxon: Routledge. pp. 317–328. Giving an account of how journalism education has provided an attempt to professionalize in the second half of the twentieth century, this ponders the gains and drawbacks of such a process.

Deuze, M. (2005) 'What is journalism? Professional identity and ideology of journalists reconsidered', *Journalism: Theory, Practice and Criticism*, 6 (4): 442–464. Based on research on interview accounts of how journalists themselves view their practice in the present, this gives a rigorous grounding in the contemporary theoretical debate surrounding the state of journalism as public communication.

Elliott, P. (1978) 'Professional ideology and organisational change: the journalist since 1800', in G. Boyce, J. Curran and P. Wingate (eds), *Newspaper History: From the 17th Century to the Present Day*. London: Constable. pp. 172–191. This gives a well-balanced account of the tensions inherent in the professionalization process.

Gopsill, T. and Neale, G. (2008) *Journalists: 100 Years of the NUJ*. London: Profile. This gives an account of the increasing political and cultural engagement of journalists from a perspective which tends towards the 'heroic', but which is nevertheless an important contribution to the organizational history of journalists in the UK as well as an interesting demonstration of their collective identification through their practice.

11

Local Journalism

Introduction

We shall finish this book by having a brief look at local journalism. For the purposes of clarity we will use the term 'local' to incorporate all forms of journalism which are not the London-based, British, national variant. The location of local journalism at the end of the book is intended to draw attention to the plight of this variety of journalism as an exception to the book's general narrative. This chapter will claim that local journalism differs in its development to that of other forms of journalism across the twentieth century. Whereas the main argument here has been that journalism has not declined from a golden age but is merely mutating to adapt to changing, technological, political and economic circumstances, it will now be asserted that local journalism is not only in a qualitative as well as a quantitative decline, but also in danger of eradication with drastic consequences for democracy at the level of the local community.

Through the twentieth century, local newspapers had played a profitable part in the articulation of local politics and local identities, as well as providing the typical first step on the career ladder for many aspiring journalists. However, their exploitation by large media monopolies, wanting to maximize advertising revenue, has reached a point where the journalism itself has come under severe pressure to fulfil the role which had provided its unique selling point – namely providing the sort of information and commentary at a local level which is unavailable elsewhere. Yet online developments, which are destroying the traditional business model for advertising on which these newspapers depended, have meant that even this restricted function of the local newspaper as a carrier of local advertising is in jeopardy. The chapter will also consider the changing roles of both local BBC and commercial broadcasters and the pressures on them to maintain a counterpart to the national output.

The Arrival of the Local

The localness of local newspapers lay in nothing other than the fact that they were printed locally (Franklin, 1997: 76). For almost one hundred years, from their first regular appearance at the start of the eighteenth century, their journalism was anything but local. Throughout most of that century they comprised a weekly digest of news from London, brought in on the posts, astutely combined with a selection of adverts for local products. Walker (2006: 376–377) has observed that it was only from the 1780s onwards that local news began being refracted through the political opinions of a wide selection of local politicians across the land. One of the first newspapers to do this was Benjamin Flower's *Cambridge Intelligencer* from 1793 which developed an editorial on the cause of Reform at this time. Complementary to this trend, Cranfield (1978: 188–189) has charted the rise of radical, working-class, provincial newspapers which made a vibrant contribution to political debate. Soon all major towns and cities and rural areas with a common identity were able to boast their own politically-affiliated newspapers, and as their commercial success grew so they shifted towards a more moderate range of political views.

By the middle years of the nineteenth century, the local newspaper was providing increasingly opinionated local news to a locally targeted readership (Walker, 2006: 378). When these newspapers were able to add access to national and international news via the telegraph from the late 1850s to their unrivalled local coverage, they reached their commercial and political peak with many becoming daily publications. The setting-up of the Press Association in 1868 consolidated this supply of news. By 1907 there were 1,338 provincial newspaper titles outside London according to *Mitchell's Newspaper Press Directory* for that year, and these had developed a characteristic local commitment couched in terms of 'a parish-pump patriotism' (Franklin and Murphy, 1991: 56). From this peak we can witness a decline, not just in the number but also in the quality and impact of the journalism of local newspapers. As in many other aspects of modern journalism's history, this came as a direct consequence of the growth in mass popular newspapers from the 1890s onwards.

The Peak of the Market: Consolidation

On the cusp of the twentieth century, local newspapers were a flourishing business and one which had developed a blend of local politics and national news that was attractive and useful to their target audience. The arrival of a mass circulation daily press from 1896 was to lead to a rapid decline in both the number and eventually a scaling back of the ambition of these local newspapers (Walker, 2006: 384). This trend was consolidated as the new mass market press barons began to acquire titles across the country and to bring these together as part of a rationalization of news provision. But what was the effect on the journalism these newspapers contained? The content of those papers which did adapt to survive reduced their coverage of national news, tailored for a local readership, and began to concentrate much more on local news. Another significant aspect of these newspapers had been that they had functioned as the prime source of political information for working-class readers (Franklin and Murphy, 1991: 55). The innovations in production methods and distribution under the corporate control of the press barons began to erode both their success and their popularity with this traditional base.

It was the scale of the success of these newspapers which from the end of the First World War made them so attractive to powerful business interests, yet inevitably the intensification in the chain ownership of local newspapers by the press barons – seeking economies of scale to further increase the profitability of their press holdings – had the effect of reducing the number and range of titles. As an illustration of this trend it has been calculated that, while in 1920, local morning and evening papers still sold a third more than the nationals, by 1923 these had been overtaken by the nationals and by 1945 were selling only half as many (Seymour-Ure, 1991: 16–17). Every area of newspaper provision during this period was hit by a reduction in titles, but while national morning newspapers were reduced from 12 to 9 the steepest decline by far came in the number of provincial morning newspapers which had borne the brunt of competition with the sleeker, more commercially honed national titles – these declined from 41 to 28 between 1927 and 1938 (Royal Commission, 1947–1949: 188). The number of provincial evening titles controlled by the five big chains (Harmsworth, Rothermere, the Berry brothers, and Lords Camrose and Kemsley) rose from 8 to 40 per cent between 1921 and 1937, while their ownership of the provincial morning titles increased from 12 to 44 per cent during the same period (Curran and Seaton, 2003: 39). The consequences of this process of consolidation were not only increased efficiency and profitability for the owners but less choice for local readers. The elimination of local competition meant that between 1921 and 1937 the number of towns with a choice of local evening paper fell from 24 to 10, while towns with a choice of morning paper declined from 15 to 7 (Curran and Seaton, 2003: 39).

The Royal Commission (1947–1949: 4) recorded that the national British titles tended to reflect the life and interests of three or four regions rather than the whole of the country, which meant that it was all the more important for the maintenance of a strong local press tradition to off-set this centralizing tendency. In 1947 Manchester's *Daily Dispatch* (475,000), the *Yorkshire Evening Post* (204,000), the *Birmingham Mail* (200,000) and the *Newcastle Journal* (146,000) (Seymour-Ure, 1991: 20) all gave authority and regional identity to their editorial content, as well as delivering this to a substantial readership base which underpinned their credibility. In 1947 all the London daily newspapers except *The Times*, the *Daily Mirror* and the *Daily Worker* maintained the tradition of printing large editions in Manchester, while the *Daily Mail* and *Daily Express* went one better and printed editions from Scotland with considerable differences in domestic news content. These two continued with their Scottish operations until 1966 and 1974 respectively (Seymour-Ure, 1991: 19).

However, a significant moment for the strength and prestige of local newspapers came when the *Manchester Guardian* moved its headquarters from Manchester to London and removed 'Manchester' from its title in 1959 – in recognition of the fact that it was read by more people outside the Manchester region than within it – and allied to this was the realization that advertisers would pay a higher premium for inclusion in a national title. Further erosions came as other editorial and production facilities outside England were closed down. The *Scottish Daily Express* closed in

1974 under pressure from the *Daily Record* (acquired by the Mirror Group in 1955) and the *Daily Mail* withdrew from its Edinburgh offices in 1966. The emerging tendency over the middle decades of the century was for a national journalism which reinforced the impression that the affairs of the UK were those of the inhabitants of the South East of England in general and London in particular. After 1955 regional commercial television provided further competition for local newspapers, both in its attractiveness to advertisers and its need to develop its own style of authenticity and intimacy with local audiences in its local news bulletins and magazines as a competitor to the style of the local newspaper.

New Technology and the Local Press

Murdoch's move to Wapping in 1986 changed the national and local newspaper scene, but it was encouraged if not enabled by changes first established in 1983 on a group of local free newspapers. The National Graphical Association closed-shop dispute with the free-newspaper Messenger Group in Warrington in 1983 demonstrated how a newspaper proprietor could take on the hitherto intimidatingly powerful print unions and introduce new technologies into the printing process on his own terms. Eddie Shah emerged from his industrial confrontation with the pickets with exactly what he wanted, and the printers were placed on new and more restrictive contracts. As a direct consequence of Shah's entrepreneurial dynamism and his ability to feed off a political atmosphere which was hostile to organized labour, between December 1985 and autumn 1987 direct input facilities were introduced into all Thomson regional news centres (Franklin and Murphy, 1991: 14).

These cumulative changes in the technological and employment environment meant that by the mid-1990s, as entrepreneurial proprietors saw the potential for increased profitability in the local newspaper market, there was a very rapid consolidation of the sector into large multi-media groups (Aldridge, 2003: 498). Local newspapers were ripe for a second wave of consolidation which ultimately had implications for the quality of local journalism overall. This period also witnessed an abrupt move away from a long tradition of local ownership with a social informative goal, paid for by local and often classified advertising to a conglomerate ownership with less interest in the specifics of local communities. By the mid-1990s, for example, over 60 per cent of the British local press had come to be owned by the ten largest companies, with more than 80 per cent owned by the top 15 companies (Franklin, 1997: 108). Making local newspapers more profitable came at the cost of staffing-level reductions and more reliance on news agencies and public-relations sources (Cole and Harcup, 2009: 54–55). Local newspapers have, as a consequence, quickly come to have less local news and to contain less news overall.

The situation for local newspapers was exacerbated by the growth in free newspapers from the late 1960s which – driven by the technological and political factors mentioned above – had by the mid-1980s mushroomed to the extent that they were outselling the paid-for weeklies (Seymour-Ure, 1991: 54). They peaked at 42 million in 1989 (Franklin, 2006: 154) and were to provide the model for the successful launch of the *Metro* in London in 1999 and its subsequent regional variants, with a highly standardized product that was wholly reliant on information accessible from a computer terminal, wrapped around its advertising core and described eloquently by Franklin as 'McDonaldized papers' (2006: 160).

As well as technological changes and changing patterns of ownership, there were also wider social and cultural changes behind the demise of a local newspaper readership. These papers, particularly the local evening newspapers, had relied heavily on patterns of behaviour that were rapidly becoming obsolete (i.e. large numbers of men leaving work at the same hour each day and either buying an evening paper and reading it on the way home or sitting down to read a home-delivered copy while waiting for their evening meal) (Aldridge, 2003: 492). Once this vanishing constituency came into contact with the collapse of the local small ad market, especially under the impact of online advertising, then a vicious circle of decline had set in.

Local newspapers are still an essential, if diminishing, element of local democracy, and they continue to provide both at least the potential for an extended sense of community (Aldridge, 2003) and a greater empathy with the sensibilities of their readers than the national press (Aldridge, 2007: 143), but despite this their content has been marked by a reduced coverage of local politics, particularly at the time of local elections (Franklin and Richardson, 2002; Franklin et al., 2006). This reduction has been assessed as diminishing overall local accountability. The contemporary crisis pertaining to the journalism of local newspapers is expressed by Franklin et al. when we read:

> *while local newspapers are highly successful businesses, the contribution of critical local journalism to local political communications and a flourishing local democracy is less evident than it was a decade ago. (2006: i).*

Regional Television Journalism

The BBC has never been quick to move in the direction of providing a fully local variety of journalism. This is probably rooted in its historical drive to encapsulate a more inclusive national constituency. It was only after the Beveridge Report's 1951 criticisms of the BBC's centralized complacency that the corporation began, belatedly, to engage with journalism produced for and within local communities. Yet even this forced-conversion to local programming was only truly energized by the creation of the ITV regional network from 1955. Despite the fact that the ITV regions were demarcated less according to popular needs than by the convenience of the market (Curran and Seaton, 2003: 182), ITV had regional broadcasting at the heart of its operation from its inception. The quality and ambition of the licensees' regional programming, particularly news and current affairs, had always been key determinants in the award and retention of licences (Tait, 2006: 28), and these institutions used their regional news programmes to develop strong local identities which were good for branding the specificity of their service, and had the additional advantage of holding viewers into their early evening schedules and thus stealing a march on the ratings of their public service rival, the BBC. It was as late as 1964 that the BBC launched the first of its own regional news magazines with BBC Midlands. In fact, ITV remained the dominant player in regional broadcasting from its creation in 1955 until the end of the 1990s, by which point the deregulation set in train by the Broadcasting Acts of 1990 and 1996 had had inevitable effects on the quality of their provision, especially in terms of current affairs journalism.

One other consequence of the deregulatory broadcast acts of 1990 and 1996 was the increasing unaffordability of providing as much regional news and current affairs coverage as had once been the case, given that the new licence holders had been forced into providing bids based on cost-effectiveness rather than the quality or range of provision. Regulatory requirements that each regional station of ITV must provide programming of a quality and range that could demonstrate an ability to 'inform, educate and entertain' its particular regional audience have been interpreted with an increasingly lighter touch since the 1990 Broadcasting Act. In an attempt, for commercial reasons, to reshape the timing of their news services at both national and local levels in 1997, the ITV networks shifted their news to later in the evening, across the board, with disastrous consequences for viewing figures. Audiences, by choosing to tune in elsewhere in increasing numbers, intuitively followed the trend of a disinvestment in commercial television's provision of journalism which was clearly being reflected in the quality of the output. As a direct consequence, by the early twenty-first century the BBC was reported by Ofcom to be spending more on its regional news provision than ITV for the first time since the latter's creation (Ofcom, 2004: 57–62). This dramatic turnaround came shortly after (from December 1998), according to the trade magazine *Broadcast*; the BBC had invested £21 million in building up its news and current affairs operations so as to match the new national constitutional arrangements. A new newsroom and 40 additional staff were placed with the Welsh Assembly; an extra 50 staff were located to cover the Scottish parliament; and an additional 30 staff were allocated to cover the Northern Ireland operations (7 July 2000, 16).

In a comparative analysis of two northern competitors – the BBC's *Look North* and ITV's *Calendar* – Gillian Ursell found that while sharing a chatty style, a man–woman celebrity presenter format and content which avoids overloading the programme with negative stories about the region, the commercial variant is inferior in the number of items as well as the length and depth of reports (2001: 189–190). Under pressure to make a profit in an increasingly difficult economic environment, the quality of journalism on commercial television is in a demonstrable decline, and given the historical role which ITV had hitherto played in catalysing the BBC's own quality of output it will, in all probability, lead to a reduction in quality at the BBC in the longer term. The implications of light regulatory control of a commercial journalism under pressure to reduce costs in order to maintain profitability during a period of starkly reduced advertising revenue are laid out by Julian Petley:

Ofcom's track record in holding ITV to any of its PSB obligations is not exactly encouraging, to put it at its mildest. Nor is a comparison between The Ownership of News *and Ofcom's* Annual Report 2007/2008, *which were published virtually simultaneously. For while the former repeatedly recommends that Ofcom plays a stronger role in protecting the public interest in broadcasting matters, the latter, with its breathless bromides about 'citizens and consumers reaping the benefits of competition' and paeons to the communications cornucopia in which apparently we all now live, reads like souped-up Comet or Curry's catalogues with intellectual pretensions. (2008: 24)*

Local Radio Journalism

It was another critical report on the performance of the BBC in relation to its provision of local and regional journalism (Pilkington, 1962) which recommended the development of a series of local radio broadcasters under the organization of the BBC. This would eventually lead to the introduction of local radio stations starting with Radio Leicester in 1967. Until then, radio journalism had remained an almost exclusively London-centred exercise despite the advances of FM technology in the late 1950s and early 1960s which could have provided local broadcasting significantly earlier. By 1970, 20 local stations were broadcasting to approximately 70 per cent of the population. The Sound Broadcasting Act 1972 made provision for an Independent Local Radio, with 60 licences granted by the end of 1973 and a regulatory watchdog to monitor its quality – the Independent Broadcast Authority. Regionally, these provided less hard-news and more light good-news about 'your area' and given that the imperative for these stations was to earn advertising revenue, talk and music were cheaper options that sustained and serious journalism.

Since 2003, according to Starkey and Crisell (2009: 48), there has been an emerging Ofcom policy of judging the performance of the local stations by 'output' rather than 'process'. The consequence of this is that if local issues and events are covered to the satisfaction of the audience (a consumer- rather than a criteria-approach to quality control), then it matters little how the information has been gathered. This has encouraged the outsourcing of news-gathering to 'news-hubs' which are able to provide cheaper customized bulletins to large numbers of different stations across whole regions of the country. They provide a journalism which is less likely to have been compiled via any sort of engagement with local people and much more likely to have been generated through the recycling of press release material.

The Scottish Experience

Scotland has had a distinct range of journalism, from the *Scottish Dove* of the civil war of the seventeenth century through to the political reviews of the early nineteenth century. The *Edinburgh Review* (1802–1929) and *Blackwood's Magazine* (1817–1980) both played a significant part in the shaping of the tradition of the great intellectual reviews of the nineteenth century which did so much to generate a journalism which was to crystallize political opinions and literary tastes in Britain and beyond. A radical tradition in Scottish journalism continued into the twentieth century with the weekly *Forward* (1906–1956) and the *People's Journal*, printed in Dundee, which was selling 250,000 copies a week at the time of the First World War. The *West Highland Free Press*, founded in 1972, was a youthful addition to this tradition both in its editorial personnel and its populist approach to a regional weekly newspaper which combined local news with fresh perspectives on broader issues. Including its best known national metropolitan titles, the *Glasgow Herald* (launched as the *Glasgow Advertiser* in 1783) and the *Scotsman* (1817), Scotland has retained, as noted by McNair, 'a public sphere of exceptional richness' (2006: 38), with ten newspapers possessing a national reach and further morning and evening newspapers serving all the major cities as well as a wide range of more local papers. Television services include BBC Scotland, as well as the commercial Borders TV, Grampian TV and Scottish TV. BBC Radio Scotland provides a distinct Scottish public service broadcasting, and the commercial Saga and Clyde FM provide the usual minimal amount of local news we have come to expect on commercial stations for Scottish audiences.

The *Scottish Record* became the leading Scottish morning newspaper in the 1970s with a circulation of over 700,000. Two elite Sunday papers were also launched and still continue successfully – *Scotland on Sunday* (1988) and the *Sunday Herald* (1999). In general, though, the picture is one of a declining market for Scottish national titles, often on account of ownership changes and related business strategies. In the 1970s Scottish-based titles accounted for 64 per cent of a daily sale of 1.7 million and 66 per cent of Sunday sales of 2.7 million in Scotland. However, by 2006 these sales had reduced to 1.5 and 1.6 million respectively (Hutchison, 2008: 66). This was in large part due both to the aggressive inroads made by English-based newspapers creating their own 'tartanized' editions and to the arrival of a localized version of the free newspaper, the *Metro*. All the Murdoch titles plus the *Scottish Daily Mail* were the chief players in this trend. By 2006 the *Scottish Sun* had overtaken its rivals in Scotland, particularly the traditionally Labour-inclined *Daily Record*, reflecting what McNair has summarized as 'a change in the country's political culture' (2008b: 229). The change in emphasis – inevitable within such a shift from Scottish-based titles to London-based ones – has also (according to a 2006 survey conducted by Michael Higgins on the elections to the devolved Scottish parliament) demonstrated that it was in the diminishing Scottish-based press that there was a discussion of the ongoing process of political representation, whereas the London-based titles were more concerned about the bare facts of the outcome itself.

It has become a common and understandable reaction to interpret the decline in Scotland's national press as having dramatic consequences for the post-devolution political debate on the future of the country. At a time when one might expect leading national newspapers to be at the forefront of such discussions, the *Scotsman* and the *Glasgow Herald* had historic low-points in terms of circulation and *Scotland on Sunday* is currently being outsold in Scotland by the *Sunday Times* (ABC, February 2008). Macmillan (2008: 36) puts this down to the new owners, the Johnston Press (*Scotsman*) and Newsquest (*Herald*), having stripped resources to the point where quality journalism is practically impossible to sustain. He quotes Tom Devine – the Sir William Fraser Professor of Scottish History at Edinburgh University and a widely acknowledged authority on modern Scotland – as saying that there is a grave danger that this may lead to a democratic deficit in discussions about Scotland's political future (2008: 41).

Broadcasting Devolution in Scotland

The early BBC had developed regionally-based transmitters but their location had much more to do with the physical logistics of broadcasting throughout the British Isles and therefore did little but pay lip service to any local or regional agendas, let alone anything approaching alternative national audiences within what was still presented as an unproblematically homogeneous nation. It was only after 1945 that the Scottish Home Service was granted its own wavelength (McDowell, 1992: 92).

After the 1954 Broadcasting Act STV was the first Scottish franchise and from 1957 this was followed by Border and Grampian in 1961, meaning that ITV's service was from this point available across the whole of Scotland. In 1978, again under pressure from commercial developments, BBC Radio Scotland was launched. Yet there have always been legitimate concerns about the implications of centralizing tendencies for Scottish journalism as the SNP's submission to the Annan Committee in 1974 made clear:

> *So long as BBC London and the ITV Big Five dominate programme schedules and sign the cheques, Scottish broadcasting will remain provincial. (McDowell, 1992: 225)*

One illustration of the persistence of these concerns about London-centrism in the provision of broadcast journalism for Scotland came a year before formal devolution in 1999, when there was a heated controversy which has continued to define the BBC's attitude and that of the British government to Scottish autonomy over its national broadcast journalism. The 'Scottish Six' would have entitled Scotland to its own hour of news from six until seven in the early evening, but it was feared that this would fatally compromise the common experience of UK news which the BBC feels it needs to provide as part of its statutory obligations as a national broadcaster (Schlesinger et al., 2001). Although Scotland has *Reporting Scotland* on the BBC and *Scotland Today* on commercial television as regional appendages, centralization has financial as well as political implications, meaning that resources for Scottish journalism continue to be dominated by decision making in London with regard to the BBC and hard market compromises regarding the commercial sector.

Journalism in Wales: Community and Identity

It is perhaps not surprising that similar issues have plagued the development of broadcast journalism in Wales. Beveridge (1951) recommended the strengthening of regional development towards the other constituent nations of the UK after the 1945 restructuring of the BBC. Northern Ireland, Wales and Scotland were to be allowed more public service provision relating to their areas, culminating in the eventual launch of BBC Radio Wales in 1964. Given the importance of the Welsh language to national and cultural identities in Wales, it was disappointing that the first sustained experiments in Welsh-language broadcasting had to wait for a commercial broadcaster – Swansea Sound – to begin to pioneer Welsh-language transmissions from 1974. The BBC eventually responded in 1977 and Radio Cymru was launched as a dual Welsh/English service. Currently, Radio Ceredigion and Champion FM are the commercial stations with the highest profile Welsh-language provision. However, in addition to the language question, a further challenge for both state and commercial broadcasters in Wales has been in finding a means to encompass the national aspirations within the framework of local requirements, since regional and local broadcasting in Wales has always been interpreted on a national level thus leaving the more localized aspects of community life in the country neglected. These gaps in broadcast provision are largely down to similar concerns to those of the Scots – that ultimately these cultural and political decisions are driven by finance and controlled from a London-centric media world (Lewis and Booth, 1989), reflecting a history of subservience to London-based decision making which has been understandably interpreted as directly undermining the appreciation of a distinctive Welsh identity (Bevan, 1984: 109).

Welsh provision was not a priority for ITV so it was not until 1958 that Television Wales and West started broadcasting. ITV provided Television Wales and the West (TWW) from 1958 for South Wales and the west of England, and Granada covered parts of North Wales. Wales (West and North) Television Ltd (WWN), or *Teledu Cymru* as it was known in Welsh, was the Independent Television company (ITV) that broadcast to the west and north of Wales between 1962 and 1963 (Medhurst, 2004: 119). From as far back as the 1950s, however, there had been pressure for a separate Welsh provision in television which was applied over two decades of direct political action and included the switching off of broadcast transmitters and the threat of a hunger strike by *Plaid Cymru* politician Gwynfor Evans. This was to eventually persuade the government to accede and launch S4C from 1982 (Barlow et al., 2005: 134–136). This was also to lead to an increase by the BBC in Welsh language provision. S4C (*Sianel Pedwar Cymru*) was built on the belief that a mediated form of communication could help save the Welsh language from its historical decline and in doing so this would boost the self-esteem of the national community (Bevan, 1984: 128–151).

From 1999 the Welsh Assembly provided the beginnings of a route to public accountability for the news media in Wales, which are making attempts to address the long heritage of cultural and communicative deficits there (Barlow et al., 2005: 22). Thomas (2006: 57) has charted the discrepancy between print journalism and broadcast journalism in representing a national and linguistic identity, with the press by-and-large restricted to local and regional coverage while broadcast journalism is predominantly national without much in the way of a regional or local focus. Jones (1993) has accounted historically for the demise of the Welsh language newspaper tradition and the overwhelming influence of English-based newspapers on the development of journalism in Wales, from the incursions of the major English chains in the last decades of the nineteenth century, especially from Liverpool and Manchester in the north of the country, and from 1869 the *Western Mail* in the south. In Wales journalism appears to have been the victim of a technological divide in the provision of newspapers and broadcasting. Thomas cites studies which conclude that there is a worryingly high reliance on English-based newspapers (Mackay and Powell, 1996; Talfan Davies, 1999) and that this is in stark contrast to the positive role of broadcast journalism in boosting a sense of Welsh national identity particularly through the medium of the Welsh language (Davies, 1994). Yet as an illustration of the potential of print at the other end of the range from the macronational, at a micronational level, one unique feature of the Welsh journalism landscape is the strength of the *papura bru*, the Welsh-language community newspapers, 13 of which were established between 1973 and 2001 (Barlow et al., 2005: 40) to provide a local, vernacular take on community and even family affairs. The *Western Mail* and the *Daily Post* have often claimed to have a remit as national newspapers but they do not have nationwide readerships and have traditionally been short on discussions of national political life. In terms of contemporary political discussion through the press the Welsh *Mirror* was launched in the 1990s with a remit to represent the whole of Wales, but this folded in 2003 with the consequence that there is now an absence of any newspaper coverage of Welsh political and cultural life in its totality – a situation which further disengages the electorate from Welsh policy makers (Thomas, 2003/4: 27).

Conclusion

There is widespread evidence that regional, local and other national communities within the UK are vanishing from the agenda of both state-funded and commercial providers of journalism. Profit or the desire for easy audience satisfaction is driving this provision towards a lowest-common-denominator approach which tends to serve actual existing communities or localities less and less and prefers to provide for commercially constructed communities instead. In terms of local newspapers Aldridge (2003: 492) has remarked, for instance, on the absence of an ethnic identification or discussion of the complexities of national identity despite the composition of the British population having shifted dramatically over the last fifty years. There is consequently little attempt being made to engage in a real news agenda with actual inhabitants of towns and cities in the way of the USA experiment with public journalism (Haas, 2005). Despite sharing the scepticism of the traditional claims of the local press to enhance local democracy, given its in-built preference for solutions which favour the status quo (Murphy, 1976: 31), Aldridge (2003: 506) still maintains that these newspapers can have a unique potential in the local public sphere with a capacity to influence the terms of popular debate. Losing them would impact on the abilities of local people to have their real concerns aired and debated in a public forum, and localities would rapidly become homogenized towards a flatter version of a commercially acceptable variant of Britain with less and less local or regional differentiation.

Broadcasting has suffered a similar fate with local and regional commitments being scaled back and little investigative current affairs work being undertaken. Cosy local identifications are preferred to challenging stereotypical depictions of communities while reductions in overall budgets reduce the range of perspectives on offer, leaving the least controversial to predominate. Local and regional broadcasting had been allowed through regulatory supervision to develop strong current affairs programming as well as strong regional identities. The decline in commercial provision under contemporary financial pressures will ultimately scale back the perceived need for the BBC to compete in this area and damage the provision of local journalism overall.

FURTHER READING

Aldridge, M. (2007) *Understanding the Local Media.* Maidenhead: Open University Press. This is a first-rate account of the processes and politics at stake in this vital area of journalism.

Barlow, D.M., Mitchell, P. and O'Malley, T. (2005) *The Media in Wales: Voices of a Small Nation.* Cardiff: University of Wales Press, and Blain, N. and Hutchison, D. (eds) (2008) *The Media in Scotland.* Edinburgh: Edinburgh University Press. These give authoritative overviews of the history, debates and policies which have shaped journalism in these countries.

Franklin, B. (ed.) (2006) *Local Journalism and Local Media: Making the News Local.* Abingdon, Oxon: Routledge. This continues the work of this author in highlighting an area of journalism which would otherwise be a neglected backwater despite its importance for the democratic process.

Walker, A. (2006) Special Issue on provincial journalism, *Journalism Studies*, 7 (3). This is an interesting range of essays which shed light on the development of local journalism across two centuries, with due consideration for the variety of its manifestations and motivations.

Conclusion

History and the Spectrum of Journalism

So what has this book attempted to do? It has charted the history of journalism over the twentieth and the beginning of the twenty-first centuries. In doing so it has argued that we should begin our survey a little earlier than the century itself, to look at a longer twentieth century. It has taken this approach in order to consider the build up to the launch of the first mass market daily newspaper in 1896 as a key date in the evolution of journalism. It is hoped that the book has shown that many of the continuities, as well as many of the changes, which help us in defining journalism predate even the pivotal year of 1896. These processes of change and resistance to change in journalism have always been fundamentally anchored within the cultural and economic expectations that owners and consumers have had of them. From mass literacy and Northcliffe's exploitation of the tastes of the new reading public, to the incorporation of the rise of the permissive society and the permeation of a celebrity culture, journalism has continued to respond to popular markets based on profitability for increasingly corporatized ownerships and also as a factor in shaping the contours of the society we live in.

It would be tempting for simplicity's sake to align with certain contemporary anxieties which claim that we have moved from a period of great stability in journalism to one of great turmoil – that is to say, to contrast a coherent past with a fragmenting present. The only problem is that even an introductory history of journalism such as this clearly demonstrates that it is simply not the case. Journalism has consisted of a diverse, competing and sometimes contradictory set of practices over the past one hundred years, and while there are elements of cohesion within some of those individual and institutional narratives there is simply no overriding uniformity across what are multiple paths of development.

The schematic nature of the book was designed to place particular narratives of journalism within an overall chronology. This was to provide useful comparisons between the mainstream and the margins and between technological and cultural questions of how journalism has adapted to challenges over time. Throughout, there has been an emphasis on bringing these historical accounts into contact with the latest research on contemporary discussions on the nature and future of journalism.

The book started from the view that economics have determined the shape of journalism and have indeed driven the changes within its mainstream practices. Ownership and control of journalism institutions have certainly played their part in ensuring that journalism fits as efficiently as possible within the machinery of advanced capitalism. At the same time this commercialized operation has needed to provide a variety of output aimed at a range of national audiences. While doing this it has had to maintain profitability as well as its reputation in providing what its audience will pay for. It was noted throughout the book that it is in this variety of offering that journalism's resilience lies. At the same time as providing market appeal, journalism has had to live up to expectations of its practice which have developed in stature over time – as a means of challenging the powerful in society, righting wrongs, and exposing both scandal in high places as well as crime and destitution in the dark corners of our society.

Recent changes in the formats of media output generally have led some to observe that there has been a blurring of genres and even an erosion of the distinctions between journalism and non-journalism (Blumler and Gurevitch, 2000: 155–172). Yet the evidence provided by a historical perspective demonstrates that this diversity and interaction between news media genres is part of a longer process of what we might term 'spectrum journalism'. However, while acknowledging that this range of communication styles has existed over a long period, at the same time we might qualify this by acknowledging that contemporary journalism is characterized by a spectrum which blurs rather than stabilizes.

An early appreciation of the range of that spectrum journalism – from serious political campaigning and investigative reporting to a form of popular entertainment at the end of a hard day's work – came in the note from Newnes to Stead in 1890, as mentioned at the start of the book, so it is appropriate that we finish by considering some of the implications for this spectrum as it has evolved during the course of over a hundred years. It start as a two-dimensional spectrum in print media where journalism could be found at the elite end of this spectrum or at any point across it. First technology, and with it speed, added two more dimensions to the spectrum reach of journalism, and the way in which this evolves in a market economy has been the story of journalism's adaptation to the twentieth century. In the present, informed by a knowledge of the key events and discussions of the past, we can conclude – to borrow a phrase from Steel's highly insightful summary of the history of journalism – that not only has journalism changed but more importantly the 'idea of journalism' has changed, which means that by the time we reach our present considerations the topic under discussion will have shifted subtly but significantly. A historical perspective allows us to consider both the continuities and the changes within what we currently think of as journalism.

Journalism has up until very recently depended on centralizing our taste and consumption on behalf of large organizations. Now audiences are fragmenting. Yet the contemporary challenges that journalism faces threaten to take it beyond the spectrum and into unchartered territory. The interesting thing about the internet in its impact on journalism is that it has been introduced in the same historically grounded way as other previous technologies but with one difference – it threatens the destruction of the very public and the coherence of communication upon which journalism has been founded, from the business paradigm which was pioneered from

1896 as the high-point of Chalaby's profitable form of public discourse. Yet, much of the surviving elements of journalism would expect to be built very much in the image of what Carey defined as symbolic rather than informational forms of social communication which prioritize the community building aspects of journalism over its purely informational content. Over the past hundred years we have seen that journalism functions best when it supplements the provision of news with the construction of a sense of community and social empathy.

The longer argument of the book would be that journalism has survived by mutating according to the commercial, political and technological shifts in the society it is reporting. Journalism's claims to political and social utility have therefore not remained static. What enables journalism to be defined in particular ways at particular historical junctures, and what has enabled it to retain a certain amount of continuity across the period this book has covered while the technological and cultural conditions have changed so dramatically, have been the main issues underpinning our enquiry.

Deuze (2007: 140), a commentator very rooted in the present, claims provocatively that 'Journalism as it is, is coming to an end'. There is a deliberate ambiguity in this phrase which invites us to consider this statement in light of the events covered by this book. The commercial and technological forces which brought journalism into the particularly successful configuration which had endured for much of the twentieth century have now intensified to such a point that journalism has been required to undergo a radical reappraisal of many of the functions which it had come to consider as core to its practice. In historical terms, journalism may have always been coming to an end and it has continually been obliged to reconsider the ways it engages with technology, shifting audience demands and the imperatives of profit-making. Journalism 'as it is' in the present needs to be considered in terms of how it is able to maintain those core continuities from the past and how newer demands can be fitted within its core. This is not the end, more of a re-figuring of journalism.

This historical overview will have helped readers to focus on journalism's commercial, political and cultural potential and its achievements in those domains. It may even form part of broader discussions as to what journalism needs to be if it is to retain its ability to inform broader society across a range of communicative styles on the issues of the day as it has done so successfully in its past.

That history informs the present is perhaps a truism, but the more this book has probed journalism's past the more it has been forced into considerations of the present. As well as indicating the sedimentation of historical influences in present-day journalism and debates on its future, the book has illustrated that journalism is very much a range of communicative practices which remain rooted in the specifics of time and place.

A book such as this which attempts to provide a range of historical perspectives on contemporary journalism will, it is hoped, encourage us not only to appreciate its range and diversity but also to explore the ways it has been able to maintain a specific social function within more general media practice. Journalism has retained its identity as a form of cultural discourse (Dahlgren, 1988: 51; Langer, 1998: 155) as it has moved between different forms of output – from the mass newspapers and generalist magazines in the late nineteenth century which became so influential in the structuring of journalism overall, to the rival discourse of broadcast journalism as a public service which had a significant impact on all other forms of journalism. A longer view of lifestyle features and the popularization of mainstream journalism, for instance, culminating in the contemporary concentration on celebrity, confirms that these are common threads emanating from the nineteenth century. This sort of long view both dispels any claims that journalism is in a decline from a golden age and repositions it in the present as a much more pragmatic response to cultural, economic and technological challenges.

Chronology

1833	The word 'journalism' enters the English language
1855	Final lifting of duties on newspapers, the so-called 'taxes on knowledge'
1855	Launch of the *Daily Telegraph* to exploit the new market for newspapers
1881	George Newnes launches his revolutionary *Tit-Bits*
1884	W.T. Stead takes on the editorship of the *Pall Mall Gazette*
1896	Harmsworth launches the *Daily Mail*, which determines the future shape of journalism
1900	Influenced by the massive public success of the *Daily Mail*, Pearson launches the *Daily Express*
1903	*Motor* magazine launched
1903	*Daily Mirror* is launched, dedicated to a daily women's market
1905	Harmsworth (now Lord Northcliffe) buys the *Observer*
1907	National Union of Journalists formed
1907	*Votes for Women* first published
1908	Northcliffe buys *The Times*
1910	*My Weekly* launched as general magazine for working-class women
1911	*Daily Herald* started as a striker's news sheet
1914	*Women's Dreadnought* (Suffragettes' official paper) launched
1916	Reuters Telegram Company restructured as Reuters Limited under wartime government control
1918	*Daily Chronicle* bought by Liberal Prime Minister, Lloyd George
1922	*Good Housekeeping*
1922	Astor buys *The Times* on Northcliffe's death
1922	British Broadcasting Company – John Reith appointed as General Manager
1922	*The Times* introduces pictures, the last mainstream newspaper to do so
1923	Sykes Committee
1923	*Radio Times* first published
1924	The 'Zinoviev letter'
1925	BBC's long-wave transmitter completed at Daventry
1925	Communist Party launches the *Sunday Worker*, from 1930 as the *Daily Worker*
1925	Crawford Committee
1926	General Strike – the BBC provides news
1927	British Broadcasting Corporation

1927	Hilda Matheson Head of Talks at BBC
1928	*Daily Mail*'s insurance scheme triggers circulation wars
1929–1931	Beaverbrook and Rothermere create their own United Empire Party
1929	*The Week in Westminster* first aired on BBC
1929	*The Listener*
1930	Relaunch of *Daily Herald* by TUC and Odhams as populist, mass-market product
1932	BBC launches its Empire Service
1933	Chistiansen revolutionizes the layout of the *Daily Express*
1934	Relaunch of the *Daily Mirror*
1936	Godfrey Winn's 'Personality Parade' in the *Daily Mirror*
1936	NUJ Code of Professional Conduct approved at annual conference
1936	Listener Research Unit launched at the BBC
1936	Ullswater Committee
1936	BBC's first experiments with television broadcasting in London
1937	*Woman* relaunched, reconfiguring the commercial women's press in Britain
1937	Coronation of George VI televised
1938	*Picture Post* – photo-illustrated reporting with a social awareness
1941	*Daily Worker* suppressed
1942	BBC's News Division established to co-ordinate foreign correspondence
1944	Introduction of the '14-day rule' by the BBC to avoid encroaching upon discussions of legislation
1944	*War Report* attracts a regular audience of 10–15 million listeners
1945	'Vote for Him' campaign in the *Daily Mirror*
1946	*Woman's Hour* relaunched by the BBC to become its longest-running radio programme
1946	The return of television
1949	Royal Commission on the Press – recruitment, monopoly and complaints
1951	National Council for the Training of Journalists established
1951	Beveridge Report supports the BBC's continued monopoly
1952	More watch Coronation on television than listen to it on radio
1953	Press Council begins its work
1953	*Daily Mirror*'s coverage of Princess Margaret's relationship with Peter Townsend marks shift in reporting of Royal Family in British press
1953	The BBC introduces its current affairs flagship *Panorama*
1954	Conservatives overrule Beveridge's findings and introduce Television Bill which establishes independent commercial television
1955	Launch of ITN as populist competitor to the BBC
1956	End of newsprint rationing imposed during the war
1956	Associated Rediffusion airs *This Week* as a populist current affairs programme
1956	*Woman's Mirror*

1957	Mary Stott becomes editor of the women's pages on the *Guardian*
1957	Cliff Michelmore and *Tonight* – evening topical political magazine programme
1958	*Woman's Realm, Woman's Day*
1959	Hugh Greene appointed as Head of News at the BBC to counter ITN's innovations
1959	*Manchester Guardian* becomes the *Guardian* and is printed in London
1960	*Flair* launched as consumer-lifestyle women's magazine aimed at the youth market
1960	*News Chronicle* begins the wave of left-leaning national newspaper closures
1961	*Honey* continues the youth publication trend
1961	*Private Eye*
1962	*Sunday Times* colour supplement
1962	By this point television news has become the main news source for the majority of the country
1962	Royal Commission on the Press – finances and the concentration of ownership
1962	Pilkington Committee
1962	The *Scotsman* becomes the first newspaper to offer a Saturday magazine supplement
1962	Telstar satellite launched
1963	*Sunday Times* introduces magazine-style in-depth analysis with 'Insight'
1963	Granada broadcasts its own populist current affairs programme *World in Action*
1963	Television Act enforces a more robust role for the ITA in monitoring the public service remit of commercial television providers
1964	*Daily Herald* is latest casualty of advertising-driven newspaper market
1965	BBC World Service launched
1966	The *Daily Worker* becomes the *Morning Star*
1966	*The Times* puts news stories on the front page
1967	Closure of *Sunday Citizen* (previously *Reynolds' News*)
1967	*News at Ten*
1967	BBC Radio Leicester becomes the first local radio station
1967	The end of anonymity for journalists on *The Times*
1968	BBC Radio Nottingham hosts first radio phone-in
1968	Murdoch buys the *News of the World*
1968	Newspaper Proprietors' Association becomes Newspaper Publishers' Association
1969	*Nationwide* – BBC's nightly news digest from around the UK
1969	BBC and ITV start regular colour broadcasting

1969	Murdoch relaunches the *Sun* and revolutionizes the tabloid newspaper
1971	*Daily Mail* merges with the tabloid *Daily Sketch* and becomes tabloid itself
1971	David English becomes editor of the *Daily Mail*
1972	British version of *Cosmopolitan* launched
1972	*Weekend World* from London Weekend Television
1972	The ITA is renamed the IBA
1972	Sound Broadcasting Act enables establishment of commercial local radio stations
1973	Frances Cairncross becomes economics correspondent on the *Guardian*
1973	*Nottingham Evening Post* first to have directly typed input from journalists
1974	Teletext
1975	Peter Preston becomes editor of the *Guardian*
1975	Angela Rippon becomes first regular BBC news reader
1976	First regular radio broadcasting of parliamentary debate
1977	Royal Commission on the Press – structure and performance, privacy versus access
1978	Publication of *The Times* and the *Sunday Times* suspended for 11 months
1979	Annan Committee Report published; recommends *Channel 4 News* with high quality PBS news provision as rival to both ITN and the BBC
1981	Murdoch buys *The Times* and the *Sunday Times*
1981	*News of the World* launches its popular *Sunday* magazine
1981	Kelvin MacKenzie becomes editor of the *Sun*
1982	Channel 4 News launched
1983	Andrew Neil becomes editor of the *Sunday Times*
1983	Breakfast television news on both the BBC and ITV
1984	*Counter Information* – Edinburgh-based anarchist news sheet
1984	First woman political editor on a national daily – Julia Langdon on the *Daily Mirror*
1984	Messenger Group dispute with the NGA over electronic publishing technology
1985	Televising of the proceedings of the House of Lords
1985	Attempt to ban *Real Lives – At the Edge of the Union*
1986	Peacock Report published
1986	Wapping dispute
1986	Launch of the *Independent* and the *Sunday Sport* and *Today*
1987	John Birt takes over at the BBC – integrates news and current affairs
1987	Conrad Black takes over the Telegraph Group

1988	The *Daily Mail* overtakes the *Daily Mirror* as the second most read paper
1988	Patsy Chapman becomes editor of the *News of the World*
1988	The *Sun* pays £1 million in libel damages to Elton John
1988	*Death on the Rock* broadcast
1988 – 1994	Broadcasting ban on Irish 'extremists' on ITV and the BBC
1989	*Daily Express* and *Sunday Express* are the last newspapers to leave Fleet Street
1989	Televising of the House of Commons
1990	*Independent on Sunday* launched – heat-set printing on cheaper paper
1990	Calcutt Commission
1990	Broadcasting Act
1990	BSkyB launched
1991	Press Complaints Commission
1991	World Service Television (BBC World) launched
1992	Paul Dacre succeeds David English as editor of the *Daily Mail*
1992	Publication of BBC's paper 'Extending Choice'
1992	'It's the Sun Wot Won It' – general election
1992	Relaunch of a more dynamic, human-interest-oriented *News at Ten*
1992	*The Big Breakfast* on Channel 4
1992	*No Fixed Abode* on Granada
1993	IBA replaced by 'lighter touch' Independent Television Commission
1993	*Channel 4 News* to gain its own advertising revenue independent of ITV
1993	The *Observer* sold to the *Guardian*
1994	*The Day Today* – television news satire
1994	*SchNEWS* first published as weekly organ of radical journalism
1994	Radio Five Live
1996	Broadcasting Act established framework for digital developments, liberalized cross-ownership, introduced Broadcasting Standards Commission
1997	*BBC News 24*
1997	Chris Morris' news satire *Brass Eye*
1997	Channel Five launched – main news at 8.30, rolling hourly bulletins, lighter and more personal emphasis
1997	The 'journalism of attachment' debate – Martin Bell
1998	The BBC invests £21 million in preparing news and current affairs for devolved nations
1998	Devolution for Wales and Scotland
1999	*Metro* launched as the first national free newspaper
1999	*Indymedia* emerges from Seattle G8 protests to become leading alternative news site
2000	ITV *24 Hour News*

2002	The BBC 'dumbing down' debate
2002	BBC's digital television initiative
2003	*Independent* produced in tabloid format
2003	Communications Act
2003	First woman editor of a national popular daily – Rebekah Wade on the *Sun* – and *Tonight With Trevor McDonald* Launched
2007	Ofcom's 'New News, Future News' report

Bibliography

Adams, W.E. (1903) *Memoirs of a Social Atom* (2 vols). London: Hutchinson.

Adburgham, A. (1972) *Women in Print: Women Writing and Women's Magazines from the Restoration to the Accession of Victoria*. London: Allen and Unwin.

Aldridge, M. (2003) 'The ties that divide: regional press campaigns, community and populism', *Media, Culture and Society*, 25 (4): 491–509.

Aldridge, M. (2007) *Understanding the Local Media*. Maidenhead: Open University Press.

Allan, S. (1999) *News Culture*. Milton Keynes: Open University Press.

Allen, R. (2005) 'Preparing reflective practitioners', in R. Keeble (ed.), *Print Journalism: A Critical History*. Abingdon, Oxon: Routledge. pp. 317–328.

Anderson, P.J. and Weymouth, A. (1999) *Insulting the Public? The British Press and the European Union*. London: Longman.

Angell, N. (1923) 'The problem of the press: salvation through the trust?', *The Nation and the Athenaeum*, 17 November: 269–270.

Arnold, M. (1887) 'Up to Easter', *The Nineteenth Century*, CXXIII (May): 627–648.

Atton, C. (1999) 'A reassessment of the alternative press', *Media, Culture and Society*, 21: 51–76.

Atton, C. (2002a) *Alternative Media*. London: SAGE.

Atton, C. (2002b) 'News cultures and new social movements: radical journalism and the mainstream media', *Journalism Studies*, 3 (4): 491–505.

Atton, C. (2003) 'Organisation and production in alternative media', in S. Cottle (ed.), *Media, Organization and Production*. London: SAGE. pp. 41–55.

Atton, C. and Hamilton, J.F. (2008) *Alternative Journalism*. London: SAGE.

Baehr, H. (1996) *Women in Television*. London: University of Westminster Press.

Baehr, H. and Dyer, G. (eds) (1987) *Boxed In: Women and Television*. London: Pandora.

Baehr, H. and Spindler-Brown, A. (1987) 'Firing a broadside: a feminist intervention into mainstream TV', in H. Baehr and G. Dyer (eds), *Boxed In: Women and Television*. London: Pandora. pp. 117–130.

Baistow, T. (1985) *Fourth Rate Estate*. London: Comedia.

Bardoel, J. (1996) 'Beyond journalism: a profession between information society and civil society', *European Journal of Communication*, 11 (3): 283–302.

Barlow, D.M., Mitchell, P. and O'Malley, T. (2005) *The Media in Wales: Voices of a Small Nation*. Cardiff: University of Wales Press.

Barnett, S. (2006) 'Reasons to be cheerful', *British Journalism Review*, 17 (1): 7–14.

Barnett, S. (2008) 'On the road to self–destruction', *British Journalism Review*, 19 (2): 5–13.

Barnett, S. and Gaber, I. (2001) *Westminster Tales: The Twenty-first Century Crisis in British Political Communication*. London: Continuum.

Barnett, S. and Seymour, E. (1999a) 'Blurred vision: how bureaucrats and focus groups stifle creativity', *Guardian*, 25 October, p C3.

Barnett, S. and Seymour, E. (1999b) *A Shrinking Iceberg Travelling South*. London: Campign for Quality Television.

Baylen, J.O. (1972) 'The "New Journalism" in late Victorian Britain', *Australian Journal of Politics and History*, 18 (3): 367–385.

Beetham, M. (1996) *A Magazine of Her Own? Domesticity and Desire in the Women's Magazine 1800–1914*. London: Routledge.

Bell, A. (1984) 'Language style as audience design', *Language in Society*, 13: 145–204.

Bell, A. (1996) 'Texts, time and technology in news English', in S. Goodman and D. Graddol (eds), *Redesigning English: New Texts, New Identities*. Milton Keynes: Open University Press. pp. 3–26.

Bell, M. (1997) 'TV news: how far should we go?', *British Journalism Review*, 8 (1): 7–16.

Bell, M. (2002) 'Bell accuses ITN of dumbing down', *Guardian*, 19 February.

Bennett, A. (1898) *Journalism for Women: A Practical Guide*. London: John Lane.

Benwell, B. (ed.) (2003) *Masculinity and Men's Lifestyle Magazines*. Oxford: Blackwell.

Bevan, D. (1984) 'The mobilisation of cultural minorities: the case of Sianel Pedwar Cymru', *Media, Culture and Society*, 6: 128–151.

Beveridge, W. (1951) *Report of the Broadcasting Committee*. (Beveridge Report). [Cmnd 8116].

Bevins, A. (1990) 'The Crippling of the Scribes', *British Journalism Review*, 1 (2): 13–17.

Billig, M. (1995) *Banal Nationalism*. London: SAGE.

Bingham, A. (2004) *Gender, Modernity and the Popular Press in Inter-War Britain*. Oxford: Oxford University Press.

Bingham, A. (2007) 'Drinking in the last chance saloon: the British press and the crisis of self-regulation, 1989–95', *Media History*, 13 (1): 79–92.

Bingham, A. (2009) *Family Newspapers? Sex, Private Life and the British Popular Press 1918–1978*. Oxford: Oxford University Press.

Bingham, A. and Conboy, M. (2009) 'The *Daily Mirror* and the creation of a commercial popular language: a people's war and a people's paper?', *Journalism Studies*, 10 (5): 639–654.

Bird, S.E. (1992) *For Enquiring Minds: A Cultural Study of Supermarket Tabloids*. Tennessee: University of Tennessee Press.

Bird, S.E. (2000) 'Audience demand in a murderous market: tabloidization in US television news', in C. Sparks and J. Tulloch (eds), *Tabloid Tales*. Oxford: Rowman and Littlefield. pp. 213–228.

Biressi, A. and Nunn, H. (eds) (2008) *The Tabloid Culture Reader*. Maidenhead: Open University Press.

Black, J. (2001) *The English Press 1622–1855*. Stroud: Sutton.

Blain, N. and Hutchison, D. (eds) (2008) *The Media in Scotland*. Edinburgh: Edinburgh University Press.

Blumler, J. and Gurevitch, M. (1995) *The Crisis in Public Communication*. London: Routledge.

Blumler, J. and Gurevitch, M. (2000) 'Rethinking the study of political communication', in J. Curran and M. Gurevitch (eds), *Mass Media and Society* (3rd edn). London: Edward Arnold. pp 155–172.

Born, G. (2005) *Uncertain Vision: Birt, Dyke and the Reinvention of the BBC*. London: Vintage.

Boston, R. (1990) *The Essential Fleet Street: Its History and Influence*. London: Blandford.

Bourdieu, P. (1998) *On Television and Journalism*. London: Pluto.

Boyce, G. (1978) 'The Fourth Estate: the reappraisal of a concept', in G. Boyce, J. Curran and P. Wingate (eds), *Newspaper History: From the 17th Century to the Present Day*. London: Constable. pp. 19–40.

Boyce, G. (1986) 'Crusaders without chains: power and the press barons, 1896–1951', *Impacts and Influences*, pp. 97–111.

Boyd-Barrett, O. (1970) 'Journalism recruitment and training: problems in professionalization', in J. Tunstall (ed.), *Media Sociology: A Reader*. London: Constable. pp. 181–201.

Braithwaite, B. (1995) *Women's Magazines: The First 300 Years*. London: Peter Owen.

Brake, L. (1988) 'The old journalism and the new: forms of cultural production in London in the 1880s', in J. Wiener (ed.), *Papers for The Millions: The New Journalism in Britain 1850–1914*. London: Greenwood.

Briggs, A. (1961) *The History of Broadcasting in the United Kingdom (Vol. I): The Birth of Broadcasting*. Oxford: Oxford University Press.

Briggs, A. (1965) *The History of Broadcasting in the United Kingdom (Vol. II): The Golden Age of the Wireless*. Oxford: Oxford University Press.

Briggs, A. (1970) *The History of Broadcasting in the United Kingdom (Vol. III): The War of Words*. Oxford: Oxford University Press.

Briggs, A. (1979) *The History of Broadcasting in the United Kingdom (Vol. IV): Sound and Vision*. Oxford: Oxford University Press.

Briggs, A. (1995) *The History of Broadcasting in the United Kingdom (Vol. V): Competition*. Oxford: Oxford University Press.

Briggs, A. and Burke, P. (2002) *A Social History of the Media*. Cambridge: Polity.

Broadcast (2000) 7 July, p. 16.

Bromley, M. (1998) 'The "tabloiding" of Britain: quality newspapers in the 1990s', in H. Stephenson and M. Bromley (eds), *Sex, Lies and Democracy*. Harlow: Longman. pp. 25–38.

Bromley, M. and Tumber, H. (1997) 'From Fleet Street to cyberspace: the British "popular" press in the late twentieth century', *European Journal of Communication, Studies*, 22 (3): 365–378.

Brookes, R., Lewis, J. and Wahl-Jorgensen, K. (2004) 'The media representation of public opinion: British television news coverage of the 2001 general election', *Media, Culture and Society*, 26 (1): 63–80.

Burnett, R. and Marshall, P.D. (2003) *Web Theory*. London: Routledge.

Cadman, E., Chester, G. and Pivot, A. (1981) *Rolling Our Own: Women as Printers, Publishers and Distributors*. London: Minority.

Campbell, K. (2000) 'Journalistic discourses and constructions of modern knowledge', in L. Brake, B. Bell and D. Finkelstein (eds), *Nineteenth Century Media and the Construction of Identities*. Basingstoke: Palgrave. pp. 40–55.

Carey, J.W. (1987) 'Why and how? The dark continent of American journalism', in R.K. Manoof and M. Schudson (eds), *Reading the News*. New York: Pantheon. pp. 162–166.

Carey, J. (1989) *Communication as Culture: Essays on Media and Society*. Boston, MA: Hyman.

Carey, J. (1996) 'Where journalism education went wrong'. Presentation to the Seigenthaler Conference at the Middle Tennessee State University, USA. Available at http://www.mtsu/~masscom/seig96/carey/carey.htm

Carter, C. (1998) 'When the extraordinary becomes ordinary. Everyday news of sexual violence', in C. Carter, G. Branston and S. Allen (eds), *News, Gender and Power*. London: Routledge. pp. 219–232.

Carter, C. (2005) 'Gendered news?', *Journalism: Theory, Practice and Criticism*, 6 (3): 259–263.

Chalaby, J. (1998) *The Invention of Journalism*. Basingstoke: Macmillan.

Chalaby, J. (2000) 'Northcliffe: proprietor as journalist', in P. Caterall, C. Seymour-Ure and A. Smith (eds), *Northcliffe's Legacy: Aspects of the British Popular Press 1896–1996*. Basingstoke: Macmillan. pp. 27–44.

Chambers, D., Steiner, L. and Fleming, C. (2004) *Women and Journalism*. London: Routledge.

Chippendale, P. and Horrie, C. (1992) *Stick It Up Your Punter*. London: Mandarin.

Christiansen, A. (1961) *Headlines All My Life*. London: Harper Row.

Christmas, L. (1997) *Chaps of Both Sexes? Women Decision-makers in Newspapers: Do They Make a Difference?* London: BT Forum/Women in Journalism.

Clarke, T. (1931) *My Northcliffe Diary*. London: Victor Gollancz.

Cockerell, M. (2000) 'Lifting the lid off spin', *British Journalism Review*, 11 (3): 6–15.

Cockett, R. (1989) *The Twilight of Truth: Chamberlain, Appeasement and the Manipulation of the Press*. London: Weidenfeld and Nicholson.

Cole, P. and Harcup, T. (2009) *Newspaper Journalism*. London: SAGE.

Coleridge, N. (1994) *Paper Tigers: The Latest, Greatest Newspaper Tycoons and How They Won the World*. London: Mandarin.

Collins, J. and Glover, R. (2002) *Collateral Language: A User's Guide to America's New War*. New York: New York University Press.

Comedia (1984) 'The Alternative Press: the development of underdevelopment', *Media, Culture and Society*, 6: 95–102.

Conboy, M. (2002) *The Press and Popular Culture*. London: SAGE.

Conboy, M. (2004) *Journalism: A Critical History*. London: SAGE.

Conboy, M. (2006) *Tabloid Britain: Constructing a Community through Language*. London: Routledge.

Conboy, M. (2007) 'Permeation and profusion: popular journalism in the new millennium', *Journalism Studies*, 8(1): 1–12.

Conboy, M. (2008) 'Foreword', in A. Biressi and H. Nunn (eds), *The Tabloid Culture Reader*. Maidenhead: Open University Press. pp. xv–xvi.

Conboy, M. (2009) 'A parachute of popularity for a commodity in freefall?', *Journalism: Theory, Practice and Criticism*, 10 (3): 302–304.

Conboy, M. and Steel, J. (2008) 'The future of journalism: historical perspectives', *Journalism Studies*, 9 (5): 650–661.

Conboy, M. and Steel, J. (2010) 'From "we" to "me": the changing construction of popular tabloid journalism', *Journalism Studies*, 11 (4): 500–510.

Connell, I. (1992) 'Personalities in the popular media', in P. Dahlgren and C. Sparks (eds), *Journalism and Popular Culture*. London: SAGE. pp. 64–83.

Connell, R. (1978) *Gender and Power*. Stanford: Stanford University Press.

Cooper, D. (2000) 'Missing Manchester values', *The Guardian*, 22 December.

Cottle, S. (1999) 'From BBC Newsroom to BBC Newscentre: on changing technology and journalist practices', *Convergence*, 5 (3): 22–43.

Cottle, S. (2001) 'Television news and citizenship: packaging the public sphere', in M. Bromley (ed.), *No News is Bad News*. Harlow: Pearson.

Cottle, S. (2003a) *Media, Organization and Production*. London: SAGE.

Cottle, S. (2003b) 'Media organisation and production: mapping the field', in S. Cottle (ed.), *Media, Organization and Production*. London: SAGE. pp. 3–24.

Couldry, N. (2000) *The Place of Media Power: Pilgrims and the Witnesses of the Media Age*. London: Routledge.

Covert, C.L. (1981) 'Journalism history and women's experience: a problem in conceptual change', *Journalism History*, 4: 2–6.

Coward, R. (1987) 'Women's Programmes: why not?', in H. Baehr and G. Dyer (eds), *Boxed In: Women and Television*. London: Pandora. pp. 96–106.

Coward, R. (2007) 'What the butler started: relations between British tabloids and monarchy in the fall-out from the Paul Burrell trial', *Journalism Practice*, 1 (2): 245–260.

Craik, J. (1994) *The Face of Fashion: Cultural Studies in Fashion*. London: Routledge.

Cranfield, G.A. (1962) *The Development of the Provincial Newspaper 1700–1760*. Oxford: Clarendon.

Cranfield, G.A. (1978) *The Press and Society*. London: Longman.

Creedon, P. (ed.) (1989) *Women in Mass Communication: Challenging Gender Views*. London: SAGE.

Crewe, B. (2003) 'Class, masculinity and editorial identity in the reformation of the UK men's press', in B. Benwell (ed.), *Masculinity and Men's Lifestyle Magazines*. Oxford: Blackwell. pp. 91–111.

Crisell, A. (1994) *Understanding Radio*. London: Routledge.

Crisell, A. (1997) *An Introductory History of British Broadcasting*. London: Routledge.

Crisell, A. and Starkey, G. (2009) *Radio Journalism*. London: SAGE.

Cronkite , W. (1997) *The Guardian*, Media Supplement, 27 January, p. 2.

Cudlipp, H. (1953) *Publish and Be Damned*. London: Andrew Dakers.

Cudlipp, H. (1980) *The Prerogative of the Harlot: Press Barons and Power*. London: Bodley Head.

Cuff, A. (1994) 'The mickey-take on news', *The Guardian*, Media Supplement, 10 January, p. 9.

Culf, A. (1996) 'Angry Wakeham rounds on MPs in media row', *Guardian*, November 8, p. 7.

Curran, J. (1986) 'The boomerang effect: the press and the battle for London, 1981–6', in J. Curran, A. Smith and P. Wingate (eds) *Impacts and Influences: Essays on Media Power in the Twentieth Century*. London: Methuen. pp. 113–140.

Curran, J., Petley, J. and Gaber, I. (2005) *Culture Wars: The Media and the British Left*. Edinburgh: Edinburgh University Press.

Curran, J. and Seaton, J. (2003) *Power Without Responsibility*. 2nd edition. London: Routledge.

Cutlip, S. (1994) *The Unseen Power: Public Relations – A History*. Hillsdale, NJ: Erlbaum.

Dahlgren, P. and Sparks, C.(1988) 'What's the meaning of this? Viewers' plural sense-making of TV news', *Media, Culture and Society*, 10 (3): 285–301.

Dahlgren, P. (1992) *Journalism and Popular Culture*. London: SAGE.

Dahlgren, P. (1995) *Television and the Public Sphere*. London: SAGE.

Dancyger, I. (1978) *A World of Women*. Dublin: Gill and Macmillan.

Dates, J.L. (2006) 'Rethinking journalism education', *Journalism Studies*, 7 (1): 144–146.

Davies, J. (1994) *Broadcasting and the BBC in Wales*. Cardiff: University of Wales Press.

Davies, N. (2008) *Flat Earth News*. London: Chatto and Windus.

Day, R. (1989) *The Grand Inquisitor*. London: Weidenfeld and Nicholson.

De Bruin, M. (2000) 'Gender, organisational and professional identities in journalism', *Journalism: Theory, Practice and Criticism*, 1 (2): 217–238.

De Burgh, H. (2000) *Investigative Journalism*. London: Routledge.

Delano, A. (2003) 'Women journalists: what's the difference?', *Journalism Studies*, 4 (2): 273–286.

Delano, A. (2008) 'Different horses, different courses', *British Journalism Review*, 19 (4): 68–74.

Delano, A. and Henningham, J. (1995) *The News Breed: British Journalists in the 1990s*. London: London Institute.

Deuze, M. (2005a) 'What is journalism? Professional identity and ideology of journalists reconsidered', *Journalism: Theory, Practice and Criticism*, 6 (4): 442–464.

Deuze, M. (2005b) 'Popular journalism and professional ideology: tabloid reporters and editors speak out', *Media, Culture and Society*, 27 (6): 861–882.

Deuze, M. (2006a) 'Liquid journalism'. Working paper available at https://scholarworks.iu.edu/dspace/handle/2022/3202?mode=simple (last accessed 22/6/09).

Deuze, M. (2006b) 'Global journalism education: a conceptual approach', *Journalism Studies*, 7 (1): 19–34.

Deuze, M. (2007) *Media Work*. Cambridge: Polity.

DiCenzo, M. (2000) 'Militant distribution: votes for women and the public sphere', *Media History*, 6 (2): 115–128.

Dimbleby, J. (1975) *Richard Dimbleby*. London: Hodder and Stoughton.

Doig, A. (1992) 'Retreat of the investigators', *British Journalism Review*, 3 (4): 44–50.

Donovan, P. (1997) *All Our Todays: Forty Years of Radio 4's 'Today' programme*. London: Cape.

Dougary, G. (1994) *The Executive Tart and Other Myths*. London: Virago.

Downing, J., Ford, T.M., Gil, G. and Stein, L. (2001) *Radical Media: Rebellious Communication and Social Movements*. London: SAGE.

Doyle, G. (2003) *Media Ownership*. London: SAGE.

Easley, A. (2000) 'Authorship, gender and power in Victorian culture: Harriet Martineau and the periodical press', in L. Brake, B. Bell and D. Finkelstein (eds), *Nineteenth Century Media and the Construction of Identities*. Basingstoke: Palgrave. pp. 154–164.

Edelman, M. (1966) *The Mirror: A Political History*. London: Hamish Hamilton.

Ehrlich, M. (2006) *Journalism in the Movies*. Champaign, IL: University of Illinois Press.

Ekström, M. (2002) 'Epistemologies of TV journalism: a theoretical framework', *Journalism: Theory, Practice and Criticism*, 3 (3): 259–282.

Eldridge, J., Kitzinger, J. and Williams, K. (1997) *The Mass Media and Power in Modern Britain*. Oxford: Oxford University Press.

Elliott, P. (1972) *The Sociology of the Professions*. London: Macmillan.

Elliott, P. (1978) 'Professional ideology and organisational change: the journalist since 1800', in G. Boyce, J. Curran and P. Wingate (eds), *Newspaper History: From the 17th Century to the Present Day*. London: Constable. pp. 172–191.

Engel, M. (1996) *Tickle the Public: One Hundred Years of the Popular Press*. London: Gollanz and Prentice-Hall.

English, D. (1996) 'Legend of the chief', *British Journalism Review*, 7 (2): 6.

Ensor, R. (1968) *The Oxford History of England (Vol IV) 1870–1914*. Oxford: Oxford University Press.

Errico, M., April, J., Asch, A., Khalfani, L., Smith, M. and Ybarra, X. (1997) 'The evolution of the summary news lead', *Media Monographs*, I (1). Available at http://www.scripps.ohiou.edu/mediahistory/mhmjour1–1.htm (last accessed 14/07/2009).

Escott, T.H.S. (1917) 'Old and new in the daily press', *Quarterly Review*, CCXXVII: 368.

Esser, F. (1999) 'Tabloidization of news: a comparative account of Anglo-American and German press journalism', *European Journal of Communication*, 14 (3): 291–324.

Evans, H. (2002) 'Attacking the devil', *British Journalism Review*, 13 (4): 6–14.

Fairclough, N. (1995) *Critical Discourse Analysis*. London: Routledge.

Fairlie, H. (1957) 'Brilliance skin-deep', *Encounter*, July: 8–14.

Featherstone, M. (1993) *Global Culture: Nationalism, Globalization and Modernity*. London: SAGE.

Ferguson, M. (1983) *Forever Feminine*. London: Gower.

Fleeman, J.D. (ed.) (1970) *Boswell: Life of Johnson*. 3rd edition. Oxford: Oxford University Press.

Foucault, M. (1974) *The Archaeology of Power* (transl. A.M. Sheridan). London: Tavistock.

Fountain, N. (1988) *Underground: The London Alternative Press, 1966–74*. London: Comedia/Routledge.

Fowler, R. (1991) *Language in the News: Discourse and Ideology in the Press*. London: Routledge.

Francis, J. (2003) 'White culture, black mark', *British Journalism Review*, 14 (3): 67–73.

Franklin, B. (1992) 'Televising the British House of Commons', in B. Franklin (ed.), *Televising Democracies*. London: Routledge. pp. 3–28.

Franklin, B. (1994) *Packaging Politics*. London: Edward Arnold.

Franklin, B. (1996) 'Keeping it "bright, light and trite": changing newspaper reporting of Parliament', *Parliamentary Affairs*, 49: 299–315.

Franklin, B. (1997) *Newszack and News Media*. London: Arnold.

Franklin, B. (ed.) (2001) *British Television Policy: A Reader*. London: Routledge.

Franklin, B. (ed.) (2006) *Local Journalism and Local Media: Making the News Local*. Abingdon, Oxon: Routledge.

Franklin, B. and Murphy, D. (1991) *What News? The Market, Politics and the Local Press*. London: Routledge.

Franklin, B. and Richardson, J.E. (2002) '"A journalist's duty?" Continuity and change in local newspaper reporting of recent UK General Elections', *Journalism Studies*, 3 (1): 35–52.

Franklin, B., Court, G. and Cushion, S. (2006) 'Downgrading the local in local newspapers': reporting of the 2005 UK General Election', in B. Franklin (ed.), *Local Journalism and Local Media: Making the News Local*. Abingdon, Oxon: Routledge. pp. 256–269.

Friederichs, H. (1911) *The Life of Sir George Newnes*. London: Hodder and Stoughton.

Frost, C. (2000) *Media Ethics and Self-Regulation*. Harlow: Longman.

Frost, C. (2004) 'The Press Complaints Commission: a study of ten years of adjudications on press complaints', *Journalism Studies*, 5 (1): 101–114.

Fyfe, H. (1930) *Northcliffe: An Intimate Biography*. London: Allen and Unwin.

Gaber, I. (2005) 'Dumb and dumber: does TV count?', *British Journalism Review*, 16 (1): 24–28.

Galtung, J. and Ruge, M. (1965) 'The structure of foreign news: the presentation of the Congo, Cuba and Cyprus crises in four Norwegian newspapers', *Journal of International Peace Research*, 1: 64–91.

Gannon, F.R. (1971) *The British Press and Germany, 1936–1939*. Oxford: Oxford University Press.

Gardiner, A.G. (1923) 'The Rothermere press and France', *The Nation and the Athenaeum*, 33, 4 August: 567–569.

Gardiner, A.G. (1932) 'C.P. Scott and Northcliffe – a contrast', *The Nineteenth Century and After*, 111, February, pp. 247–256.

Geary, J. (2006) 'In praise of the tabs (sort of)', *British Journalism Review*, 17 (1): 41–44.

Giddens, A. (1991) *Modernity and Self-Identity: Self and Society in the Late Modern Age*. Cambridge: Polity Press.

Giles, D. (2000) *Illusions of Immortality: A Psychology of Fame and Celebrity*. London: Macmillan.

Gill, R. (2003) 'Power and the production of subjects', in B. Benwell (ed.), *Masculinity and Men's Lifestyle Magazines*. Oxford: Blackwell. pp. 34–56.

Glasser, T. (2006) 'Journalism studies and the education of journalists', *Journalism Studies*, 7 (1): 146–149.

Glover, S. (ed.) (1999) *Secrets of the Press: Journalists on Journalism*. Harmondsworth: Penguin.

Gough-Yates, A. (2003) *Understanding Women's Magazines: Publishing, Markets and Readerships*. London: Routledge.

Good, H. (ed.) (2008) *Journalism Ethics Goes to the Movies.* Lanham, MD: Rowman and Littlefield.

Goodbody, J. (1985) 'The *Star*: its role in the rise of popular newspapers, 1888–1914', *Journal of Newspaper and Periodical History*, 1 (2): 20–29.

Goodhart, D. and Wintour, P. (1986) *Eddie Shah and the Newspaper Revolution.* London: Coronet.

Greater London Authority (2007) 'The search for common ground: Muslims, non-muslims and the UK media'. A report commissioned by the Mayor of London. Available at: www.london.gov.uk/mayor/equalities/doc/commonground-report. pdf (accessed 14.07.2009).

Greenslade, R. (1996) 'The telling selling game', *Guardian 2.* 12 August. p. 17.

Greenwood, F. (1890) 'The newspaper press', *The Nineteenth Century*, 27 (May): 833–842.

Greenwood, F. (1897) 'The newspaper press: half a century's survey', *Blackwood's Edinburgh Magazine*, 161 (May): 704–720.

Grieve, M. (1964) *Millions Made my Story*. London: Gollancz.

Gripsrud, J. (2000) 'Tabloidization, popular journalism and democracy', in C. Sparks, and J. Tulloch (eds), *Tabloid Tales*. Oxford: Rowman and Littlefield. pp. 285–300.

Haas, T. (2005) *The Idea of Public Journalism*. Abingdon, Oxon: Routledge.

Habermas, J. (1984) *The Theory of Communicative Action: Reason and the Rationalization of the Lifeworld*. Cambridge: Polity.

Habermas, J. (1987) *The Theory of Communicative Action: The Critique of Functionalist Reason*. Cambridge: Polity.

Habermas, J. (1992) *The Structural Transformation of the Public Sphere*. Cambridge: Polity.

Halascz, A. (1997) *The Marketplace of Print*. Cambridge: University of Cambridge Press.

Hall, J. (2001) *Online Journalism: A Critical Primer*. London: Pluto.

Hall, S. and Jacques, M. (1983) 'Introduction', in M. Jacques (ed.), *New Times: The Changing Face of Politics in the 1990s*. London: Wishart and Lawrence. pp. 11–20.

Hampton, M. (2001) '"Understanding media": theories of the press in Britain, 1850–1914', *Media, Culture and Society*, 23 (2): 213–231.

Hampton, M. (2004) *Visions of the Press in Britain, 1850-1950*. Urbana and Chicago: University of Illinois Press.

Harcup, T. (1994) *A Northern Star: Leeds Other Paper and the Alternative Press 1974–1994*. London and Pontefract: Campaign for Press and Broadcasting Freedom.

Harcup, T. (2002) 'Journalists and ethics: the quest for a collective voice', *Journalism Studies*, 3 (1): 101–114.

Harcup, T. (2003) 'The unspoken – said', *Journalism: Theory, Practice and Criticism*, 4 (3): 356–376.

Harcup, T. and O'Neil, D. (2001) 'What is news? Galtung and Ruge revisited', *Journalism Studies*, 2 (2): 261–80.

Hargreaves, I. (2001) 'Why is the *Sun* hot for Tony?', *Financial Times*, Creative Industries Supplement, 5 December, p. 5.

Hargreaves, I. and Thomas, J. (2002) *New News, Old News*. London: I.T.C. Viewer Relations Unit.

Harrington, S. (2008) 'Popular news in the 21st century: time for a new critical approach', *Journalism: Theory, Practice and Criticism*, 9 (3): 266–284.

Harrison, J. (2006) *News*. Abingdon, Oxon: Routledge.

Harrison, S. (1974) *Poor Men's Guardians*. London: Lawrence and Wishart.

Hartley, J. (1996) *Popular Reality*. London: Arnold.

Hartley, J. (2000) 'Communicative democracy in a redactional society: the future of journalism studies', *Journalism: Theory, Practice and Criticism*, 1 (1): 39–48.

Hartley, J. (2007) 'Documenting Kate Moss: fashion photography and the persistence of photojournalism', *Journalism Studies*, 8 (4): 555–565.

Hastings, M. (2002) *Editor*. London: Macmillan.

Heller, Z. (1999) 'Girl columns', in S. Glover (ed.), *Secrets of the Press: Journalists on Journalism*. Harmondsworth: Penguin. pp 10–17.

Hendy, D. (1994) '… But is it too fast for its own good?', *British Journalism Review*, 5 (2): 15–17.

Henningham, J.P. and Delano, A. (1998) 'British journalists', in D.H. Weaver (ed.), *The Global Journalist: News People Around the World*. Cresskill, NJ: Hampton.

Herd, H. (1952) *The March of Journalism: The Story of the British Press from 1622 to the Present Day*. London: Allen and Unwin.

Higgins, M. (2006) 'Substantiating a political public sphere in the Scottish press: a comparative analysis', *Journalism: Theory, Practice and Criticism*, 7 (1): 25–44.

Hill, A. (2005) *Reality Television*. London: Routledge.

Hirsch, F. and Gordon, D. (1975) *Newspaper Money*. London: Hutchinson.

Hobsbawm, J. (ed.) (2006) *Where the Truth Lies: Trust and Morality in PR and Journalism*. London: Atlantic.

Hodge, R. and Kress, G. (1993) *Language as Ideology*. London: Routledge.

Hoggart, R. (1958) *The Uses of Literacy*. Harmondsworth: Pelican.

Holland, P. (1983) 'The Page 3 Girl speaks to women too', *Screen*, 24 (3): 84–102.

Holland, P. (1987) 'When a woman reads the news', in H. Baehr and G. Dyer (eds), *Boxed In: Women and Television*. London: Pandora. pp. 133–150.

Holland, P. (1998) 'The politics of the smile: "soft news" and the sexualization of the popular press', in C. Carter, G. Branston and S. Allen (eds), *News, Gender and Power*. London: Routledge. pp. 17–32.

Holland, P. (2001) 'Authority and authenticity: redefining television current affairs', in M. Bromley (ed.), *No News is Bad News*. Cambridge: Pearson.

Holland, P. (2006) *The Angry Buzz: This Week and Current Affairs Television.* London: I.B. Taurus.

Hollingsworth, M. (1986) *The Press and Political Dissent*. London: Pluto.

Hollis, P. (1970) *The Pauper Press*. Oxford: Oxford University Press.

Holmes, T. (2007) 'Guest editor's introduction – Special Issue: Mapping the Magazine', *Journalism Studies*, 8 (4): 510–521.

Hood, S. (1967) *A Survey of Television*. London: Heinemann.

Hood, S. and O' Leary, G. (1990) *Questions of Broadcasting*. London: Methuen.

Hughes, C. (1986) 'Imperialism, illustration and the *Daily Mail*: 1896–1904', in M. Harris and A.J. Lee (eds), *The Press in English Society from the Seventeenth*

Century to the Nineteenth Century. London and Toronto: Associated University Presses.

Hunt, L. (1998) *British Low Culture: From Safari Suits to Sexploitation*. London: Routledge.

Hunter, F. (2000) 'Hilda Matheson and the BBC, 1926–1940', in C. Mitchell (ed.), *Women and Radio: Airing Differences*. London: Routledge. pp. 41–47.

Hunter, J. (1977) 'The lady's magazine and the study of Englishwomen in the eighteenth century', in D.H. Bond and R. McLeod (eds), *Newsletters to Newspapers: Eighteenth Century Journalism*. West Virginia: University Press. pp. 103–117.

Hutchison, D. (2008) 'The history of the press', in N. Blain and D. Hutchison (eds), *The Media in Scotland*. Edinburgh: Edinburgh University Press. pp. 55–70.

Hutton, Lord (2004) *Report of the Inquiry into the Circumstances Surrounding the Death of Dr. David Kelly C.M.G.* London: HMSO.

Isaacs, J. (1989) *Storm Over 4: A Personal Account*. London: Weidenfeld and Nicholson.

Jackson, K. (2000) 'Perceptions of journalism', in K. Campbell (ed.), *Journalism, Literature and Modernity*. Edinburgh: Edinburgh University Press. pp. 1–14.

Jackson, K. (2001) *George Newnes and the New Journalism in Britain, 1880–1910: Culture and Profit*. Aldershot: Ashgate.

Jacob, I. (1947) 'The European Service holds the mirror up to British opinion', *BBC Yearbook 1947*. London: BBC. Cited in A. Webb (2006) 'Auntie goes to war', *Media History*, 12 (2): 117–132.

Jameson, F. (1985) 'Postmodernism and consumer society', in H. Foster (ed.), *Postmodern Culture*. London: Pluto. pp. 111–125.

Jenkins, S. (2006) 'PR and the press: two big guns', *British Journalism Review*, 17 (1): 45–49.

Jones, A. (1993) *Press, Politics and Society: A History of Journalism in Wales*. Cardiff: University of Wales Press.

Jones, A. (1996) *Powers of the Press: Newspapers, Power and the Public in Nineteenth Century England*. Aldershot: Ashgate and Scolar Press.

Jones, N. (1995) *Soundbites and Spin Doctors: How Politicians Manipulate the Mass Media and Vice Versa*. London: Cassell.

Jones, N. (1997) *Campaign 1997: How the General Election Was Won and Lost*. London: Indigo.

Journalism Training Forum (2002) *Journalists at Work*. London: NTO/Skillset.

Kadritzke, S. (2000) 'Reporting the news: does the targeting of an audience affect the informational value of television news?' MA thesis, Trinity and All Saints University College, Leeds, quoted in Ursell (2001).

Kaplan, J. (2003) 'Convergence not a panacea', *Journalism Studies*, 4 (4): 515–518.

Kaufman, G. (1996) *Guardian*, 8 November, p. 7.

Keeble, R. (ed.) (1994) *The Newspapers Handbook*. London: Routledge.

Keeble, R. (1997) *Secret War: Silent Press*. Luton: University of Luton Press.

Keeble, R. (2001) 'Orwell as war correspondent: a reassessment', *Journalism Studies*, 2 (3): 393–406.

Keeble, R. (2005a) 'New militarism, massacrespeak and the language of silence', *Ethical Space: The International Journal of Communication Ethics*, 2 (1/2): 39–45.

Keeble, R. (2005b) *Print Journalism: A Critical History*. London: Routledge.

Kettle, M. (2009) 'The true patrons of this greed are our over-mighty press', *The Guardian*, 15 May, p. 33.

Khiabany, G. (2000) '*Red Pepper*: a new model for the alternative press?', *Media, Culture and Society*, 22 (4): 447–463.

Kidd, D. (2003a) 'The Independent Media Center: a new model', *Media Development*, 4: 7–10.

Kidd, D. (2003b) 'Indymedia.org: a new communication commons', in M. McCaughey and M.D. Ayers (eds), *Cyberactivism: Online Activism in Theory and Practice*. New York: Routledge. pp. 47–69.

Kitzinger, J. (1998) 'The gender politics of news production: silenced voices and false memories', in C. Carter, G. Branston and S. Allen (eds), *News, Gender and Power*. London: Routledge. pp. 186–203.

Knightley, P. (1982) *The First Casualty, from the Crimea to Vietnam: The Correspondent as Hero, Propagandist and Myth-maker*. London: Quartet.

Koss, S. (1981 and 1984) *The Rise and Fall of the Political Press in Britain* (2 vols). Chapel Hill, NC: University of North Carolina Press.

Kovach, W. and Rosenstiel, T. (2001) *The Elements of Journalism*. New York: Three Rivers.

Lamb, L. (1989) *Sunrise: The Remarkable Rise and Rise of the Best-selling Soaraway Sun*. London: Papermac.

Landry, C., Morley, D., Southwood, R. and Wright, P. (1985) *What a Way to Run a Railroad: An Analysis of Radical Failure*. London: Comedia.

Langer, J. (1998) *Tabloid Television: Popular Journalism and the 'Other News'*. London: Routledge.

Lasica, J. (2002) 'The promise of the Daily Me', *Online Journalism Review*, available at http://www.ojr.org/ojr/lasica/1017779142.php (last accessed 14/07/2009).

Leavis, Q.D. (1932) *Fiction and the Reading Public*. London: Bellew.

Lee, A.J. (1976) *The Origins of the Popular Press 1855–1914*. London: Croom Helm.

Lee, A.J. (1978) 'The structure, ownership and control of the press, 1855–1914', in G. Boyce, J. Curran and P. Wingate (eds), *Newspaper History: From the 17th Century to the Present Day*. London: Constable. pp. 117–129.

LeMahieu, D.L. (1988) *A Culture for Democracy: Mass Communication and the Cultivated Mind in Britain Between the Wars*. Oxford: Clarendon.

Leslie, A. (2004) 'If the BBC is wrecked or ever weakened by bullying politicians, then we WILL all be losers', *Daily Mail*, 30 January, p. 12.

Lewis, D. (2003) 'Online news: a new genre?', in J. Aitchison and D. Lewis (eds), *New Media Language*. London: Routledge. pp. 95–104.

Lewis, J. (2004) 'Television, public opinion and the war in Iraq: the case of Britain', *International Journal of Public Relations Research*, 16 (3): 295–310.

Lewis, J., Cushion, S. and Thomas, J. (2005) 'Immediacy, convenience or engagement? An analysis of 24-hour news channels in the UK', *Journalism Studies*, 6 (4): 461–477.

Lewis, J., Williams, A. and Franklin, B. (2008a) 'A compromised fourth estate?', *Journalism Studies*, 9 (1): 1–20.

Lewis, J., Williams, A. and Franklin, B. (2008b) 'Four rumours and an explanation: a political economic account of journalists' changing newsgathering and reporting practices', *Journalism Practice*, 2 (1): 27–45.

Lewis, P.M. and Booth, J. (1989) *The Invisible Medium: Public, Commercial and Community Radio*. London: Macmillan.

Livingstone, S. and Lunt, P. (1994) *Talk on Television*. London: Routledge.

Lloyd, J. (2004) *What the Media Are Doing to Our Politics*. London: Constable.

Lovelace, C. (1978) 'British press censorship during the First World War', in G. Boyce, J. Curran and P. Wingate (eds), *Newspaper History: From the 17th Century to the Present Day*. London: Constable. pp. 309–319.

Lowry, W. (2006) 'Mapping the journalism–blogging relationship', *Journalism: Theory, Practice and Criticism*, 7 (4): 477–500.

Lusoli, W. (2005) 'A second-order medium? The internet as a source of electoral information in 25 European countries', *Information Polity*, 10 (3–4): 247–265.

MacArthur, B. (1988) *Eddy Shah,* Today *and the Newspaper Revolution*. London: David and Charles.

Macdonald, M. (2000) 'Rethinking personalization in current affairs journalism', in C. Sparks and J. Tulloch (eds), *Tabloid Tales*. Oxford: Rowman and Littlefield. pp. 251–266.

MacGregor, S. (2002) *Woman of Today*. London: Headline.

Mackay, H. and Powell, A. (1996) 'Wales and its media: production, consumption and regulation', *Contemporary Wales*, 9: 8–39.

McManus, H.R. (1994) *Market-Driven Journalism: Let the Citizen Beware*. London: SAGE.

MacMillan, A. (2008) 'Scots on the rocks', *British Journalism Review*, 19 (3): 35–42.

Marquand, D. (1995) 'After Whig imperialism? Can there be a British identity?', *New Community*, 21 (2): 183–193.

Marr, A. (2005) *My Trade: A Short History of British Journalism*. London: Pan.

Marsh, K. (2004) 'Power but scant responsibility', *British Journalism Review*, 15 (4): 17–21.

Mass Observation (1949) *The Press and Its Readers*. London: Art and Technics.

Matheson, D. (2000) 'The birth of news discourse: changes in news language in British newspapers, 1880–1930', *Media, Culture and Society*, 22 (5): 557–573.

Matheson, H. (1933) *Broadcasting*. London: Thornton Butterworth.

McChesney, R. (2000) *Rich Media, Poor Democracy: Communication Politics in Dubious Times*. New York: New Press.

McChesney, R. (2003) 'Corporate media, global capitalism', in S. Cottle (ed.), *Media Organisation and Production*. London: SAGE. pp. 27–40.

McDowell, P. (1998) *The Women of Grub Street*. Oxford: Oxford University Press.

McDowell, W.H. (1992) *The History of BBC Broadcasting in Scotland, 1923–1983*. Edinburgh: Edinburgh University Press.

McGuigan, J. (1993) *Cultural Populism*. London: Routledge.

McKee, A. (2005) *The Public Sphere: An Introduction*. Melbourne: Cambridge University Press.

McKnight, D. (2003) ' "A world hungry for a new philosophy": Rupert Murdoch and the rise of neo–liberalism', *Journalism Studies*, 4 (3): 347–358.

McLachlan, S. and Golding, P. (2000) 'Tabloidization in the British press: a quantitative investigation into changes in British newspapers', in C. Sparks and J. Tulloch (eds), *Tabloid Tales*. Oxford: Rowman and Littlefield. pp. 75–90.

McNair, B. (1996) *News and Journalism in the UK* (2nd edn). London: Routldge.

McNair, B. (1998) *The Sociology of Journalism*. London: Routledge.

McNair, B. (2000) *Journalism and Democracy: An Evaluation of the Political Public*

McNair, B. (2002) 'Journalism and democracy: a millennial audit', *Journalism Studies*, 1 (2): 197–211.

McNair, B. (2003a) *An Introduction to Political Communication*. London: Routledge.

McNair, B. (2003b) 'From control to chaos: towards a new sociology of journalism', *Media, Culture and Society*, 25 (4): 547–555.

McNair, B. (2004) 'PR must die: spin, anti-spin and political public relations in the UK, 1997–2004', *Journalism Studies*, 5 (3): 325–338.

McNair, B. (2006) 'News from a small country: the media in Scotland', in B. Franklin (ed.), *Local Journalism and Local Media*. Abingdon, Oxon: Routledge. pp. 37–48.

McNair, B. (2008a) '"I, Columnist"', in B. Franklin (ed.), *Pulling Newspapers Apart*. Abingdon, Oxon: Routledge. pp. 112–120.

McNair, B. (2008b) 'The Scottish media and politics' in N. Blain and D. Hutchison (eds), *The Media in Scotland*. Edinburgh: Edinburgh University Press. pp. 227–242.

McRobbie, A. (1991) *Feminism and Youth Culture from* Jackie *to* Just Seventeen. Basingstoke: Macmillan.

Medhurst, J. (2004) '"Wales Television – Mammon's Television"? ITV in Wales in the 1960s', *Media History*, 10 (2): 119–131.

Meikle, G. (2003) 'Inymedia and the New Net news', *Media Development*, 4: 3–6.

Meyer, T. with Hinchman, L. (2002) *Media Democracy: How the Media Colonize Politics*. Cambridge: Polity.

Minority Press Group (1980) *Here Is The Other News: Challenges to the Local Commercial Press*. London: Minority Press Group.

Mitchell, C. (2000) *Women and Radio: Airing Differences*. London: Routledge.

Monck, A. (2008) 'Dangerous obsession', *British Journalism Review*, 19 (2): 14–18.

Moore, M. (2006) 'In news we trust', *British Journalism Review*, 17 (4): 45–51.

Mort, F. (1996) *Cultures of Consumption: Masculinities and Social Space in Late Twentieth Century Britain*. London: Routledge.

Murdock, G. (2004) 'Past the posts: rethinking change, retrieving critique', *European Journal of Communication*, 19 (19): 19–38.

Murdock, G. and Golding, P. (1978) 'The structure, ownership and control of the press, 1914–76', in G. Boyce, J. Curran, and P. Wingate (eds), *Newspaper History: From the 17th Century to the Present Day*. London: Constable. pp. 130–151.

Murphy, D. (1976) *The Silent Watchdog*. London: Constable.

Murray, G. (1972) *The Press and the Public: The Story of the British Press Council*. Carbondale, IL: Southern University Press.

Murphy, D. (1988) 'The alternative local press'. Unpublished paper presented to the annual conference of the Political Studies Association. Plymouth. 12–14 April. Cited in Franklin, B. (1997) p. 110.

Negrine, R. (1994) *Politics and the Mass Media in Britain*. London: Routledge.

Negrine, R. (1998) *Parliament and the Media: A study of Britain, Germany and the Media*. London: Pinter.

Negrine, R., Mancini, P., Holtz–Bacha, C. and Papthanassopoulos, S. (eds) (2007) *The Professionalization of Political Communication*. Bristol: Intellect.

Negroponte, N. (1995) *Being Digital*. New York: Vintage.

Neil, A. (1996) *Full Disclosure*. London: Macmillan.

Neil, R., Benson, G., Boaden, H. Tait, R., van Klaveren, A and Whittles, S. (2004) *The Report of the Neil Review Team*. London: BBC. http://www.bbc.co.uk/info/policies/pdf/neil_report.pdf (accessed 14/07/2009).

Nelson, E. (1989) *The British Counter-Culture, 1966–73: A Study of the Underground Press*. London: Macmillan.

Newspaper Press Directory (1907) London: Charles Mitchell and Co.

Niblock, S. and Machin, D. (2007) 'News values for consumer groups: the case of Independent Radio News, London, UK', *Journalism: Theory, Practice and Criticism*, 8 (2): 184–204.

Nixon, S. (1996) *Hard Looks: Masculinities, Spectatorship and Contemporary Consumption*. London: UCL Press.

O'Connor, T.P. (1889) 'The new journalism', *New Review*, 1, October: 423–434.

Ofcom (2004) *The Communications Market – Television*. London: Ofcom.

O'Hagan, J. and Jennings, M. (2003) 'Public broadcasting in Europe: rationale, license fee and other issues', *Journal of Cultural Economics*, 27 (1): 31–56.

O'Malley, T. (1994) *Closedown: The BBC and Government Broadcasting Policy 1979–1992*. London: Pluto.

O'Malley, T. (2001) 'The decline of public service broadcasting in the UK, 1979–2000', in M. Bromley (ed.), *No News is Bad News*. Harlow: Pearson.

O'Neill, D. and O'Connor, C. (2008) 'The passive journalist: how sources dominate local news', *Journalism Practice*, 2 (3): 487–500.

Osgerby, B. (2003) 'A pedigree of the consuming male: masculinity, consumption and the American "leisure class"', in B. Benwell (ed.), *Masculinity and Men's Lifestyle Magazines*. Oxford: Blackwell. pp. 57–85.

Paletz, D.L. (1998) *The Media in American Politics*: *Contents and Consequences*. New York: Longman.

Pavlik, J. (2001) *Journalism and the New Media*. New York: Columbia University Press.

Paxman, J. (2000) 'All is not what it seems', *Guardian*, Media Section, 8 May, pp. 10–11.

Pebody, P. (1882) *English Journalism and the Men Who Have Made It*. London: Cassell, Petter, Galpin and Co.

Perkin, H. (1981) *The Structured Crowd: Essays in English Social History*. Brighton: Harvester.

Petley, J. (2003) ' Last chance revisited', *British Journalism Review*, 14 (3): 80–83.

Petley, J. (2006) 'Public Service Broadcasting in the UK', in D. Gomery and L. Hockley (eds), *Television Industry*. London: British Film Institute. pp. 42–45.

Petley, J. (2008) 'Bleak outlook on the news front', *British Journalism Review*, 19 (3): 19–25.

Pilkington, H. (1962) *Report of the Committee on Broadcasting* (Pilkington Report) [cmnd 1753].

Platell, A. (1999) 'Institutionalized sexism', in S. Glover (ed.), *Secrets of the Press: Journalists on Journalism*. Harmondsworth: Penguin. pp. 140–147.

Pinkus, P. (1968) *Grubstreet Stripped Bare*. London: Constable.

Porter, H. (1985) *Lies, Damned Lies and Some Exclusives*. London: Coronet.

Postman, N. (1986) *Amusing Ourselves to Death: Public Discourse in the Age of Showbusiness*. London: Methuen.

Pöttker, H. (2003) 'News and its communicative quality: the inverted pyramid – when and why did it appear?' *Journalism Studies*, 4 (4): 501–511.

Press Council (1974) *Press Council 21st Annual Report*. London.

Preston, P. (2004) 'Tabloids: only the beginning', *British Journalism Review*, 15 (1): 50–55.

Pugh, M. (1998) 'The *Daily Mirror* and the revival of Labour', *Twentieth Century British History*, 9 (3): 420–438.

Putnis, P. (2008) 'Share 999', *Media History*, 14 (2): 141–165.

Quinn, S. (2005) 'Convergence's fundamental question', *Journalism Studies*, 6 (1): 29–38.

Raboy, M. and Dagenais, B. (eds) (1992) *Media, Crisis and Democracy*. London: SAGE.

Raymond, J. (1996) *The Invention of the Newspaper: English Newsbooks, 1641–1649*. Oxford: Oxford University Press.

Reed, D. (1997) *The Popular Magazine in Britain and the United States, 1880–1960*. London: The British Library.

Reese, S., Rutigliano, L., Kidewk, H. and Jeong, J. (2007) 'Mapping the blogosphere: citizen-based media in the global news era', *Journalism: Theory, Practice and Criticism*, 8 (3): 235–262.

Reith, J. (1924) *Broadcast over Britain*. London: Hodder and Stoughton.

Report of the Broadcasting Committee 1949 (1951) [The Beveridge Report], Cmd 8116. London: HMSO.

Rhoufari, M.M. (2000) 'Talking about the tabloids', in C. Sparks and J. Tulloch (eds), *Tabloid Tales*. Oxford: Rowman and Littlefield. pp. 163–176.

Richards, H. (1997) *The Bloody Circus: The* Daily Herald *and the Left*. London: Pluto.

Richardson, J.E. (2004) *(Mis) Representing Islam: The Racism and Rhetoric of the Broadsheet Press*. Amsterdam: John Benjamins.

Rojek, C. (2001) *Celebrity*. London: Reaktion.

Rooney, D. (1998) 'Dynamics of the British tabloid press', *Javnost*, 5 (3): 95–107.

Rooney, D. (2000) 'Thirty years of competition in the British tabloid press: the *Mirror* and the *Sun*', in C. Sparks and J. Tulloch (eds), *Tabloid Tales*. Oxford: Rowman and Littlefield. pp. 91–110.

Royal Commission on the Press 1947–1949 (1949) *Report*, Cmnd 7700. London: HMSO.

Royal Commission on the Press 1961–1962 (1962) *Report*, Cmnd 1811. London: HMSO.

Royal Commission on the Press 1974–1977 (1977) *Report*, Cmnd 6810. London: HMSO.

Rowbotham, S. (1996) *Hidden from History: 300 Years of Women's Oppression and the Fight Against It*. London: Pluto.

Runnymede Trust (April 2008) 'A tale of two Englands: "race" and violent crime in the press'. London: Runnymede Trust. Available at. www.runnymedetrust.org/.../race-and-violent-crime-in-the-press.htm (accessed 14.07.2009).

Rusbridger, A. (2005) 'The Hugo Young Memorial Lecture'. University of Sheffield, 9 March.

Salmon, R. (2000) '"A simulacrum of power": intimacy and abstraction in the rhetoric of the New Journalism', in L. Brake, B. Bell and D. Finkelstein (eds), *Nineteenth Century Media and the Construction of Identities*. Basingstoke: Palgrave. pp. 27–39.

Salter, L. (2005) 'The communicative structures of journalism and public relations', *Journalism: Theory, Practice and Criticism*, 6 (1): 90–106.

Savage, G. (1998) 'Erotic stories and public decency: newspaper reporting of divorce proceedings in England', *Historical Journal*, 41: 511–528.

Scannell, P. (1979) 'The social eye of television, 1946–1955', *Media, Culture and Society*, 1: 97–106.

Scannell, P. (1996) *Radio, Television and Modern Life: A Phenomenological Approach*. Oxford: Blackwell.

Scannell, P. and Cardiff, D. (1991) *A Social History of Broadcasting, 1922–1939: Serving the Nation* (Vol. 1). Oxford: Blackwell.

Schlesinger, P. (1978) *Putting Reality Together*. London: Routledge.

Schlesinger, P. (1992) 'From production to power', in P. Scannell, P. Schlesinger and C. Sparks (eds), *Culture and Power*. London: SAGE.

Schlesinger, P., Miller, D. and Dinan, W. (2001) *Open Scotland? Journalists, Spin Doctors and Lobbyists*. Edinburgh: Polygon.

Schudson, M. (1978) *Discovering the News: A Social History of American Newspapers*. New York: Harper.

Sebba, A. (1994) *Battling for the News: The Rise of the Woman Reporter*. London: Sceptre.

Self, W. (1997) 'Chris the saviour', *Observer*, Review Section, 9 March, p. 9.

Seymour-Ure, C. (1991) *The British Press and Broadcasting Since 1945*. Oxford: Blackwell.

Seymour-Ure, C. (2000) 'Northcliffe's legacy', in P. Caterall, C. Seymour-Ure and A. Smith (eds), *Northcliffe's Legacy*. Basingstoke: Macmillan. pp. 9–25.

Shawcross, W. (1992) *Rupert Murdoch*. London: Chatto and Windus.

Shevelow, K. (1989) *Women and Print Culture*. London: Routledge.

Siebert, F.S. (1965) *Freedom of the Press in England, 1476–1776: The Rise and Fall of Government Control*. Urbana, IL: Urbana University Press.

Simpson, P. (1993) *Language, Ideology and Point of View*. London: Routledge.

Singer, J.B. (2007) 'Contested autonomy: professional and popular claims on journalistic norms', *Journalism Studies*, 8 (1): 79–95.

Smith, A. (1973) *The Shadow in the Cave*. London: Allen and Unwin.

Smith, A. (1975) *Paper Voices*. London: Chatto and Windus.

Smith, A. (1978) 'The press and popular culture: an historical perspective', in G. Boyce, J. Curran and P. Wingate (eds), *Newspaper History from the Seventeenth Century to the Present Day*. London: Constable. pp. 41–50.

Smith, A. (1979) *The Newspaper: An International History*. London: Thames and Hudson.

Smith, C. (2007) 'Pornography for women, or what they don't show you in *Cosmo!*', *Journalism Studies*, 8 (4): 529–38.

Smith, R. (1976) 'Sex and occupational role in Fleet Street', in D. Leonard-Barker and S. Allen (eds), *Sexual Divisions and Society*: *Process and Change*. London.

Snoddy, R. (1992) *The Good, The Bad and the Unacceptable*. London: Faber and Faber.

Snow, J. (1997) 'Is TV news telling the whole story?' *Guardian*, Media Supplement, 27 January, p. 3.

Society of Editors (2004) *Diversity in the Newsroom*. London: Society of Editors. Available at: www.societyofeditors.co.uk/userfiles/file/Diversity%20inthe%20News room%20Report%20PDF (accessed14/07/2009).

Sommerville, J. (1996) *The News Revolution*. Oxford: Oxford University Press.

Southwell, T. (1998) *Getting Away With It: The Inside Story of Loaded*. London: Ebury.

Sparks, C. (1998) 'Introduction: tabloidization and the media', *Javnost – The Public*, 5 (3): 5–10.

Sparks, C. (2000) 'Introduction: the panic over tabloid news', in C. Sparks and J. Tulloch (eds), *Tabloid Tales*. Oxford: Rowman and Littlefield. pp. 1–40.

Sparks, C. and Tulloch, J. (eds) (2000) *Tabloid Tales*. Oxford: Rowman and Littlefield.

Spiers, J. (1974) *The Underground and Alternative Press in Britain: A Bibliographical Guide with Historical Notes*. Brighton: Harvester.

Stanyer, J. (2001) *The Creation of Political News: Television and British Party Political Conferences*. Brighton: Sussex Academic Press.

Starkey, G. and Crisell, A. (2009) *Radio Journalism*. London: SAGE.

Stead, W.T. (1886) 'Government by journalism', *Contemporary Review*, XLIX, May: 653–674.

Steel, J. (2009) 'The idea of journalism', in W. Eadie (ed.), *21st Century Communication*. Thousand Oaks, CA: SAGE. pp. 583–91.

Stephens, M. (2006) 'Rethinking journalism education', *Journalism Studies*, 7 (1): 150–53.

Stephenson, H. and Bromley, M. (eds) (1998) *Sex, Lies and Democracy: The Press and the Public*. Harlow: Longman.

Stevenson, N., Jackson, P. and Brooks, K. (2001) *Understanding Men's Magazines*. Cambridge: Polity.

Street, S. (2002) *A Concise History of British Radio*. Tiverton: Kelly.

Sutton Trust (2006) 'The educational background of leading journalists', http://www.suttontrust.com/reports/Journalists-backgrounds-final-report.pdf (accessed on 14/07/2009).

Strick, H. (1957) 'British Newpaper Journalism, 1900–1956'. University of London, Unpublished PhD thesis.

Sweeney, M. (2008) Broadcasting: from birth to devolution ... and beyond', in N. Blain and D. Hutchison (eds), *The Media in Scotland*. Edinburgh: Edinburgh University Press. pp. 87–103.

Swithinbank, T. (2001) *Coming Up From the Streets: The Story of the* Big Issue. London: Earthscan.

Tait, R. (2006) 'What future for regional television news?', in B. Franklin (ed.), *Local Journalism and Local Media: Making the Local News*. Abingdon, Oxon: Routledge. pp. 27–36.

Talfan Davis, G. (1999) *Not By Bread Alone: Information, Media and the National Assembly*. Cardiff: Wales Media Forum.

Taylor, A.J.P. (1976) *English History, 1914–1945*. Oxford: Clarendon.

Taylor, H.A. (1940) *Through 50 Years: An Outline History of the Institute of Journalists*. London: Institute of Journalists.

Taylor, P. (2003) *Munitions of the Mind: A History of Propaganda from the Ancient World to the Present Day*. London: Routledge.

Taylor, S.J. (1992) *Shock! Horror! The Tabloids in Action*. London: Black Swan.

Temple, M. (2008) *The British Press*. Maidenhead: Open University Press.

Thomas, J. (2003/4) 'Buried without tears: the death of the *Welsh Mirror*', *Planet*, 162: 23–27.

Thomas, J. (2005) *Popular Newspapers, The Labour Party and British Politics.* London: Routledge.

Thomas, J. (2006) 'The regional and local media in Wales', in B. Franklin (ed.), *Local Journalism and Local Media: Making the News Local*. Abingdon, Oxon: Routledge. pp. 49–59.

Thompson, E.P. (1979) *The Making of the English Working Classes*. Harmondsworth: Penguin.

Thumin, J. (1998) '"Mrs Knight *Must* Be Balanced": methodological problems in researching early British television', in C. Carter, G. Branston and S. Allan (eds), *News, Gender and Power*. London: Routledge. pp. 91–104.

Thurman, N. (2007) 'The globalization of journalism online: a transatlantic study of news websites and their international readers', *Journalism: Theory, Practice and Criticism*, 8 (3): 285–307.

Tomalin, N. (1975) *Nicholas Tomalin Reporting*. London: Andre Deutsch.

Traber, M. (1985) *Alternative Journalism, Alternative Media* (Communication Resource No. 7), World Association for Christian Communication.

Tuchman, G. (1978) *Making News: A Study in the Construction of Reality*. New York: Free Press.

Tulloch, J. (2000) 'The eternal recurrence of New Journalism', in C. Sparks and J. Tulloch (eds), *Tabloid Tales*. Oxford: Rowman and Littlefield. pp. 131–146.

Tumber, H. and Palmer, J. (2004) *Media at War: The Iraq Crisis*. London: SAGE.

Tunstall, J. (ed.) (1970) *Media Sociology: A Reader*. London: Constable.

Tunstall, J. (1971) *Journalists at Work*. London: Constable.

Tunstall, J. (1983) *The Media in Britain*. London: Constable.

Tunstall, J. (1996) *Newspaper Power: The New National Press in Britain*. Oxford: Clarendon.

Turner, G. (2003) *Understanding Celebrity*. London: SAGE.

Tusan, M. (2005) *Women Making News: Gender and Journalism in Modern Britain*. Urbana and Chicago: University of Illinois Press.

Ursell, G.D.M. (2001) 'Dumbing down or shaping up? New technologies, new media, new journalism', *Journalism: Theory, Practice and Criticism*, 2 (2): 174–196.

Van Dijk, T. (1991) *Racism in the Press*. London: Routledge.

Van Dijk, T. (1993) *Elite Discourse and Racism*. London: SAGE.

Van Zoonen, L. (1994) *Feminist Media Studies.* London: SAGE.

Van Zoonen, L. (1998) '"One of the girls": the changing gender of journalism', in C. Carter, G. Branston and S. Allan (eds), *News, Gender and Power*. London: Routledge. pp. 33–46.

Walker, A. (2006) 'The development of the provincial press in England c. 1780–1914', *Journalism Studies*, 7 (3): 452–462.

Wallis, R. and Baran, S.J. (1990) *The Known World of Broadcast News: International News and the Electronic Media*. London: Routledge.

Ward, J. (2002) *Journalism Online*. Oxford: Focal.

Whale, J. (1969) *The Eye Half-Shut*. Basingstoke: Macmillan.

Wheaton, B. (2003) 'Lifestyle sport magazines and the discourses of sporting masculinity', in B. Benwell (ed.), *Masculinity and Men's Lifestyle Magazines*. Oxford: Blackwell. pp. 193–221.

White, C.L. (1970) *Women's Magazines' 1693–1968*. London: Michael Joseph.

Whitehorn, K. (1997) 'We never had orgasms on the front page ... Of course, it's all changed now', *Observer Review*, 7 December, p. 1.

Whitlow, S. (1977) *Inside Women's Magazines*. London: Pandora.

Whittaker, B. (1981) *News Ltd: Why You Can't Read All About It*. London: Minority Press Group.

Wiener, J. (ed.) (1988a), *Papers For the Millions: The New Journalism in Britain, 1850–1914*. New York: Greenwood.

Wiener, J. (1988b) 'How new was the New Journalism?', in J. Wiener (ed.), *Papers For the Millions: The New Journalism in Britain, 1850–1914*. New York: Greenwood. pp. 47–72.

Wiener, J. (1996) 'The Americanization of the British press', in M. Harris and T. O'Malley (eds), *Studies in Newspaper and Periodical History: 1994 Annual*. Westport, CT: Greenwood. pp. 61–74.

Wilby, P. (2006) 'Brave new world?', *British Journalism Review*, 17 (4): 15–21.

Williams, K. (1998) *Get Me a Murder a Day! A History of Mass Communication in Britain*. London: Arnold.

Williams, R. (1961) *The Long Revolution*. Harmondsworth: Penguin.

Williams, R. (1990) *Television, Technology and Cultural Form*. London: Routledge.

Winship, J. (1987) *Inside Women's Magazines*. London: Pandora Press.

Winston, B. (1998) *Media Technology and Society*. London: Routledge.

Winston, B. (2002) 'Towards tabloidization? Glasgow revisited, 1975–2001', *Journalism Studies*, 3 (1): 5–20.

Wintour, C. (1972) *Pressures on the Press*. London: Deutsch.

Worcester, R.M. (1998) 'Demographics and values: what the British public reads and what it thinks about its newspapers', in H. Stephenson and M. Bromley (eds), *Sex Lies and Democracy: The Press and the Public*. Harlow: Longman. pp. 39–48.

Wright, J. (2003) 'The myth in the *Mirror*', *British Journalism Review*, 14 (3): 59–66.

Wyndham Goldie, G. (1977) *Facing the Nation: Television and Politics, 1936–1976*. London: Bodley Head.

Young, H. (1984) 'Rupert Murdoch and the *Sunday Times*: a lamp goes out', *Political Quarterly*, 55 (4): 382–390.

Index